THREADED INTERPRETIVE
LANGUAGES

THREADED INTERPRETIVE LANGUAGES

LANGUAGES

THEIR DESIGN AND IMPLEMENTATION

R. G. LOELIGER

BYTE BOOKS
70 Main St
Peterborough, NH 03458

Threaded Interpretive Languages

Library of Congress Cataloging in Publication Data

Loeliger, R G

    Threaded interpretive languages.

    Bibliography: p.
    Includes index.
    1. Programming languages (Electronic computers) 2. Interpreters (Computer programs) I. Title.
QA76.7.L63   001.64'24   80-19392
ISBN 0-07-038360-X

567890 HALHAL 89876543

To Sandi, Jill and Guy
with love

PREFACE

This manuscript is the outgrowth of a sequence of events that began in July 1978. I had a very basic microcomputer with a very basic BASIC. Not the most exciting combination. What I really wanted at that point was a compiler. I had more or less decided that C looked like a reasonable language to implement. My essential problem was how to bootstrap a C compiler. Clearly it could be booted in BASIC, but the very thought appalled my sense of rightness.

At the July 1978 National Computer Conference (NCC) at Disneyland, I picked up a copy of *Dr. Dobb's Journal of Computer Calisthenics & Orthodontia* that had an article on FORTH.* "Aha," I said, "an *extensible* interpreter." Clearly a much better approach than BASIC to bootstrap a compiler. The problem then was how to get my hands on FORTH. After a quick trip to Manhattan Beach for a copy of FORTH, Inc's *Microforth Primer* for the Z80 and a two-week wait for the DECUS (DEC User's Society) FORTH manual for the PDP-11, I had the ammunition for my own threaded interpretive language (TIL) design.

By August 1978, six weeks after the NCC, I had an up and running version of a TIL called ZIP (Z80 Interpretive Processor) merrily extending itself in all directions. I had not built the initial C bootstrap compiler simply because ZIP was so much fun to play with.

Because there was so much controversy about languages for microcomputers during this time period, I decided to join the fray with a short article on TILs and their advantages for small microcomputers. A call to *BYTE* magazine resulted in a request for a 200-page book manuscript rather than an article! Months later, a 500-page manuscript resulted. TILs are not the only extensible things in this world.

The main point is that TILs are fun. They are easy to write, easy to use, and very useful tools for the small computer user. I have built several versions of

*FORTH is a registered trademark of FORTH, Inc, 2309 Pacific Coast Highway, Hermosa Beach CA 90254.

ZIP, some in as little as twenty hours. All have been fun and all have been used. When I bought UCSD Pascal for my system, I used ZIPD (a disk-based version of ZIP) to examine the Pascal files, specialize the I/O for my system, and generate the disks to boot the compiler. The simple utility of threaded interpretive languages is one of their nicest attributes.

There's no need to be a software guru to write and code a TIL. I certainly don't fit in the guru class, and yet I managed. I hope that others will also manage, and on something other than a Z80-based system. I have attempted to explain what I did as well as how. When using the system, be inventive. That's precisely how ZIP evolved.

As a final note, special thanks go to Shirley Kalle, Carol Lee, Vicki Haas, and Velva Hinkle for typing the manuscript.

Dayton, Ohio
August 1979

CONTENTS

FIGURES

TABLES

LISTINGS

THREADED INTERPRETIVE LANGUAGES

1 | Overview

This text is intended for people owning either a microcomputer or minicomputer with minimal peripherals, those who write software for these types of systems, and those who are interested in learning about such systems.

1.1 Introduction

The topic of this book is the design of TILs (threaded interpretive languages). The goal is to reverse the trend toward language standardization advocated by the users of large computer complexes. Using FORTRAN to write a program is fine if the compiler fits on the machine you own and produces *efficient* code. In general, this is not true for microcomputers and is only marginally true for most minicomputers. If you have a real-time application, you may have trouble. A threaded interpreter can solve your problem without resorting to assembly language programming.

A threaded interpreter approach is a way of developing a standard, nonstandard language. This is not quite as strange as it sounds. Embedded in the language is a compiler which allows the user to extend the language and redefine operators and data types. If you know what someone else's program does, you can simply modify your existing language to encompass the definitions of the other program and then directly execute it. The modifications may be done by using either existing language constructs or machine language. In either event the extensions are done using the existing language.

One point must be stressed. There is no right threaded interpretive language and no right way to implement the language. It is strictly applications-dependent. TILs can be used to write a program for a microcomputer monitor, a general-purpose language, an editor, or a real-time program for sorting widgets. I shall concentrate on developing an interactive interpreter which will include some of the above as a subset and will support the generation of the others.

This text is tutorial in nature. It presumes a nonextensive familiarity with computers and programming terminology. It is not for the rank amateur, nor is it for the PhD in computer science. The former will not find it easy going and the latter will not find anything new.

The examples in the text are directed toward the Zilog Z80 instruction set simply because I own a Z80-based microcomputer. Any other microcomputer would serve as well for illustration purposes.

1.2 What is a TIL?

To define a TIL, it is necessary to view it in the context of translation. A translator is a computer program which converts *source language* into *target language*. Each language has well-defined semantic and syntactic constructs. If the source language is FORTRAN or Pascal and the target language is assembly language or machine language, the translator is known as a *compiler*. If the source language is assembly language and the target language is machine language, the translator is known as an *assembler*.

An *interpreter* for a source language accepts the source language as input and executes it directly. It does not produce a target language but translates directly to an action. A *pure interpreter* will analyze a source language statement each time it is executed. Fortunately, these beasts are rare. Most interpreters actually employ two phases. The first phase translates the source language to an intermediate language or *internal form*. The second phase then interprets or executes the internal form. The internal form is designed to reduce subsequent analysis and execution times. Most BASIC interpreters do exactly this, with the first phase occurring during program input/edit and the second phase occurring at run time.

A *threaded code interpreter* produces a fully analyzed internal form. The internal form consists of a *list of addresses* of previously defined internal forms. The list is *threaded* together during the first translation phase. This first phase is remarkably similar to that of a compiler and is generally called the *compile mode*. During execution the interpreter executes consecutive internal forms without performing any analyses or searches, since both were completed before execution was evoked.

If the concept is extended to include a broad class of internal forms and a method of interacting with the interpreter, a *threaded interpretive language* (*TIL*) results. TILs are characterized by *extensibility* since they have the full power of the compile mode to augment their existing internal forms. Our TIL will also allow pure interpretation directly from the input line. Most TILs resort to *stacks* and *reverse Polish notation* to achieve an acceptable level of efficiency. I shall consider this class of threaded interpretive languages.

If the full scope of the desired TIL is known, the compile mode may be deleted (since all internal forms are known), producing a threaded interpretive program. This type of program is useful for real-time, fixed process controllers and system monitors with a fixed scope. These types of programs are generally placed in read-only memory but require a minimal amount of programmable memory to support system variables and stacks. It sounds impressive. Let's see if it is!

1.3 The Elements

There are certain elements that characterize any language implementation. The elements that characterize threaded interpretive languages will be extended to include those of an interactive terminal-directed implementation. The presumptions will be based on a minimum system consisting of a keyboard, a video display, a microcomputer with at least 8 K bytes of programmable memory and some type of mass storage. An operating system or monitor which supports program generation and modification is presumed to be available.

The visible attribute of any language is the man-machine interface. The keyboard and display device are critical since they are the means of interacting with the system. The inputs to the system will be *tokens* separated by spaces. A token may be composed of any sequence of ASCII (American Standard Code for Information Interchange) characters that your system supports. A token may be any of the following:

- a number (integer, real, etc)
- an operand (constant, variable, etc)
- an operator (logical or arithmetic, such as $+$, $-$, $<$, $>$, etc)
- a function (fixed subprogram that returns a result)
- a subroutine (subprogram which performs some action but does not necessarily return a result)
- a directive (system control command)
- a program (desired operation or action)

Examples of tokens could include @, $+$, TOKEN, Rumplestiltskin, $<$R, or "," . Token lengths are only limited by the line length of your input device or your own personal preference. The only *token separator* is an ASCII space (■ in this text).

Consider a *line-oriented* I/O (input/output) scheme. An input line consists of a sequence of tokens (separated by spaces) terminated by a *carriage return*. In order to correct input errors, the I/O routine must recognize a *rubout* or *backspace* to erase the last character on the line and a *line delete* command to erase the entire input line and return to the input mode. The input is implemented using an *input line buffer*. Output is also line-oriented. Successful completion of an input operation is usually followed by the system echoing a message to the operator. The usual "OK" may be used, or any other sequence you wish to use. If the system does not recognize a token, it will echo the token followed by a question mark (?). I prefer this to the somewhat ubiquitous "WHAT?" employed by others. A simple question mark seems less threatening. Internal errors detected by the system result in an error message after which control reverts to the operator.

This is about as simple an operator's interface as can be devised. It is also extremely effective and flexible. Several extensions to the above I/O scheme can be implemented. I usually allow lowercase alphabetic characters as input, but they are stored in the input buffer as uppercase. All system responses are in uppercase. This clearly separates commands from responses. I also display a marker at the end of any line that has been deleted. These are niceties that make life easier.

A central element that characterizes our TIL is a *dictionary*. Almost all of the language is composed of dictionary entries. There is an entry for every token defined in the system. Tokens other than input numbers are called *keywords*. The dictionary is the medium that allows the system to locate keywords. The dictionary is segmented into *vocabularies* that contain keywords associated with a particular function. A *core vocabulary* exists that contains the primary language keywords. The core coexists with any specific vocabulary such as an assembler or an editor vocabulary.

This TIL will contain *defining words* which create new dictionary entries. The keyword attributes may be specified using machine or assembly code or may be defined in terms of previously defined keywords using the compile mode. The TIL will also contain defining words which create dictionary entries of a generic type. Examples of these include constant and variable defining words and other more complex operations.

Defining words are defined using more primitive defining words. Defining words always create dictionary *headers* for the keyword being defined. The headers form a linear *linked list* to facilitate identifying a specific keyword when the dictionary is searched. One or more vocabularies may be searched during a given dictionary search. I will consider several header forms and search policies in greater detail later in the text.

Another central element in this TIL will be the use of *stacks*. These are the standard LIFO (last-in, first-out) push-down stacks supported by many microcomputers and minicomputers. Specifically there are two stacks used to implement the TIL. A *data stack* is used to store numbers and addresses of operands. Operators generally expect data on the stack in a predefined order and return results to the stack. A second stack called the *return stack* is used to store program flow-control parameters. This stack can also be used for temporary data storage (carefully). Two stacks are used to separate data from control parameters. The data stack, commonly called just the stack, is always 16 bits wide. The return stack will always be called just that and is usually 16 bits wide. Sometimes the return stack is only 8 bits wide.

The element which is most unusual is the use of RPN (reverse Polish notation) to represent arithmetic or logic expressions. RPN specifies simply and exactly the order in which expressions are to be evaluated. The operators come *after* the operands. The general rules are:

- The identifiers, operands or numbers appear in the same order in both infix notation and reverse Polish notation.
- The operators appear in the same order (from left to right) as they are to be applied.
- The operators appear immediately after the identifiers.

For example:

$7 \times 6/4 \quad \rightarrow \quad 7 \blacksquare 6 \blacksquare \times \blacksquare 4 \blacksquare /$

$3+\{4 \times 6-2\}/7 \quad \rightarrow \quad 3 \blacksquare 4 \blacksquare 6 \blacksquare \times \blacksquare 2 \blacksquare - \blacksquare 7 \blacksquare / \blacksquare +$

The use of the data stack and reverse Polish notation allows an easy left-to-right scan of an input line. As each number is scanned, its value is pushed onto the stack. Binary operators pop two values from the top of the stack and push the result onto the top of the stack. Unary operators simply replace the top stack value.

One of the most common programming errors is mismanagement of the stack because operators expect values on the stack. During interactive program execution, stack underflow should be checked by testing for underflow. Stack overflow can be tested using the "." keyword. This keyword displays the top stack value, destroying its value in the process. If the stack is empty, it results in a stack underflow message. If a value should be on the stack, this makes it available for verification. Gross stack overflow can cause the program to self-destruct as I have proven many times.

The most useful element of the TIL is its compile mode. Keywords may be defined in terms of previously defined keywords using the compile mode. This produces a threaded list definition of the new keyword. In point of fact, a program is nothing more than such a list produced by compiling the definition. When the program is compiled, ie: the program keyword is defined, the compiler produces a list of the addresses of the previously defined keywords and stores them in a dictionary entry. This list may also include *literal handlers* followed by *literals* or *program control directives* followed by *relative jump constants*. Literals allow numbers and labels to be embedded in the program. Control directives allow program branches to be mechanized. *Dictionary* searches to locate keywords associated with tokens, handlers, and directives occur only during compilation. Execution of a program involves only a single dictionary search to find the program since the threaded list contains all the data required to execute the program. This also explains why a pure interpretive mode is required. Without this mode it is impossible to execute a program or keyword.

1.4 The Attributes

There are several advantages to a TIL as well as several disadvantages. It all depends on whose side you are on. The general trade-offs will be discussed briefly.

A threaded interpretive language is generally fast compared to most interpreters available for microcomputers, and in some applications it is faster than compiled code. My current TIL is about three times as fast as an integer BASIC. TILs are slow relative to *optimal* assembled code. The very best compilers are about 10 to 15% inefficient given a reasonable processor instruction set. The very best microcomputer compilers are probably 15 to 50% inefficient if they are cross-compilers hosted on a large computer and if significant code optimization is included. Microcomputer compilers are not as efficient, particularly if they are hosted on the microcomputer. The instruction sets of most microcomputers do not support easy code optimization. Depending on the application, a 100% inefficiency is not unusual in a microcomputer compiler. This is roughly the inefficiency of a TIL. In a purely number crunching application, however, a threaded interpretive language is nearly as efficient as assembled code.

A major advantage of a TIL is the memory required to implement the language. The core language can be contained in less than 4 K bytes, and an assembler, editor, and virtual memory system requires an additional 2 or 3 K bytes. Compare this to the 24 to 32 K bytes required to host a compiler on a microcomputer or minicomputer. Once the core language is available, an application keyword can be added in an incredibly small space because the full power of the core language is available. For example, a keyword to evaluate an expression of the form $Ax^2 + Bx + C$ normally requires less than 40 bytes.

If a real-time, stand-alone program is required, the program can be developed and tested in an interactive mode. Then the program can be *cross-compiled* to leave only the keywords needed for the application in the cross-compiled version. All dictionary search bytes (the headers) may be removed, leaving a minimal set of code. The resulting program can be placed in read-only memory for dedicated machine hosting.

One of the nicest features of a TIL is the simplicity with which programs can be developed and tested. A top-down approach is assumed since the TIL is fully structured. Each function or subroutine is a keyword. In the interactive mode, numbers in the input line are pushed to the stack. The keyword follows and expects its parameters on the stack. The keyword leaves its results on the stack where they can be popped and examined by the user with the "." keyword. A separate driver program is never needed to test a TIL keyword.

TIL coding ease is somewhere between that of a higher-order language and an assembly-language—more difficult than the former and easier than the latter. The only difficult feature is tracking the order and number of items on the stack. Checkout is so easy, however, that the total time to develop and test a program is shorter than the time needed for either a higher-order language or an assembly-language program.

It should be noted that designing and implementing a TIL is quite simple. My first design took about six weeks of evenings to implement in machine code. Don't panic! My preference is to hand-assemble and machine-code short routines. A TIL is nothing more than a sequence of very short routines. Few of the keyword routines, including the dictionary headers, are longer than 20 bytes.

1.5 Implementation Notes

Technically, the type of threaded interpretive language considered here is a *tree-structured*, threaded code interpreter. There are two types of keyword structures: *primitives* and *secondaries*. Primitives have *code bodies* that consist of the *machine code* which implements the action. Secondary code bodies are *lists of addresses* of previously defined primitives and secondaries. It is obvious that secondaries cannot be directly executed by the processor.

Primitives are closely akin to *subroutines*. Secondaries are akin to a *list of subroutines*. The outer loop or executive of any TIL program is a secondary. Each call to a primitive from a secondary causes the machine code of the primitive to be executed and then control is returned to the next instruction in the secondary (ie: the next address in the threaded list). If the next instruction to be executed is a secondary, the following instruction's address is stored on the return stack as the *return address*. When this new secondary completes all of its threaded instructions, it retrieves the return address and returns to execute the next instruction following its call location. This effectively creates a tree structure, the end nodes of which are always primitives. This will be explained in much greater detail later in the text, since it is central to the operation of a threaded interpretive language.

There are many ways to implement a threaded interpretive language. A typical TIL can be implemented using as few as forty to sixty primitives and defining all other keywords as secondaries using this minimal set of primitives. This is the technique used in FORTH, a typical TIL. A secondary does, however, require more overhead time to execute than a primitive. Using a minimal set of primitives results in a slower, less efficient language. It does produce a much more portable language. These types of implementations are also extremely memory conservative. Depending on the application, you may be interested in defining a minimal set of primitives. I tend to make all user-available operator definitions primitives. This results in faster programs at a slight memory penalty.

The heart of the TIL is the *inner interpreter*. The inner interpreter contains the routines which step from address to address in the threaded list of instructions, saving return addresses when a secondary is encountered, and retrieving return addresses when a secondary completes. The inner interpreter code must take as little time as possible since it determines how quickly the TIL can operate. This is a case where time efficiency is far more important than memory minimization.

The *outer interpreter* is the system executive used to implement the interactive, terminal-directed operator's interface. The outer interpreter supports both a pure interpretive mode similar to a BASIC calculator mode and a compile mode to extend the language. The outer interpreter will be written, oddly enough, in TIL. Several variations on the outer interpreter theme will be considered, but all will be endless loops. How else can we return to the operator?

Some dictionary entries need not be contained in any vocabulary. These entries fall into two general catagories. Certain system routines used to implement the outer interpreter are of absolutely no earthly use to the operator. Other routines such as the literal handlers and program-control directives are available to the operator only indirectly. These routines are invoked by the system only in the compile mode. It makes little sense to include header bytes to locate something which cannot be used.

There are several ways to handle different data types. FORTRAN, for example, treats all variables starting with I, J, K, L, M, or N as integers unless the variable is specifically declared to be a real type. The operators then resolve the data types based on a predefined precedence rule. The philosophy adopted for the TIL will be substantially different. All operators will presume operands of a given type. For example, the operator "+" presumes two 16-bit integers on the stack and will replace the top two elements by their sum. If floating-point addition is desired, an operator such as F+ must be used and it will presume two floating-point number arrays on the stack. This places the burden of data type resolution squarely on the programmer. What could be simpler?

The threaded interpretive language I will investigate will be fully structured. It supports branching and loop structures but not an unconditional jump (GOTO). An experienced programmer can defeat this structured goal, but not easily. I have no intention of telling anyone how this can be done.

The implementation will be directed toward defining a minimum threaded interpretive language that supports self-generation of the remaining language. Since the language contains a compiler, only a minimal amount of the language need be hand-coded. The rest can be coded using the TIL itself. About 2 K bytes of code are usually sufficient to allow this self-generation capability.

2 | How a TIL Works

*A fundamental difficulty in explaining how a threaded in-
terpreter works is the interdependence of the various
language elements. If there is a single unifying explanation,
it has escaped me. My approach is simply to draw sabers
and charge — not elegant, but usually effective.*

2.1 Operator's View

The system operator has a rather myopic view of the inner workings of any
program, but the operator has the only seat in the house for interacting with
the system. All of the operator's input to the system consists of *input lines*,
generally composed of as many characters as the display will support on a
single display line. In the *input submode*, the system will indicate the input
point on the video display by a *cursor* symbol. I often use a blinking
underscore (an ASCII "_" alternating with a ■) as a cursor. Since my editor
insists that the typesetter does not have a blinking character font, I will ignore
the input point and only consider entire lines of input in the text. Any subsequent system response will be underlined.

The input submode is called a submode because the system is devoting its
full resources to filling an input buffer. The system mode may be in either the
execute or compile mode during the input submode. Until the carriage return
key is pressed, the system will stay in the input submode. The system will
recognize three distinct commands in the input submode:

Backspace — This command will enter a space (■) at the cursor point and
move the cursor left one character position. If the cursor is at the first
character position of the line it will remain at the first position and not move.
Line Delete — This command will enter a line delete symbol at the current cursor point, output a carriage return and line feed, and leave the cursor at the
first position of the next line.

Carriage Return — This command causes the system to enter a space at the cursor point, move the cursor right one character, and exit the input submode.

Any other character entered by the operator is simply displayed on the video display at the current cursor location and the cursor is moved right one character place. Concurrently, the character is moved to the line buffer which is a one-for-one duplication of the display line (with one exception) up to the point where the carriage return key is pressed. The exception is, of course, the lowercase alphabet. Lowercase alphabetic entries are displayed as lowercase but stored in the line buffer as uppercase. As previously mentioned, this allows separation of commands from any later system response which will always be in uppercase.

One other point is worth mentioning. When the last available character place of the display line is entered, the input submode remains in effect. The next entry will simply replace the last character on the line. The cursor will not advance. Only a carriage return terminates the input submode.

Although this line buffer and display line scheme may seem complex, it is well worth the trouble. It allows easy editing of the line. The line delete function, for example, eliminates the need to enter multiple backspaces to reach the left end of a line in which there is an input error when the current entry point is on the right end. It is easier to start over. My first microcomputer had a read-only memory monitor without a line delete, backspace, or carriage return. The last character in a command caused immediate execution of the command. This crazy scheme required pressing the system master reset button to recover from input errors and almost destroyed my index finger. Worse still, I occasionally hit the power button instead of master reset, totally destroying the resident programs. Be advised!

Consider that the execute mode and input submode are in effect, and the cursor is at the first character position of a display line. The carriage return key is pressed. The system will respond:

$$\blacksquare\text{OK}$$

The cursor will then advance to the first entry position of the next line.

The line buffer is cleared (filled with blanks) until a keyboard printing character key is depressed. In the example, depressing the carriage return key causes the system to enter the execution mode. The system then scans the input buffer from left to right looking for a *token*: a sequence of ASCII characters terminated by a space. Finding nothing in the buffer in the example, it displays a message to the operator indicating successful completion of all requested actions and returns to the input mode for the next command. Any time you see ■OK, you know the line buffer is empty.

Now consider the following input and response:

$$1\blacksquare. \quad \blacksquare1\blacksquare\blacksquare\text{OK}$$

In this case, the system will first find the token "1" in the buffer. Its first response is to presume the token is a keyword. It searches the dictionary looking for the keyword named 1. It finds such a keyword (since regardless of the number base a 1 is a 1). The keyword 1 is a primitive which pushes a 1 to the data stack. Since the system is in the execution mode the system executes the keyword to affect its action, tests for stack errors, finds none, and returns to scan the next token. The next token it finds is the ".". This token is a secondary keyword which pops the top data stack, converts it to a string of ASCII characters that represent the number in the current system number base, and echo displays these characters followed by a space to the operator. The system executes the "." keyword, which results in the 1■ action. Again, no errors are detected, so the system returns to scan the next token. Finding nothing further in the line buffer, it displays ■OK and returns to the input mode.

In the following sequence a slightly more complex action occurs:

DECIMAL■10■HEX■.■A■■OK

The keyword DECIMAL is the keyword which sets the system number base to the decimal (or base 10) mode. This token is scanned and executed. The token "10" ASCII will not be found in the dictionary. Since it is not a dictionary keyword, the system will attempt to convert it to a number. Because all characters in the token are in the valid decimal character set (0 thru 9) and the execution mode is in effect, the system will convert the input from ASCII to a string of binary numbers equivalent to the values of each character and then convert this string to a single binary number using the current system number base. The result is pushed to the stack. The system returns to scan the token HEX. The keyword HEX sets the system number base to the hexadecimal or base 16 mode. The token is scanned, located, and executed. The "." token, when executed, uses the hexadecimal number base to convert the top stack value resulting in A■ . The character A in hexadecimal is exactly equal to the character 10 in decimal.

If the system detects a stack error, it will advance one display line and echo some message, such as ■SP■ERROR (or ■STK , or whatever you like) instead of ■OK . It will then proceed to reset the stack pointer and system variables to evoke the execute mode under operator control (ie: it enters the input submode, where the operator must respond).

If the operator enters a keyword which is neither an existing keyword nor a valid number in the current number base, the system will advance one display line, echo the token followed by "?" and revert to the input submode. Any error of this type detected in the compile mode will result in the partially compiled keyword being deleted from the dictionary. The upshot of this is that forward references are not allowed. A keyword cannot be referenced before it is defined.

Obviously there is more to the operator's interface than has been illustrated to this point. All of the essential features of the interface have been described. What is lacking is a complete syntactic and semantic description of the language. This is the subject of Chapter 4, "The Tower of Babel Revisited." At this point, I will pursue the subject of how the TIL works, not what it does.

2.2 Dictionary Format —————————————————————

Since approximately 90% of a threaded interpretive language consists of dictionary entries, an explanation of their general form is in order. Most dictionary entries consist of a *header* and a *body* located in consecutive memory. The header is optional. The header is used by a *search* algorithm to locate the address of the first word in the body of a specific keyword. This address (where the keyword is located) is called the *word address* of the keyword. The headers form a linear *linked list* to facilitate location of the word address in a reasonable length of time.

Several alternate header formats can be realized. The form I use for a microcomputer consists of 6 bytes: the number of characters in the keyword name (1 byte), the ASCII code for the first three characters in the keyword name (3 bytes), and a pointer to the first header location of the preceding dictionary entry (2 bytes). The pointer is called the *link address* or *link*. A typical dictionary organization for this type of implementation is shown in figure 2.1.

Note that 3 bytes are always allocated in this format for keyword names. If there are fewer than three characters in the keyword name — < R, for example — the unused characters can be anything since the search algorithm will be designed to test only the length plus the number of characters specified by the length up to a maximum of three. If there are more than three characters in the keyword name, those characters in excess of three are not used to identify the keyword. Thus DROP and DROX identify the same keyword but DROP and DROPIT identify different keywords because their lengths are different.

The link address allows the search algorithm to step to the preceding header if the current header does not match the token scanned from the input buffer. The link address of the last dictionary entry has a value of zero. This is an easy value to test for and indicates that the search has terminated unsuccessfully. The zero value is unlikely to prove restrictive.

Some dictionary entries do not have headers. A typical example of this type of entry is the literal handler for numbers. The system knows the word address, but the operator does not. If a number is input to a keyword being defined in the compile mode, the system will automatically load the word address of the number literal handler to the threaded-code listing and then the number. The operator has no reason to know the word address of the literal handler. Header bytes are superfluous in this case.

Clearly, alternate header formats are possible. A common extension is to allocate storage for up to five characters of the keyword name. This increases the header requirements from 6 to 8 bytes. Although this does not appear to cost much in terms of memory, it does. A 4 K-byte TIL usually contains about 150 keywords with headers. At 2 bytes extra per header, a 300-byte memory penalty occurs. (For the more mathematically inclined, the answer is

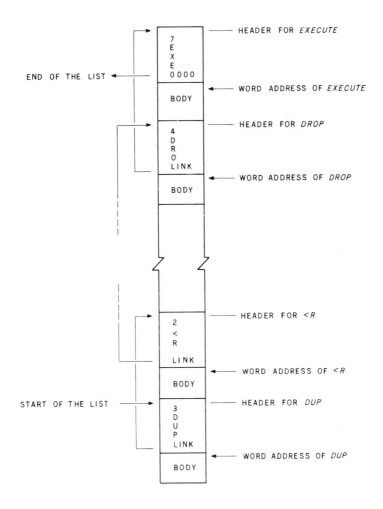

HEADER FOR *EXECUTE*

WORD ADDRESS OF *EXECUTE*

HEADER FOR *DROP*

WORD ADDRESS OF *DROP*

HEADER FOR *<R*

WORD ADDRESS OF *<R*

HEADER FOR *DUP*

WORD ADDRESS OF *DUP*

END OF THE LIST

START OF THE LIST

Figure 2.1: *Typical dictionary organization.*

4 K-bytes/150 keywords = 27 bytes/keyword. Few keywords exceed 20 bytes in length, including the header bytes. The less than 30-byte average keyword length is correct. The difference is due to a few long routines used to mechanize the outer interpreter and the headerless routines.)

The 2-byte link is standard as is the single token-length byte. Since the keyword names are rarely over ten characters long, one bit of the length character can be used to identify immediate keywords (keywords that are executed in the compile mode). I will expand my comments on this when vocabularies are discussed.

The body of the dictionary entry contains the implementation details of the keyword. The body may be *active* or *passive*. An active body produces an action and is associated with operands, directives, programs, and similar functions. A passive body contains data of some type. The first word (16 bits) of the code body (ie: the contents of the word address) implicitly specifies the code body type. This word is called the *code address* of the keyword, and it always points to executable machine code. This routine either initiates the action of an active body or manipulates the data of a passive body.

Active keywords (primitives or secondaries) have a body which consists of a *code address*, a *code body*, and a *return address*. The code body of a primitive always consists of machine code. The code body of a secondary always consists of a list of word addresses of previously defined primitive or secondary keywords. Embedded in this list may be literal handler word addresses followed by literal data, or program-control directive-word addresses followed by relative jump constants. Literals may be numbers or lists of ASCII data. The relative jump constants allow the program sequence to be modified so that loop and branch constructs can be mechanized.

The code address and return address of the code bodies control the tree-structured nature of the language via the inner interpreter. The controlling program or *executive* for the threaded interpretive language or program must be a secondary. The code address of a primitive points to the first byte of the code body of the primitive. The return address of the primitive transfers control to an inner interpreter routine which extracts the next word address of the current secondary.

The consequence of this sequence is that a primitive is analogous to a subroutine with a return terminating the machine code that implements the keyword action. The code address of a secondary points to an inner interpreter routine which saves the address of the next word address of the current secondary on the return stack and makes the first word address of the new secondary current. In effect, this is nesting down one level: looking for a primitive in the new secondary to execute. The return address of a secondary points to an inner interpreter routine which retrieves the word address on the return stack and makes it current. This is in effect de-nesting one level: returning to the next word address of the secondary that called the terminating secondary.

If all of this sounds confusing, don't panic — it is. Actually, it will all be discussed again in this chapter when the inner interpreter is investigated and when an implementation scheme is considered. To add a sense of mystery, the passive code body discussion will be delayed until later.

2.3 Outer Interpreter

If the inner interpreter is the heart of a threaded interpretive language, the outer interpreter is its soul. The outer interpreter establishes the *man-machine interface*. All of the external attributes of the language are affected by the design of this routine. The outer interpreter is written in TIL. A simple flow diagram of the outer interpreter will suffice at this stage.

Figure 2.2 is one possible realization of an outer interpreter. The routines perform the following tasks:

START/RESTART — Initializes the stack pointers and system variables to establish the *execution mode* under operator control. It is entered on start-up or in the event a system-detected error occurs.

INLINE — This routine fills and displays the input line buffer via the input keyboard. It recognizes backspace, the line delete command and terminates on carriage return.

MASS — Fills the input line buffer from a mass storage device. A virtual memory mechanization is usually used.

TOKEN — Scans the next token from the input line buffer and moves it to the end of the *dictionary space* (the place where new routines will be added) in *extended header form*. (It must include all token characters in case it is a number or cannot be recognized.)

OK — If the line buffer is empty and the terminal is the input device, a successful end-of-line message is displayed to the operator.

SEARCH — Searches the dictionary looking for a keyword header that matches the token. Returns the word address of the token, if it is located, by pushing it to the stack. Always returns a flag on the stack indicating success or failure.

?EXECUTE — If the system is in the *execute mode*, the keyword is executed. Note that both active and passive keywords have code addresses that point to routines which perform some action. Control normally returns to ?EXECUTE unless an unconditional jump to the START/RESTART routine or system monitor is executed or unless the keyword itself contains an endless loop. If the system is in the *compile mode*, two events are possible. If the keyword is an *immediate keyword*, it is executed. Immediate keywords are either *compiler directives* which implement literals and program control directives or a *compile mode termination directive*. If the keyword is not immediate, its word address is added to the threaded list of the new keyword being compiled. ?EXECUTE tests for stack underflow or overflow errors before exiting.

?STACK — If a stack error is detected following execution, an error message is displayed and control is passed back to the operator via the START/RESTART routine. If the error is detected while the compile mode is in effect, the partially completed keyword defintion being compiled is deleted.

NUMBER — If the token is neither a carriage return nor a keyword, this routine attempts to convert the token to a binary number using the current system *number base*. (Number bases are in the set 2 thru 9, A thru Z with A = 10, B = 11, etc.) If a successful conversion occurs, one of two events can result: if the compile mode is in effect, a literal handler followed by the number is added to the keyword threaded list being compiled. If the execution mode is in effect, the number is pushed to the stack.

QUESTION — If the token is not a carriage return, an existing keyword, or a number, somebody goofed. The offending token is echo displayed to the operator followed by "?" or WHAT? (or whatever) and control reverts to the operator.

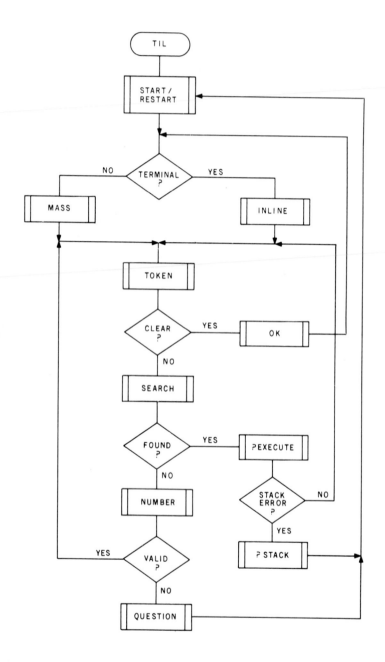

Figure 2.2: *Outer interpreter example.*

It is obvious from the description of the routines that two separate system modes exist, a *compile mode* and an *execution mode*. In the execution mode, each token scanned from the input line is tested as follows:

- If the line buffer is empty and the operator mode is in effect, an OK is printed. Control is returned to get the next input line.
- If it is a keyword, it is executed.
- If it is a valid number, it is pushed onto the stack.
- If it is not recognized, it is echoed to the operator followed by "?".

During the compile mode a slightly more complex scheme is used. The compile mode is building a new dictionary entry which may have branches or literal data embedded in the threaded code. Two classes of keywords are important. *Immediate* keywords are executed when encountered to allow the system to generate appropriate sequences of threaded code to append to the keyword being defined or to terminate the compiler mode. That is, when an immediate keyword is encountered in the compile mode, it is executed immediately. All keywords which are not immediate are not executed. Their word addresses are simply added to the definition being compiled. In the compile mode, each token scanned from the input line is tested as follows:

- If the line buffer is empty and the operator mode is in effect, an OK is printed. Control is returned to get the next input line.
- If it is located and is an immediate keyword, it is executed.
- If it is found and it is not an immediate keyword, its word address is added to the threaded list of the keyword being defined.
- If it is a valid number, the number literal is added to the threaded list of the word being defined followed by the number.
- If it is not recognized, it is echoed to the operator followed by "?" and the partially completed keyword being defined is deleted.

Clearly, the method of re-establishing the execution mode is through the use of an immediate keyword which terminates the definition.

The dictionary space for the system must be in programmable memory as must be the input line buffers and the stack areas. The inner and outer interpreter and the core language may be in read-only memory, but normally they are also in programmable memory. One possible system configuration is shown in figure 2.3. The *dictionary pointer* points to the next available memory area where language extensions can be added. As definitions are added, the language grows upward in memory.

As each token is scanned from the input buffer, its length plus all of its characters are moved to the dictionary space. This is a convenient place to hold temporary data. The use of an extended dictionary format to hold tokens is designed to allow easy enclosure of the characters to form a dictionary header, but all characters must be moved in case it is a number or cannot be located.

The data stack area builds downward and the language builds upward in the free memory area. When the two meet, the ball game is over. Stack overflows are fatal since they inevitably overwrite the language. Not much can be done about this situation since a runaway stack will eventually overwrite the program no matter where you initially hide the stack pointer.

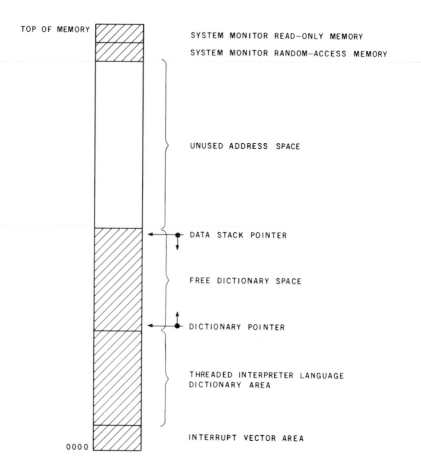

Figure 2.3: *Typical memory configuration.*

2.4 Inner Interpreter

The crux of a threaded interpreter is the inner interpreter. The inner interpreter controls the order of execution of the machine code which mechanizes the language. It is composed of three short, fast routines, one of which has three entrances as shown in figure 2.4. The layout of the bodies of dictionary entries is predicated on the inner interpreter routines. The dictionary bodies of a primitive and a secondary are shown in figure 2.5 for a byte-addressed computer.

All secondaries except the secondary which forms the outer loop of the threaded program have a code address and a return address. The outer loop of the program is a loop. The last word address of the outer loop causes a jump back to the first word address of the loop. In the threaded interpreter being discussed, this outer loop is the outer interpreter. A glance back to figure 2.2 will verify this endless loop aspect of the outer interpreter. This outer loop is the executive for the program.

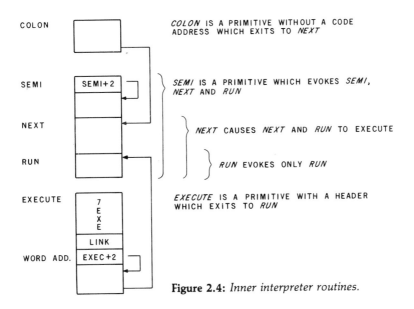

Figure 2.4: *Inner interpreter routines.*

The code body of the outer loop is a list of the word addresses of previously defined keywords. The inner interpreter maintains a register called the *instruction register*. It contains the address of the next secondary instruction to be executed. Since the outer loop is a secondary, there will always be a next secondary address to be executed. The inner interpreter routine which will execute the next secondary instruction is called NEXT.

The routine NEXT extracts the word address of the next instruction pointed to by the instruction register, places it in a *word address register* and increments the instruction register by two. In figure 2.5 if the instruction register contained WA+2, the routine NEXT would extract WA#1 and leave the instruction register containing WA+4. It is desired to run the routine WA#1 which is now the current instruction. WA#1 is the word address of the routine to be executed. WA#1 may point to either a primitive or a secondary.

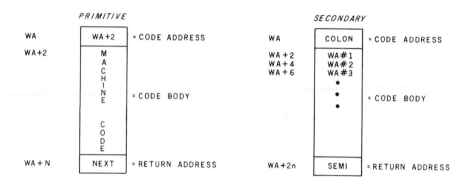

Figure 2.5: *Code body descriptions.*

When NEXT completes, it falls through to the routine called RUN to run the routine. The routine RUN extracts the code address pointed to by the word-address register (WA#1 in our example), increments the word-address register by two, and loads the code address to the program counter in the central processing unit. The next machine code instruction to be executed will be the contents of the word address of routine WA#1, ie: its code address. The code address of both primitives and secondaries *must* point to executable machine code.

If the word address was that of a primitive, the code address extracted by RUN points to the first instruction in the code body of the primitive. Thus, the primitive's machine code will be executed. The return address of the primitive is an instruction which jumps back to the routine NEXT. In the example, if WA#1 was the word address of a primitive, it will return to NEXT after the primitive executes. The instruction register now contains WA+4 so that the next secondary instruction to be run will be WA#2.

If the word address was that of a secondary, the code address extracted by RUN points to the inner interpreter routine COLON. Note that the RUN routine incremented the word address by two so that it points to WA#1+2. The routine COLON pushes the instruction register contents onto the return stack and moves the word address register to the instruction register. In our example, WA+4 would be placed on the return stack and WA#1+2 would be placed in the instruction register. COLON then jumps to NEXT. The address WA#1+2 is the first secondary instruction address in the now-current keyword WA#1. COLON effectively nests down one level to begin execution of the lower-level routine WA#1.

The return address of a secondary is a primitive called SEMI. SEMI simply pops the top address from the return stack and loads the address to the instruction register. In our example, it would pop the address WA+4 and load it to the instruction register. SEMI exits to NEXT so that in the example, WA#2 will be the next secondary instruction. SEMI de-nests one level to begin execution of the next instruction of the higher-level routine (WA#2 in the example).

In all of the above, the only machine codes actually executed are primitives and inner interpreter routines. Secondaries may call secondaries that call secondaries, but the bottom of the chain is always a primitive which actually executes program machine code. Structurally the procedure forms a tree, the end nodes (end branches) of which are always primitives.

All of this is well and good, but how does the outer interpreter ever execute a keyword? Actually it is simple. The search algorithm in the outer interpreter locates the word address of a valid keyword and pushes it to the data stack. If the routine is to be executed, the routine ?EXECUTE calls the primitive called EXECUTE. EXECUTE pops the word address from the data stack, loads it to the word address register and jumps to RUN. Note that the instruction register contains the address of the instruction following EXECUTE in the ?EXECUTE routine so that after the execution of the token, control reverts to the outer interpreter.

EXECUTE is the only inner interpreter routine with a header. The word addresses of SEMI and code address COLON are known by other routines within the language, as are the entrances for NEXT and RUN. The routines SEMI, NEXT and RUN are generally a single routine with three entrances while EXECUTE and COLON exist as separate entities.

Several points are important. The instruction register is the effective program counter for the interpreter. It must be carefully preserved by primitive machine-code routines. Similar caution must be exercised with regard to the return stack. When SEMI pops the top entry from the return stack, it had best be a valid word address and not some temporary value inadvertently left on the return stack. Finally, note that the word address register always points to the first location of the code body when RUN has been completed. This is not only important in the routine COLON but also will be important when passive code bodies are considered.

If this is confusing, do not despair. It will be considered in great detail in Chapter 3, "Hup, Two, Three, Four."

2.5 Defining Words and the Compile Mode

Writing a threaded interpretive program consists of defining new keywords. These definitions may be coded in machine code, assembly language, or compiled using previously defined keywords to create more complex keywords. The final program is simply another keyword.

The language contains a number of predefined *defining words*. Defining words always create a dictionary header. All defining words are evoked in the execution mode. The keyword that initiates the compiler mode (ASCII :) is a defining word (ie: it is evoked in the execution mode and creates a dictionary entry). All defining words except ":" return the system to the execution mode on completion. The compile mode is established by the keyword ":" and terminated by the keyword ";" or ;CODE, both of which re-establish the execution mode among other things. These latter two keywords are immediate keywords and are executed only in the compile mode.

All defining words create a dictionary header from the token following the defining word in the input buffer. (Note that the defining words must be defined themselves before they can be evoked. Predefinitions of some routines are necessary.)

The simplest defining word is CREATE. For example:

CREATE■GODZILLA■ ■OK

This sequence will create a primitive header for a keyword named GODZILLA. The keyword CREATE first parses the token GODZILLA from the input buffer and moves it to the dictionary space as 8GODZILLA. Next, it advances the dictionary pointer contents (a system variable called DP) by four to enclose 8GOD in the dictionary. It extracts the address of the last keyword header from the current vocabulary, encloses it in the dictionary as the link address, and then replaces the current vocabulary address with the address of the 8 in the 8GODZILLA header. Finally, CREATE encloses the address of DP+2 (the code address) at the DP address location (the word address).

CREATE simply creates a primitive dictionary header but does not reserve any bytes in the code body of the word being defined. Creating GODZILLA is far simpler than foreign film makers could possibly imagine. Basically, all defining words evoke CREATE to form the dictionary header and then replace the code address as appropriate. The compiler word ":" calls CREATE and then replaces the code address with the address of the inner interpreter COLON routine. Now you see why that funny name was selected for this inner interpreter routine.

Although CREATE appears to be useless by itself, this is not true. For example, a word could be defined to drop the top value from the data stack using the sequence:

HEX■CREATE■DROP■E1■C,■NEXT■ ■OK

First HEX establishes the system number base as hexadecimal. CREATE creates a primitive keyword named DROP. The E1 is a valid hexadecimal number and is pushed to the data stack since the execution mode is in effect. The C, pops the data stack and encloses the low-order byte in the dictionary (the E1). Finally, NEXT encloses the jump to the inner interpreter NEXT routine in the dictionary. When DROP is evoked, the machine instruction E1 is executed, which pops the top of the data stack to the HL register pair and then executes a jump to NEXT. The value popped to the HL register pair is never used. The value is simply dropped from the data stack. This is a simple example of extending the language using machine code to create a new primitive keyword.

An example of a compiling word is:

: ■2DUP ■DUP ■DUP ■ ; ■ ■OK

Here a keyword DUP has already been defined. This keyword duplicates the top stack value leaving two copies of the value on the stack. The keyword 2DUP is designed to leave three copies of the previous top stack value on the stack by calling DUP twice. Here ":" creates a 2DUP keyword dictionary entry with the COLON routine code address in its word address (ie: it creates a secondary dictionary header and then sets the system mode to the compile mode). The next token scanned is DUP. The search routine will locate its word address since it is already defined. The outer interpreter routine ?EXECUTE will enclose the word address of DUP in the dictionary since the compile mode, not the execute mode, is in effect. This will occur again when the second DUP in the input buffer is scanned. The keyword ";" is an immediate keyword which will be executed in the compile mode. It encloses the word address of the inner interpreter primitive routine SEMI in the dictionary and sets the system mode to the execute mode. Here the language extension is a new secondary keyword created from existing keywords via the compile mode.

A typical defining word is CONSTANT. CONSTANT defines a passive keyword which, when evoked, will push a constant value to the data stack. An example of its use is:

DECIMAL ■288 ■CONSTANT ■2GROSS

Here the keyword DECIMAL sets the system number base to the decimal (10) base, the 288 is pushed to the stack as a binary number and CONSTANT creates the dictionary entry for the keyword 2GROSS with a code body whose contents are 0120, the hexadecimal equivalent of 288 decimal. When 2GROSS is evoked it will always push hexadecimal 0120 to the data stack.

Obviously a definition of CONSTANT is required before 2GROSS can be defined. A formal definition of CONSTANT is:

HEX ■ : ■CONSTANT ■CREATE ■ , ■ ;CODE ■....

Here "..." indicates machine code that will be entered following ;CODE. First the ":" creates a secondary dictionary header for CONSTANT and sets the compile mode. The CREATE and "," word addresses are then placed in the code body of CONSTANT. The ;CODE keyword is an immediate keyword which places the word address of a routine called SCODE in the code body of CONSTANT and sets the system mode to the execute mode. The machine code that follows ;CODE in the definition is machine-specific, but the action it is to implement is universal. The code will extract the word pointed to by the word-address register and push it to the data stack and then jump to the inner interpreter routine NEXT. Note that this code is not executed when CONSTANT is defined, but is added to the dictionary definition of CONSTANT.

There are three levels of action: one when CONSTANT is defined, one when 2GROSS is defined, and one when 2GROSS is evoked. When 2GROSS is defined, the keyword CONSTANT is called. CONSTANT first creates a primitive header called 2GROSS by the call to CREATE. The keyword "," in CONSTANT will pop the data stack and enclose the value in the dictionary. In the example, it pops the hexadecimal 0120 (288 decimal) from the stack and places it in the body of 2GROSS. The keyword SCODE in CONSTANT replaces the code address of the word being defined by the address of the word following its location and then returns to the inner interpreter routine NEXT. The result is diagrammed in figure 2.6.

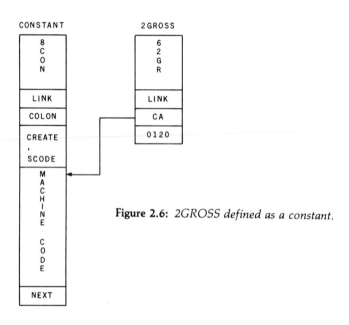

Figure 2.6: *2GROSS defined as a constant.*

When 2GROSS is evoked, its code address points to the machine code following the SCODE in CONSTANT. This code will be executed. However, the inner interpreter routine RUN will leave the word-address register contents at the address of the 0120 following the code address of 2GROSS. The machine code, as explained, will extract the word located at the word-address register location and push it to the stack (ie: it pushes hexadecimal 0120 to the stack). All constants defined using CONSTANT have code addresses which point to the machine code in CONSTANT.

The keyword ;CODE is the critical factor in defining generic data types. It allows the specification of actions (machine code) that allow the creation of data types. The machine code that follows ;CODE is a generic primitive consisting of a body and a return. The address for this primitive is always stored in the word-address location of the word being defined.

So far, examples of defining new keywords directly in machine code by compiling new definitions and using defining words have been presented. Even more examples will be given in Chapter 4, "The Tower of Babel Revisited."

2.6 Vocabularies

Although it has been mentioned that the dictionary is segmented into vocabularies, no rationale for this has been presented. There are several reasons for this segmentation. Fundamentally it presents a functional separation of the language. A full-blown text editor may be desirable sometimes, but a modest editor may be resident in the core language. By vocabulary control, keyword names that could be in contention are resolved. Another reason for different vocabularies is that certain keywords can be hidden. Compiler directives, for example, are only used in the compile mode. If the operator called these directives in the execution mode, stack errors would result and it is possible for the program to consume itself.

The basic vocabulary structure is a tree with the *core language* as the trunk. Each vocabulary is named and its location exists in a passive keyword in the core. This is illustrated in figure 2.7. Note that some vocabularies are normally hidden but may be linked to the core in special circumstances. Others may be *lost* by the simple expedient of not including headers.

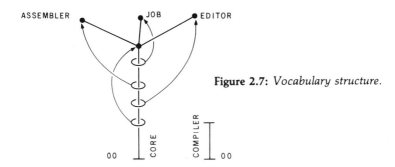

Figure 2.7: *Vocabulary structure.*

The vocabulary search order determines how keywords are located. Each vocabulary is a linear-linked list by virtue of its header format. Two keywords can have precisely the same identifying name. The first one located will terminate the search. It is this keyword that will be used by the outer interpreter. New definitions are always linked to the top of an existing vocabulary. Redefining an existing keyword will cause any subsequent reference to use the new definition. Any preexisting routine which calls the old definition will continue to use the old definition. This results from the fact that the word address of the old definition is extant in all preexisting routines. It has been compiled and will not change.

A dictionary search begins at the address contained in the variable CONTEXT. This variable is set when the name of a vocabulary is used. For example, the keyword CORE is the core language vocabulary name and its use sets CONTEXT to point to CORE which contains the address of the first dictionary header in the core language. New keyword definitions are linked to the vocabulary specified by the variable CURRENT. The keyword DEFINITIONS sets CURRENT to CONTEXT. Some defining words also affect CONTEXT. The keyword ":", which establishes the compiling mode, sets CONTEXT to CURRENT while the defining word CODE, which evokes the assembler vocabulary, sets CONTEXT to ASSEMBLER.

Keywords from different vocabularies can be interlaced in memory; they need not be contiguous. New definitions are always added to the top of the language. They build up in memory space and are linked to the CURRENT vocabulary. A keyword FORGET will cause removal of dictionary entries in a spatial sense. If the keyword name following FORGET is in the CURRENT vocabulary, the keyword and all subsequent keywords will be forgotten. FORGET sets CONTEXT to CURRENT, locates the keyword, resets CURRENT to the link address of the located keyword and resets the dictionary pointer DP to the first header byte of the located keyword. Care is advised in the use of FORGET. It is possible to forget the entire language.

The use of the keyword IMMEDIATE causes the top entry of the CURRENT vocabulary to be made an immediate keyword (ie: can be executed only in the compile mode).

Some comments are needed concerning immediate words, dictionary headers, and lost vocabulary words. A standard technique for defining an immediate keyword is to set a precedence bit somewhere in the header (generally the length-parameter, high-order bit). If this bit is set, the keyword is executed regardless of the mode. I do not like this technique. I usually establish a separate compiler vocabulary for immediate words. This vocabulary is searched only if the compile mode is in effect. This prevents compiler directives from being executed in the execute mode. The compiler directives load the word addresses of program-control directives to the dictionary and muck around with the stacks. There is never a reason for executing a compiler directive in the execution mode. The program control directives do not have headers and thus cannot be located by the search algorithm. The compiler directives know the word addresses of their associated program control directives. No other keyword needs this information. The operator does not need to know this information either.

2.7 Synthesis

Synthesizing this chapter is essential to understanding the threaded interpretive language concept. All of the elements are interdependent. The dictionary formats, the interpreters, the stacks, the defining words, the compiling mode, and the vocabularies are all predicated on the form and function of each other. If you do not feel comfortable with some element, try rereading it. If this does not work, continue to the end. You may find the answer to what's bugging you.

3 | HUP, Two, Three, Four

*Some people have been audacious enough to claim that I
march to a different tune. Regardless of the validity of that,
I tell the truth when I claim that your TIL had best march
quickly through your code. And tirelessly too!*

3.1 An Inner Interpreter For A Generic Computer —————————

To fully illustrate the actions of an inner interpreter, I'm going to resort to
the old generic computer trick. The generic computer I will construct is not
very sophisticated: the inner interpreter code will be written, a primitive and a
secondary will be written, and then we will execute some code — at least on
paper.

The computer to be built will have several registers. Registers are not all that
important, but the principles are easier to understand this way. The same end
results can be achieved using memory locations in machines with fewer
registers. The registers are all 16-bit registers as follows:

Register	Description
I	Instruction register. Contains the address of the next instruction in the threaded list of the current secondary.
WA	Word Address register. Contains the word address of the current keyword or the address of the first code body location of the current keyword.
CA	Code Address register.
RS	Return Stack register.
SP	Stack Pointer register.
PC	Processor Program Counter register.

The instruction set necessary to illustrate the inner interpreter is fairly simple. A byte-oriented addressing scheme is presumed (ie: I + 2 is the next word in memory following memory word location I). All instructions are presumed to be one word in length. The following instruction set is assumed:

Instruction	Description
@A→B	The contents of the memory location word whose address is in register A are loaded into register B (a 16-bit indirect fetch from A to B).
A = A + n	The contents of register A are incremented by the constant n.
POP S→A	The S push down stack top entry is loaded to register A and the stack pointer is adjusted.
PSH A→S	The A register contents are loaded to the S push down stack and the stack pointer is adjusted.
A→PC	The contents of the A register are loaded into the PC. The processor will fetch its next instruction from this location.
JMP XX	Unconditional jump to the address contained in the word following the jump instruction.

Note: — A and B are any of I, WA, or CA.
     — S is either RS or SP.

The inner interpreter can be written as in listing 3.1.

Location	Mnemonic	Instruction	Comment
0140	COLON	PSH I→RS	
0142		WA→I	
0144		JMP	} Jump to NEXT
0146		0104	
0100	SEMI	0102	Code address of SEMI
0102		POP RS→I	
0104	NEXT	@I→WA	
0106		I = I + 2	
0108	RUN	@WA→CA	
010A		WA = WA + 2	
010C		CA→PC	
0050		7E	} Dictionary
0052		XE	header
0054		LA	for EXECUTE
0056	EXECUTE	0058	Code address of EXECUTE

```
0058                    POP SP→WA
005A                    JMP          }
005C                    0108         }  Jump to RUN
                                     }
```

Listing 3.1: *Pseudo-code implementation of inner interpreter.*

That's it! The entire inner interpreter is just 36 bytes long.

All of this may appear hopelessly complex or ridiculously simple. Unless the details and beauty of the inner interpreter are appreciated, it is impossible to fully understand a threaded interpretive language.

Some points about this inner interpreter implementation:

- The I register is effectively the program counter for the threaded interpretive language. It must be preserved by all primitive machine code.
- Only the inner interpreter machine code and primitive machine code are ever executed.
- When the routine RUN completes, the WA register points to the address of the code body of the keyword. This fact is important in passive keyword definitions and in the COLON routine.
- The word address of SEMI, the value that terminates all secondaries, contains a word address value equal to the address of SEMI. Thus SEMI is a primitive.
- SEMI always executes NEXT and RUN; NEXT always executes RUN.
- The word address of all secondaries contains the address of the COLON routine. When the PSH I→RS instruction is executed, it saves the word address of the next instruction of the current secondary on the return stack. The instruction WA→I actually loads the word address of the first instruction of the new secondary into the instruction register (see third remark above).
- The routine EXECUTE is used by the outer interpreter to execute a keyword. The search algorithm returns the word address of a located keyword on the stack. EXECUTE pops this word address into WA and jumps to RUN. This causes the keyword to be executed but control returns to the outer interpreter at completion since the I register contains the word address of the keyword following the outer interpreter EXECUTE location.

A modestly complex but fundamentally simple scenario will be developed to illustrate several aspects of the inner interpreter. Assume that a constant with value 288 has been defined as 2GROSS. A primitive routine called DUP that duplicates the top stack exists. A secondary that duplicates the top stack value twice is desired. It is defined as:

: ■2DUP ■DUP ■DUP ■;■ ■OK

A routine named FUNNY is needed that leaves three values of 288 on the stack for some funny reason. It is defined as:

: ■FUNNY■2GROSS■2DUP■ ; ■ ■OK

Finally FUNNY will be executed as:

FUNNY■ ■OK

The resulting memory contents after this sequence will be presumed to be as shown in listing 3.2.

Location	Contents	Comments
1000	0056	EXECUTE location in
1002	XXXX	outer interpreter
2000	3D ⎫	Dictionary header
2002	UP ⎬	for the
2004	LA ⎭	primitive DUP
2006	2008	DUP's word address
2008	POP SP→CA	Code that duplicates
200A	PSH CA→SP	the stack
200C	PSH CA→SP	
200E	JMP ⎱	Jump to NEXT
2010	0104 ⎰	
2100	8C	Dictionary header
2102	ON	for the secondary
2104	LA	defining keyword CONSTANT
2106	0140	COLON Address
2108	CREATE ⎫	Actually addresses but
210A	, ⎬	not important for
210C	SCODE ⎭	the example
210E	@WA→CA	Code to extract a
2110	PSH CA→SP	constant and push it
2112	JMP ⎱	Jump to NEXT
2114	0104 ⎰	
2050	62 ⎫	Dictionary header
2052	GR ⎬	for the constant
2054	LA ⎭	2GROSS
2056	210E	Pointer to CONSTANT code
2058	0120	Decimal 288 in hexadecimal
2200	42 ⎫	Dictionary header for
2202	DU ⎬	the secondary
2204	LA ⎭	2DUP

2206	0140		COLON Address
2208	2006		DUP Address
220A	2006		DUP Address
220C	0100		SEMI Address
220E	5F	⎞	Dictionary header for
2210	UN	⎬	the secondary FUNNY
2212	2200	⎠	linked to 2DUP
2214	0140		COLON Address
2216	2056		2GROSS Address
2218	2206		2DUP Address
221A	0100		SEMI Address

Listing 3.2: *Memory contents after routine FUNNY has been compiled.*

In the dictionary header for FUNNY, the link address points to 2DUP since consecutive definitions were entered by the operator.

The scenario will begin with the word address of FUNNY (2214) on the stack and the outer interpreter just about to execute the EXECUTE word address (I contains 1000). The step-by-step march of the processor through the code is given in table 3.1.

While a careful examination of the code illustrates the principles, the example is not exactly tiptoeing through the tulips. Stomping, maybe, but tiptoeing — no. This is partially due to some not-too-neat scenario definitions. For instance, the definition of 2DUP as a primitive requires one more instruction than a DUP, or two more instructions than the 2DUP secondary form. If this were done, a NEXT-RUN-COLON, NEXT-RUN-DUP and NEXT-RUN-SEMI set of instructions would be replaced by the extra PSA CA→A instruction needed to implement a primitive 2DUP keyword. FUNNY is a funny definition simply because it is incomplete and does not do very much. If it were really required, a primitive machine-code keyword routine could be defined to both generate the hexadecimal 0120 and push it to the stack three times. This is far more efficient than the scenario definitions.

The code illustrated here uses post-indexing of the word and instruction registers. In processors with pre-indexing indirect memory fetches, or in most microcomputers, the indexing increments can occur before the fetches. This will affect the inner interpreter code and other routines which access the word and instruction registers.

3.2 An Inner Interpreter For the Z80 ————————————

In implementing any inner interpreter, careful consideration should be given

ROUTINE	PC INSTRUCTION	I	WA	CA	RS	SP	
NEXT	0104 @I→WA	1000	0056	—	—	2214	Set up to run EXECUTE
	0106 I=I+2	1002	0056	—	—	2214	
RUN	0108 @WA→CA	1002	0056	0058	—	2214	
	010A WA=WA+2	1002	0058	0058	—	2214	
	010C CA→PC	1002	0058	0058	—	2214	
EXECUTE	0058 POP SP→WA	1002	2214	0058	—	—	Run EXECUTE
	005A JMP 0108	1002	2214	0058	—	—	
RUN	0108 @WA→CA	1002	2214	0140	—	—	Set up to run FUNNY
	010A WA=WA+2	1002	2216	0140	—	—	
	010C CA→PC	1002	2216	0140	—	—	
COLON	0140 PSH I→RS	1002	2216	0140	1002	—	Nest down one level
	0142 WA→I	2216	2216	0140	1002	—	
	0144 JMP 0104	2216	2216	0140	1002	—	
NEXT	0104 @I→WA	2216	2056	0140	1002	—	Set to run 2GROSS
	0106 I=I+2	2218	2056	0140	1002	—	
RUN	0108 @WA→CA	2218	2056	210E	1002	—	
	010A WA=WA+2	2218	2058	210E	1002	—	
	010C CA→PC	2218	2058	210E	1002	—	
CONSTANT	210E @WA→CA	2218	2058	0120	1002	—	Run CONSTANT code to get the value
	2100 PSH CA→SP	2218	2058	0120	1002	0120	
	2112 JMP 0104	2218	2058	0120	1002	0120	
NEXT	0104 @I→WA	2218	2206	0120	1002	0120	Set up to run 2 DUP
	0106 I=I+2	221A	2206	0120	1002	0120	
RUN	0108 @WA→CA	221A	2206	0140	1002	0120	
	010A WA=WA+2	221A	2208	0140	1002	0120	
	010C CA→PC	221A	2208	0140	1002	0120	
COLON	0140 PSH I→RS	221A	2208	0140	221A, 1002	0120	Nest down one level
	0142 WA→I	2208	2208	1040	221A, 1002	0120	
	0144 JMP 0104	2208	2208	0140	221A, 1002	0120	
NEXT	0104 @I→WA	2208	2006	0140	221A, 1002	0120	Set up to run the first DUP
	0106 I=I+2	220A	2006	0140	221A, 1002	0120	
RUN	0108 @WA→CA	220A	2006	2008	221A, 1002	0120	
	010A WA=WA+2	220A	2008	2008	221A, 1002	0120	
	010C CA→PC	220A	2008	2008	221A, 1002	0120	
DUP	2008 POP SP→CA	220A	2008	0120	221A, 1002	—	Run the first DUP
	200A PSH CA→SP	220A	2008	0120	221A, 1002	0120	
	200C PSH CA→SP	220A	2008	0102	221A, 1002	0120,0120	
	200E JMP 0104	220A	2008	0120	221A, 1002	0120,0120	
NEXT	0104 @I→WA	220A	2006	0120	221A, 1002	0120,0120	Set up to run the second DUP
	0106 I=I+2	220C	2006	0120	221A, 1002	0120,0120	
RUN	0108 @WA→CA	220C	2006	2008	221A, 1002	0120,0120	
	010A WA=WA+2	220C	2008	2008	221A, 1002	0120,0120	
	010C CA→PC	220C	2008	2008	221A, 1002	0120,0120	
DUP	2008 POP SP→CA	220C	2008	0120	221A, 1002	0120	Run the second DUP
	200A PSH CA→SP	220C	2008	0120	221A, 1002	0120,0120	
	200C PSH CA→SP	220C	2008	0120	221A, 1002	0120,0120,0120	
	200E JMP 0104	220C	2008	0120	221A, 1002	0120,0120,0120	
NEXT	0104 @I→WA	220C	0100	0120	221A, 1002	0120,0120,0120	Set up to run SEMI in 2DUP
	0106 I=I+2	220E	0100	0120	221A, 1002	0120,0120,0120	
RUN	0108 @WA→CA	220E	0100	0102	221A, 1002	0120,0120,0120	
	010A WA=WA+2	220E	0102	0102	221A, 1002	0120,1020,0120	
	010C CA→PC	220E	0102	0102	221A, 1002	0120,0120,0120	
SEMI	0102 POP RS→I	221A	0102	0102	1002	0120,0120,0120	Denest 1 level
NEXT	0104 @I→WA	221A	0100	0102	1002	0120,0120,0120	Set up to run SEMI in FUNNY
	0106 I=I+2	221C	0100	0102	1002	0120,0120,0120	
RUN	0108 @WA→CA	221C	0100	0102	1002	0120,0120,0120	
	010A WA=WA+2	221C	0102	0102	1002	0120,0120,0120	
	010C CA→PC	221C	0102	0102	1002	0120,0120,0120	
SEMI	0102 POP RS→I	1002	0102	0102	—	0120,0120,0120	Denest 1 level
NEXT	0104 @I→WA	1002	XXXX	0102	—	0120,0120,0120	Set up to run outer interpreter routine following EXECUTE

Table 3.1: *Stepping through the pseudo-code for routine FUNNY.*

to maximizing the efficiency of the code in terms of execution speed. The faster the routines, the more efficient the TIL. The Z80 is not an ideal microcomputer for implementing a TIL. Fundamentally it does not have a high-speed, 16-bit, indirect memory-addressing mode. It does have an 8-bit, implied memory-addressing mode which can be used with a slight degree of difficulty to implement the inner interpreter.

To mechanize the inner interpreter, the Z80 registers are assigned as in table 3.2.

Register Pair Usage

AF	8-bit accumulator and program status word
BC	Instruction register
DE	Word address register and scratch register
HL	Scratch register
IX	Return stack pointer
IY	Address of NEXT
SP	Data stack pointer
AF'	
BC'	Scratch
DE'	
HL'	

Table 3.2: *Z80 register assignment.*

The HL register pair is also used as a 16-bit accumulator. The use of IY to contain the address of NEXT provides a quick way to perform a 2-byte jump to an absolute memory location (NEXT) via a JP (IY) instruction: an implied jump to the address contained in IY.

The particular method of arranging the data and return stacks affects the code used to implement the inner interpreter. The top 4 K bytes of my Z80 system are arranged as shown in figure 3.1. The system monitor uses the system 1 K bytes of programmable memory for stacks and variable storage. The threaded interpreter also uses this same area for its stacks.

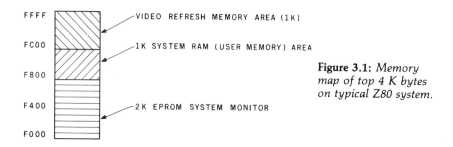

Figure 3.1: *Memory map of top 4 K bytes on typical Z80 system.*

The system programmable memory map is shown in figure 3.2. The first 128 bytes are reserved for input line buffers. The area immediately above the buffer area is reserved for the system monitor and TIL system variables. The data stack pointer is initialized to the top of this memory area and the return stack pointer to the middle of the memory. This implementation allocates 512 bytes to the data stack and about 300 bytes to the return stack with both stacks building downward in memory. Actually, I am cheating. The system monitor is a threaded interpreter which explains why the TIL system variables are located here in my system. It is more typical to locate the TIL system variables with the TIL code. The stack areas are more than adequate for any problem I have ever encountered, even though only 1 K was allocated. The data stack is used for temporary parameter storage. If great numbers of user variables are required, the top of the low-order memory should be partitioned into blocks for this data storage. (A TIL will not "create" memory. A 4 K-byte TIL and a 4 K-byte BASIC leave the same free memory space — in any given system — for programs and variables. TIL programs tend to use less memory, leaving more room for variables.)

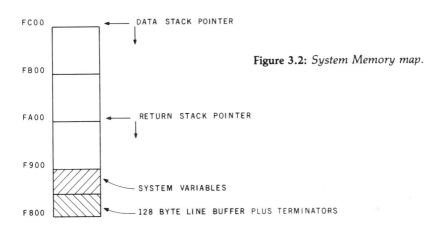

Figure 3.2: *System Memory map.*

Assume the inner interpreter is to be located in low memory. One mechanization of the inner interpreter is given in table 3.3. Several interesting features can be learned from this specific mechanization as opposed to the generic computer inner interpreter.

The Z80, as many other microcomputers, accesses the low-order byte in the first memory location and the high-order byte as the second location when an address (word) is accessed from memory. This order is maintained when the return stack is accessed. This is obvious in both the SEMI and COLON routine, as in table 3.3. It is clear from these routines that the implied, 8-bit address scheme requires at least twice the number of instructions as the generic computer with its single, indirect, 16-bit addressing instruction. Furthermore, the use of the IX register for implied addressing is substantially slower than using the main Z80 registers as may be noted from the "T" state or timing states associated with each instruction.

The time efficiency of a TIL keyword can be computed from knowledge of the inner interpreter timing and the keyword timing. Stepping from primitive

LOCATION	CONTENTS	ASSEMBLY CODE		"T" STATES
0100	0201	SEMI:	* +2	
0102	DD4E00	LD	C,{IX +0}	19
0105	DD23	INC	IX	10
0107	DD4600	LD	B,{IX +0}	19
010A	DD23	INC	IX	10 = 58
010C	0A	NEXT: LD	A,{BC}	7
010D	6F	LD	L,A	4
010E	03	INC	BC	6
010F	0A	LD	A,{BC}	7
0110	67	LD	H,A	4
0111	03	INC	BC	6 = 34
0112	5E	RUN: LD	E,{HL}	7
0113	23	INC	HL	6
0114	56	LD	D,{HL}	7
0115	23	INC	HL	6
0116	EB	EX	DE,HL	4
0117	E9	JP	{HL}	4 = 34
0118	DD2B	COLON: DEC	IX	10
011A	DD7000	LD	{IX +0},B	19
011D	DD2B	DEC	IX	10
011F	DD7100	LD	{IX +0},C	19
0122	4B	LD	C,E	4
0123	42	LD	B,D	4
0124	FDE9	JP	{IY}	8 = 74
0126	07455845	DATA	7,E,X,E	
012A	0000	DATA	00	
012C	2E01	EXECUTE:	* +2	
012E	E1	POP	HL	
012F	18E1	JR	RUN	

Table 3.3: *A Z80 inner interpreter.*

to primitive within a secondary always requires an execution of NEXT, RUN, the primitive code body, and the return to NEXT for each step. A primitive always terminates with a JP (IY) instruction as its return. Thus, for the Z80 inner interpreter:

$$\text{'T' Primitive} = \text{NEXT} + \text{RUN} + \text{body} + \text{JP (IY)}$$
$$= 34 + 34 + \text{body} + 8$$
$$= 76 + \text{body}$$

Primitive primitives are extremely inefficient. The primitive DROP requires a single POP HL instruction in its code body with a "T" state requirement of ten states. If the primitive code was simply strung together (that is, truly compiled), this keyword would require ten states rather than the eighty-six states required of the TIL definition. The "inefficiency" of the TIL is then:

$$\% \text{ Inefficiency } = \frac{\text{total} - \text{body}}{\text{body}} \times 100$$

DROP is thus 760% inefficient relative to compiled code. The arithmetic multiply routine "*" requires 384 to 464 T states to complete. Thus "*" has an inefficiency of 16 to 20% relative to compiled code.

The timing inefficiency of secondaries is more difficult to assess. It is clear, however, that each call to a secondary requires a NEXT-RUN-COLON and a NEXT-RUN-SEMI on entrance and exit. If we return to the 2DUP example of table 3.3, a DUP keyword costs thirty-two T states and a primitive 2DUP costs forty-three T states. Thus for 2DUP:

Secondary = NEXT + RUN + COLON + NEXT + RUN + DUP
        + RET + NEXT + RUN + DUP + RET + NEXT
        + RUN + SEMI
        = 34 + 34 + 74 + 34 + 34 + <u>32</u> + 8 + 34 + 34
        + <u>32</u> + 8 + 34 + 34 + 58
        = 420 + <u>64</u> = 484
Primitive = NEXT + RUN + 2DUP + RET
        = 34 + 34 + <u>43</u> + 8
        = 76 + <u>43</u> = 119

The secondary form of 2DUP requires about four times as long to execute as does the primitive form. The inefficiency of the 2DUP forms are:

$$\text{Secondary} = \frac{484 - 43}{43} = 1026\%$$

$$\text{Primitive} = \frac{76}{43} = 177\%$$

This explains why I prefer all operator-available keywords to be primitives.

The nice feature about a TIL is that the primitives can be as complex as desired. In a truly time-critical application, it is possible to resort to machine code. In applications that are not time-critical, the ease of defining keywords as secondaries is available. The speed of the outer interpreter is never a problem. Believe me, it is much quicker than the operator.

As should be clear from the Z80 inner interpreter example, care must be exercised in designing an inner interpreter. Not only must the register allocation be optimized for inner interpreter speed, but the stack location and mechanization must also be considered.

3.3 Double Time

Almost inevitably, the first thought that enters a programmer's mind about any program is: "How can I speed it up?" There are several ways to speed up a TIL. Most fundamental is to select a processor with an optimal set of addressing modes. For instance, compare my Z80 with an indirect, 16-bit, addressing machine. Naturally it helps to operate the chip at its maximum possible speed. (I run a Z80A processor at 2.5 MHz rather than its 4 MHz limit to insure reliability.) Almost all attempts to "speed up" a given processor and program combination result in the "times 2" phenomenon — careful "tuning" may increase the speed of an average routine by two. There are limits to how much is gained by optimization.

The next question almost always involves microcoding a particular machine to optimize its execution relative to a particular language. Microcode has nothing to do with microcomputer code — it is a means of implementing a usable processing instruction set through the use of a faster and more primitive internal processor. This internal processor executes microcode to implement the functions necessary to emulate the instruction set. The instruction set which the processor executes can be changed by changing the microcode.

If this approach is used to mechanize the instructions required to implement the inner interpreter, a faster TIL could result, one possibly twice as fast as the same processor without the specialized instructions. Taking things one step further, the inner interpreter and the primitives necessary to create all other keywords (say forty to sixty primitives) could be microcoded. The inflexibility of the instruction set is the disadvantage of this approach. Speed is gained in the primitives themselves, but there is no option to use "machine code" since the only "machine codes" are the primitives.

Among the 8-bit microcomputer chips available today, the Signetics 2650 probably has the best instruction set for TIL implementation. The RCA 1802 is also reasonable. The more popular Z80, 8080, 6502 and 6800 are not the best but they are viable. Integer TILs based on these microcomputers are only three to four times as fast as integer BASICs. The expected upgrades to the 8-bit microcomputers such as the 6809 should cure the speed problem. Most minicomputers are fundamentally 16-bit machines and usually have more addressing modes than microcomputers. Minicomputers are generally far more efficient than microcomputers in a threaded interpreter environment.

4 | The Tower of Babel Revisited

*A plethora of keyword actions is possible. I shall explore
a subset of the more common actions. Like a menu in a
Chinese restaurant, you have a choice from column A, column B, etc. Tea and fortune cookies will not be provided.
The typesetter does not have those fonts either.*

4.1 Naming Conventions

Keyword names in this text were selected arbitrarily and capriciously, and
sometimes simply plagiarized from existing language standards. The main purpose of the keyword names is to provide a degree of cohesiveness to the text.
Feel free to create your own language by creating your own names.

The action produced by the keyword name is the important point, not the
name itself. One, "uno," and "ber" (Turkish) are all cognates. Some
mathematical terms such as + and − are more widely used but are still not
universal. The fundamentally English keyword names I use are designed to
trigger a personal internal recognition of the associated action. A French-,
German-, or Turkish-based TIL is just as viable and just as easy to generate.
After all, isn't that what Babel was about?

Several relatively simple standards are used in my names for keywords. For
example, all of the keywords associated with bytes (as opposed to words)
prefix the equivalent word length keyword with the letter "C". This C is borrowed from FORTH, not C. (FORTH? Si!)

Keywords that always occur in pairs in a fixed order and may have other
keywords between their occurrence generally start with < if they are the left
keyword and end with > if they are the right keyword. I also use < if
something is entering the stack. This just keeps the water muddy.

A routine that has no dictionary headers but whose word address is known
by another keyword generally starts with *. The remaining characters are the
same as the calling keyword. Thus, IF knows the word address of the "lost"
keyword *IF.

Finally, subroutines used by several keywords start with a $. Some of these subroutines, such as the I/O (input/output) routines, are presumed to exist in your system's software.

4.2 Data Types ───────────────────────────

In the following paragraphs, an integer language will serve as the baseline. This is not to imply that floating-point threaded interpreters are not viable — they are. An integer baseline language is easier to explain and implement on a microprocessor that does not have floating-point hardware. Integer versions take maximum advantage of the inherently limited computational capabilities of a microprocessor.

4.2.1 Numbers ───────────────────────────

There are innumerable ways to handle numbers in a threaded interpreter. The method I shall propose is a very flexible, general method. Simpler schemes are possible.

All number tokens in the input buffer are converted to binary integers for internal usage. This conversion takes place in the outer interpreter routine NUMBER. Internally the integers may be 8 or 16 bits wide (byte or word) and occasionally 24 bits wide, except when they are on the data stack. All data stack numbers are 16 bits wide.

Numbers are converted to binary form from their input form using a system variable called BASE. The number base must be in the set 2 thru 9, A thru Z, with A = 10, etc. (BASE controls both input and output.) Keywords named BINARY, OCTAL, DECIMAL, and HEX preset the variable BASE to 2, 8, 10, and 16, respectively, since they are the most commonly used bases. Note that a leading "−" may be the first character in a number token but all other characters must be in the set $\{0, ..., BASE-1\}$, ie: decimal numbers or base 10 numbers are in the set $\{0, ..., 9\}$. The numbers 0, −1, and 1 are usually defined as constants with keyword names 0, −1, and 1, respectively, since they exist in all allowable number bases.

The internal forms of the binary number are first generated as 16-bit integers by the outer loop routine NUMBER. The integers may be signed or unsigned, depending on the application. Signed integers have the range:

$$-32768 \le n \le 32767$$

Unsigned integers have the range:

$$0 \le n \le 65535$$

A leading minus sign causes the two's complement of the number to be taken after conversion to the internal binary form. A leading plus sign is not allowed in a number.

When stored in memory as constants, variables, etc, or when stored in a definition as a number literal (preceded by the number literal handler), the full 16-bit range capability is not always required. Signed and unsigned numbers in the ranges:

$$-128 \le n \le 127$$
$$0 \le n \le 256$$

only require 8 bits. Memory utilization is minimized by storing these numbers as bytes rather than words. This does require that the routines which place these numbers on the stack have a predefined technique for expanding 8-bit numbers to 16-bit numbers. The routines that do this expansion are established by defining byte constants, byte variables, etc, and a byte-number literal handler.

There are two ways to handle the predefinition. One is to treat numbers in the range 0 to 256 as bytes and treat all negative numbers as word length integers. This is consistent with allowing only positive byte constants, etc. Although I have occasionally implemented this technique, an alternate form is also available. By defining byte numbers as having the range -128 to 127, all byte forms can be defined consistently. When byte forms are pushed to the stack, all bits of the most significant byte are set equal to the MSB (most significant bit) of the number byte. This is the standard two's complement convention.

Care must be exercised when using byte numbers. It is possible to leave a number on the stack that exceeds the predefined range. These numbers cannot be correctly stored into a byte variable. System error messages are generally not included for this type of error since the tests to discover them adversely affect execution speed. The burden is on the user to insure numeric correctness.

All of the attributes of the input number conversion are controlled by the outer loop routine NUMBER. Caution must be used in naming tokens to insure that this routine can be executed. It is possible on number entry to name a keyword "2". Any attempt to input the number two would result in the search algorithm finding the keyword "2" and performing the indicated action. As long as "2" is defined as the constant two, the system is safe. Any other definition would effectively eliminate all number bases other than binary. The number conversion routine is never reached if an existing keyword name preempts a number. For this reason it is wise to include a character not in the set {0 thru 9, A thru Z} in all keyword names of length two or less and to include high-end alphabetic characters in keyword names of length three. This allows large number bases before a collision occurs between a keyword and a potential number.

The outer loop NUMBER routine either pushes the converted binary number to the stack if the execute mode is in effect, or adds a literal handler word address and the number to the dictionary if the compile mode is in effect.

The literal-handler word address may specify either a byte number (*C#) or a word number (*#). All of this is transparent to the programmer.

When the number literal handler *C# or *# is executed, the instruction register points to the location of either the byte or the first byte of the word where the number is stored (ie: its address in the list of "instructions"). The literal handler extracts the number from the instruction list, pushes the number to the stack, and increments the instruction register to the instruction following the number in the threaded list.

Using the literal format, byte-length numbers require 3 bytes and word-length numbers require 4 bytes within the keyword being defined. The selection of the format needed is done by the system, based on the actual number entered in the definition.

In purely integer TILs, an extension to this baseline can be included to fake out the populace. Periods (decimal points) can be allowed in the input number. The number conversion routine must be designed to ignore periods but this allows "real" numbers.

4.2.2 Logical Flags

A logical flag is a parameter with two possible states, True or False. A computer cannot directly recognize these states, so the standard convention is to define True as 1 (non-zero) and False as 0 (zero). Certain relational testing keywords return logical flags which are always a zero or a 1. A constant or a variable may sometimes be treated as a logical flag. In this event any non-zero number is by definition True. Care must be used in designing keywords that expect a logical flag as an input parameter. Any non-zero number should be treated as True, so that all bits of a flag must be examined, not just the LSB (least significant bit). Flags are defined and stored in memory as variables.

4.2.3 Strings and Things

All systems that display data to the operator must have at least a rudimentary form for handling strings of ASCII data. Displaying messages to the operator implies some method of outputting an ASCII string. Displaying numbers implies converting the numbers to a sequence of positional numbers, converting these numbers to their equivalent ASCII number code, and displaying the resulting string.

In our threaded interpretive language, the tokens are ASCII strings. When the outer interpreter moves a token to the dictionary space, it appends the token length to the string as the first character of the string. This particular string format is convenient for dictionary header formation as well as for input number conversion. If the system does not recognize the token, an error message is created from the data located at the DP (dictionary pointer) contents (the location of the unknown token in extended header format). This string format has a lead number equal to the number of characters in the string, and it is followed by the string itself.

When an output number conversion is requested, an alternate method of string handling is used. In this circumstance, the unused high-order bit (except for parity in some input/output transfers) of the ASCII code format is employed to mark the *last* character in the string. This bit is one set in the last character of the string. For number output, the terminating character is always a space with the higher-order bit 1 set, which is pushed onto the stack. Numeric data is always converted by pushing successive ASCII numbers characters to the stack. During number output, the string values are displayed a character at a time as popped off the stack until the character with the high-order bit set is output.

Strings of ASCII data may be embedded within a word being compiled as a literal. The system keyword that performs this action is the immediate keyword "[".

[— This keyword adds the ASCII literal handler word address to the dictionary and encloses it in the definition being compiled. It changes the token separator to "]" from the normal ■ and scans the next token from the input buffer. Finally it encloses the scanned token in the word being defined.

This procedure encloses the ASCII literal handler, the length of the string, and all characters (starting with the character following the ■ separator for "[") until the occurrence of "]" in the word being defined. This format is very similar to the first format introduced. When the literal handler is executed, the instruction register points to the length of the string. The literal handler will echo-display the string, leaving the instruction register pointing to the next instruction in the threaded code.

Obviously the "[" keyword is very convenient for defining labels and operator messages. Other string variables and operators are not part of the core language. You can add strings and string operators if you need them for your application.

4.2.4 Constants

Constants are named passive keywords that push the *integer value* of the constant to the stack when evoked. Constant values may be internally stored as bytes or words. Constants are defined in the execute mode using defining words as follows:

n■CONSTANT■name
m■CCONSTANT■name

where:

$$\left. \begin{array}{l} -32768 \le n \le 32767 \\ -128 \le m \le 127 \end{array} \right\} = \text{the value}$$

and where name is any valid token. CONSTANTs require 10 bytes of storage and CCONSTANTs require 9 bytes of storage including the header (see figure 2.6). The numbers n and m are converted using the BASE in effect when they are defined.

Constants may be compiled into other keyword definitions using one of two techniques. For example, the sequence:

DECIMAL■288■CONSTANT■2GROSS■ ■OK
:■......■2GROSS■.....■;■ ■OK

or:

DECIMAL■:■.....■288■.....■;■ ■OK

are two techniques for compiling a keyword that contains an instruction to push the integer 288 to the stack. In the first case a CONSTANT is defined which requires 10 bytes for the dictionary entry and 2 bytes for each usage in any subsequently defined keyword that includes the constant keyword. In the second case the occurrence of a 288 in the input buffer causes the constant literal handler (2 bytes) and the number (2 bytes) to be added to the threaded code list of the word being defined rather than the word address of a constant (2 bytes).

At first it would appear that a constant which is used less than five times within a program need not be defined as a CONSTANT. For example, using 2GROSS four times in subsequent definitions costs 18 bytes total, but using 288 four times only requires 16 bytes total. There is, however, a subtle difference. The constant definition can be changed at one place (the word following its word address) and it will change the value pushed to the stack in all occurrences of its invocation. The literal handler method requires that each occurrence of the constant be located within each threaded code definition and changed. This latter procedure is much more difficult than the former. The constant forms are ideal for usage where occasional value changes are desired or where the same constant is used five or more times within a program. The values 0, 1, and −1 are actually defined as CCONSTANTs since they occur so often.

4.2.5 Variables

Variables are named passive keywords that push the *address of the variable* to the stack when evoked. Variables may be internally stored as bytes or words. Variables are defined in-line in the execute mode using defining words as follows:

n■VARIABLE■name
m■CVARIABLE■name

where:

$$-32768 \leq n \leq 32767$$
$$-128 \leq m \leq 127$$
$$\} = \text{the initial value}$$

and where name is any valid token. VARIABLEs require 10 bytes of storage and CVARIABLEs require 9 bytes of storage including the header. The variable dictionary entries are similar to the constant forms. The initial values n and m are converted using the BASE in effect when they are defined.

4.2.6 Arrays

Arrays are named passive keywords that allocate blocks of dictionary memory for data types following a dictionary header. Arrays are actually application-specific but are based on variables since variables return the address of the first location in the array. For example, the sequence:

DECIMAL■0■CVARIABLE■name■99■DP■+!■■OK

will reserve 100 bytes of storage under the keyword name. In the example, the sequence through "name" simply creates a CVARIABLE keyword and initializes the first byte to zero. The sequence 99■DP■+! advances the dictionary pointer by 99 so that 100 bytes following the header are reserved. Only the first byte is initialized. The other 99 bytes contain garbage.

If the problem under consideration requires arrays, then create the arrays. Operators to manipulate the arrays can also be defined to produce a language specifically tuned to the array problem. In general, specific entries in arrays are accessed by addressing them relative to the first address in the array. This first address is the address pushed to the stack when the array keyword is evoked.

4.2.7 User Parameters ───────────────────────

If a program is to be placed in read-only memory, a section of programmable memory must be available for user parameter storage. The variable defining words cannot be used in the generation of parameters within the program definition. The variable defining words compile the definition in-line. This would intermix code and variables. After the program is placed in read-only memory, the variable could not be changed. It would always return the value contained in the read-only memory (ie: the "variable" would become a virtual constant).

The above problem of in-line variables could be circumvented by always referencing the programmable memory address of the parameter in the keyword definitions of the program. This generally requires 4 bytes per reference: 2 bytes for the number literal handler plus 2 bytes for the variable address, unless the variable area is within the first 256 bytes of memory. An alternate approach is to define an immediate keyword called USERS. This immediate keyword expects a number in the range $0 \leq n \leq 255$ as the next token in the input buffer following its invocation. USERS encloses the user literal handler in the definition, extracts the next token, converts it to an unsigned byte constant, and encloses the number in the definition.

When executed, the user literal handler forms the address of the variable by adding the number to the base address of the users parameter area in programmable memory. This resulting address is pushed to the stack. This is usually the method used to access system variables.

In effect, the keyword USERS allows relative addressing within a 256-byte, users-memory parameter block. The block can be anywhere in the address space and still be accessed by a 3-byte reference. This is obviously not as efficient as a 2-byte in-line variable (which won't work in read-only memory), but is better than a 4-byte absolute reference. If more than the 256 bytes are needed for user variable storage, simply define 1USER, 2USER, etc. Each form has its individual base address allowing multiples of 256-byte blocks.

4.2.8 System Parameters ───────────────────────

There are a number of parameters that the system must have available to operate. These contain the critical system data. Depending on the central processing unit architecture, certain of these parameters may be stored in processor registers. Those system parameters not stored in registers are stored in programmable memory as variables. An area of programmable memory must be allocated for these variables.

For the interactive terminal-directed TIL being considered, the following system parameters are used:

IR — The Instruction Register contains the word address of the next keyword (instruction) in the current secondary keyword that the inner interpreter will execute. It is the effective program counter for the TIL machine.

WA — The Word Address variable contains the word address of the current keyword to be executed before the keyword code address is extracted by the inner interpreter. It contains the address of the keyword code body just after this event. This variable is important only for a short time following code address extraction. If the code called via the code address does not need the address of the code body, the WA variable can be overwritten. WA is most often contained in a processor register.

SP — Data Stack Pointer.

RSP — Return Stack Pointer.

MODE — The system parameter MODE is a logical flag with False (0) equal to the execute mode and True (1) equal to the compile mode. MODE is True set by the keyword ":" and False set on start/restart or by the keyword ";" or ;CODE.

STATE — The system parameter STATE is a logical flag used to control execution of immediate keywords. In the compile mode (MODE=True), the compiler vocabulary is searched and STATE is set True if the keyword is found in this vocabulary. Keywords are executed by the outer interpreter routine ?EXECUTE if, and only if, MODE equals STATE. ?EXECUTE always sets STATE false before it completes.

DP — The Dictionary Pointer is a variable containing the address of the next free location in the dictionary space.

CONTEXT — The variable CONTEXT contains the address of the vocabulary which will be searched to locate keyword word addresses.

CURRENT — The variable CURRENT contains the address of the vocabulary to which new keyword definitions will be linked.

START — The variable START contains a flag which is True if the TIL is being entered for the first time and False otherwise. It is used to distinguish a start from a restart.

LBP — The Line Buffer Pointer is a variable containing the address where token scans will begin. When the input submode completes, LBP will point to the first location of the line buffer. As each token is scanned, LBP is reset to point to the location following the token separator of the token scanned.

BASE — The variable BASE contains the current number base for input from the keyboard and output to the display.

There are several other system parameters that may be contained within the system. These are associated with virtual memory mechanizations. The parameters will be introduced in Chapter 7 where extensions to the basic mechanization will be considered.

The system MODE and STATE parameters have the following states:

Mode	State	Action
0	0	Execute keyword
0	1	Not allowed
1	0	Compile keyword
1	1	Execute immediate keyword

The MODE parameter is also used by the outer loop number routine to decide whether to compile a number or push it to the stack.

Accessing system parameters will be considered in later sections.

4.3 Operator Keywords

The operators are active keywords selected for inclusion in the threaded interpretive language. The actual list depends on what you want to do with the language. It is not smart to include operators to manipulate data types that are not used. I will present a fairly hefty cross-section of operator types. No presumptions will be made about their utility. After all, I am not the designer of your language — you are.

4.3.1 Stack Operators

The stack operator keywords are among the more important in a stack-oriented language such as our TIL. Their usage is so pervasive that these operators are almost always coded as primitives.

The stack operators always manipulate stack words. The operators implement the following actions:

DROP — Pops the top stack entry and discards it.

DUP — Duplicates the top stack entry and pushes it to the stack.

2DUP — Duplicates the top stack entry and pushes it to the stack twice.

SWAP — Interchanges the order of the top two stack entries.

OVER — Duplicates the second stack entry and pushes it to the stack (copies it over the top stack element).

RROT — Rotates the top three stack elements to the right. In infix notation A B C → C A B.

LROT — Rotates the top three stack elements to the left. In infix notation A B C → B C A.

2OVER — Duplicates the third stack entry and pushes it to the stack.

2SWAP — Interchanges the order of the first and third stack entries.

CSPLIT — Pops the top stack word and creates two 16-bit numbers from the 2 bytes which compose the word. The high-order byte is expanded to 16 bits and stored as the second stack entry. The low-order byte is the top stack entry.

CJOIN — Pops the top two stack entries and forms a 16-bit word. The high-order byte of the new words is the low-order byte of the second entry, and the low-order byte is the low-order byte of the top entry. The resulting word is pushed back on the stack.

As may be imagined, stack operators are useful in a variety of applications. The effects of some can be produced by a sequence of other operators. The ones you include in your language depend on the utility derived by their inclusion.

4.3.2 Memory-Reference Operators ───────────────

The memory-reference operator keywords always presume that the address of a parameter is the top stack entry. As a general rule, the parameters must be in programmable memory since most of the operators specifically change the numerical value of the parameter. As with stack operators these operators are usually primitives.

The memory reference operators are as follows:

! — Stores the second stack word at the address specified by the top stack entry. Removes both entries from the stack.

C! — Stores the low-order byte of the second stack word at the address specified by the top stack entry. Removes both entries from the stack.

+! — Adds the word stored at the second stack entry to the word whose address is the top stack entry. Removes both entries from the stack.

C+! — Adds the low-order byte of the second stack entry to the byte whose address is the top stack entry. Removes both entries from the stack.

0SET — Sets the word whose address is the top stack entry to zero (False). Removes the top entry.

1SET — Sets the word whose address is the top stack entry to one (True). Removes the top entry.

C0SET — Sets the byte whose address is the top stack entry to zero (False). Removes the top entry.

C1SET — Sets the byte whose address is the top stack entry to one (True). Removes the top entry.

@ — Replaces the address at the top stack entry by the word stored at that address.

C@ — Replaces the address at the top stack entry by the byte stored at that address but expanded to 16 bits.

All of the keywords except @ and C@ are applicable only to programmable memory. These two keywords can be used to access any type of memory except write-only memory — unoccupied address space. Even this works, although the results are uninteresting.

4.3.3 Interstack Operators —————————————————————

The data stack is usually used to store parameters. The return stack is usually used to store return addresses. The return stack is also used by the system to
store loop parameters (which I will explore in Section 4.4.4) and may be used
by the programmer for temporary data storage (carefully). Any data stored on
the return stack must be removed in the same keyword definition. Primary
and secondary calls can occur between the storage and removal, but there
must be a net change of zero in the return stack pointer before the definition
ends. If there is a net change in the return stack pointer within a definition, the
inner interpreter SEMI routine (which terminates the definition) will not extract the valid return address. This can lead to the self-consuming program
phenomenon mentioned earlier in which the program counter gets loaded with
fluff.

With these cautions in mind, the following primitive interstack operators
are suggested for careful usage:

<R — Pops the top data stack word and pushes it to the return stack (a 16-bit
push).
R> — Pops the top return stack word and pushes it to the data stack.
C<R — Pops the top data stack word and pushes the low-order byte to the
return stack (an 8-bit push).
CR> — Pops the top return stack byte, expands it to 16 bits and pushes the
word to the data stack.

The keywords I>, CI>, J>, CJ>, K>, and CK> duplicate loop indices
from the return stack and push the index numbers to the data stack. These
words will be considered in Section 4.4.

It should be pointed out that the interstack operators should not be used
within a loop construct that stores indices on the return stack. This can lead to
the infamous, inadvertent DO...FOREVER loop.

4.3.4 Arithmetic Operators ———————————————————

The arithmetic operators include some fairly common types and some rather
unusual types. The core language does not contain a great number of
arithmetic operators. There is sufficient power in the core language set to work
the more commonly encountered problems. Your ingenuity is required to add
additional operators for your specific problem.

All the numbers on the stack are presumed to be 16 bits wide, two's complement numbers. All byte-length numbers are presumed to be expanded to this
form. Some functions use intermediate values or generate values that are 24
bits wide. The multiply and divide operators evoke signed operations.

Divisors are restricted to the set $|n| \leq 127$. The numbers themselves may thus have 16, 8, or 7 significant bits. All arithmetic operators are coded as primitives.

Because of the unusual operator designs, the explanations of the operator functions will be fairly detailed. The arithmetic keywords are as follows:

ABS — A unary operator which leaves the absolute value (a positive integer) of the top stack value on the stack. That is, in infix, $|N|$. It is applicable to signed numbers.

MINUS — A unary operator which leaves the two's complement of the top stack entry on the stack: in infix notation, $-N$. It is applicable to signed numbers.

+ — A binary operator which replaces the top two stack entries by their two's complement sum. Neither overflow nor carry are tested. Here $N2(16) + N1(16) = N1(16)$.

− — A binary operator which replaces the top two stack entries by their two's complement differences. Neither overflow nor carry are tested. Here $N2(16) - N1(16) = N1(16)$.

S* — A binary operator which multiplies the low-order bytes of the top two stack entries and leaves a 16-bit product as the top stack entry. It is equivalent to $N2(8)*N1(8) = N1(16)$. The high-order bytes of the original stack entries are not tested to insure that valid 8-bit numbers are on the stack prior to execution.

* — A binary operator which multiplies the second stack entry word by the low-order byte of the top stack entry and returns a 16-bit product as the top stack entry. It is equivalent to $N2(16)*N1(8) = N1(16)$. No validity test is made on the high-order byte of the original top stack entry and no test is made on the result to verify 16 bits or less in the product.

D* — A binary operator that multiplies the second stack entry word by the low-order byte of the top stack entry and returns a 24-bit product. The least significant 16 bits are returned as the second stack entry and the 8 most significant bits are expanded to a 16-bit word and returned as the top stack entry. D* is equivalent to $N2(16)*N1(8) = N2,1(24)$. No validity test is made on the high-order byte of the original top stack entry.

/MOD — A binary operator which divides the second stack entry word by the low-order byte of the top entry. It returns the 8-bit quotient expanded to 16 bits as the second stack entry and the positive remainder expanded to 16 bits as the top entry. The low-order byte of the original top stack entry must be in the range $-128 \leq n \leq 127$. /MOD is equivalent to $N2(16)/N2(7) = N2(8)$ and $N2(16)_{MOD\ N1[7]} = N1(8)$. No test is made to insure that an 8-bit quotient will result from this operation.

MODU/ — Exactly the same operation as /MOD except the return order of the top two stack elements is reversed. The quotient is the top stack entry and the remainder is the second entry.

MOD — Exactly the same operation as /MOD except only the remainder is returned as the top stack entry.

D/ — Presumes a 24-bit number for the second and third stack entries with the most significant 8 bits as the second entry word. It divides this number by the low-order byte of the top entry $(-128 \leq n \leq 127)$. C/ returns a 16-bit quotient as the second stack entry and an 8-bit positive remainder expanded to 16 bits as the top entry. It is equivalent to $N3,2(24)/N1(7)=N2(16)$ and $N3,2(24)_{MODN1[7]}=N1(8)$. No validity tests are made on the original stack entries to insure a valid 16-bit quotient.

/ — Exactly the same routine as D/ except only a 16-bit number as the second stack element and an 8-bit $(-128 \leq b \leq 127)$ top entry are presumed. The 8 most significant bits of the dividend are zero set and only the 16-bit quotient is returned. It is equivalent to $N2(16)/N1(7) = N1(16)$. All other constraints are the same as with D/.

/MOD — Multiplies the third stack entry word by the low-order byte of the second stack entry yielding a 24-bit intermediate product (exactly as with D). It divides the 24-bit intermediate product by the low-order byte $(-128 \leq n \leq 127)$ of the top stack entry (exactly as with D/). */MOD returns the 8-bit positive remainder expanded to 16 bits as the second stack entry and the 16-bit quotient as the top entry. It is equivalent to $(N3(16)*N2(8))/N1(7) = N2(16)$ and $(N3(16)*N2(8))_{MOD\ N1[7]} = N1(8)$. The constraints of D* and D/ apply.

*/ — The same operation as */MOD except only the 16-bit quotient is returned.

MAX — A binary operator that leaves the larger of the two top stack entries on the stack. It assumes signed integers on the stack.

MIN — A binary operator that leaves the smaller of the two top stack entries on the stack. It assumes signed integers on the stack.

2* — A fast multiply by two unary operators. It is actually a 1-bit left shift of the top stack value. Carry and overflow are not tested.

2/ — A fast divide by two unary operators. Effectively a 1-bit right arithmetic shift of the top stack value.

1+ — Increments the top stack entry by one.

2+ — Increments the top stack entry by two.

1− — Decrements the top stack entry by one.

2− — Decrements the top stack entry by two.

The arithmetic operators are strange in a wonderful way. Operations such as */ are extremely useful. With the 24-bit intermediate product, loss of precision from truncation errors can be prevented in many operations. For example, $\pi \approx 245/78$ so that:

DECIMAL■10000■245■78■*/■.■31410■■OK

If a multiply by π is common, define a new keyword as:

DECIMAL■:■*PI■245■78■*/■;■■OK

If the numerical accuracy is insufficient, a more complex algorithm can be designed to achieve even more accurate results.

Those of you who are familiar with higher-order languages may sneer at the unsophistication of a language without a full-blown, floating-point arithmetic set. In response let me point out that data input to the system by most interface equipment is almost never in floating point. The time penalty in converting inputs to floating point format is sometimes as costly as doing the entire problem in scaled, fixed binary arithmetic. Finally, may I point out that for years most of our sophisticated military systems (including the present ICBM fleet) used scaled, binary fixed-integer arithmetic in their computer programs. High-speed, floating-point hardware exists only in modern medium-to-large size computers. Low-speed, floating point hardware is equivalent to software emulation in microcomputers. The only advantage to floating point is programming ease (and ridiculous superiority claims). After all, you are not afraid of fixed point — are you?

4.3.5 Logical Operators

The logical operators are simple. All except NOT presume two 16-bit words on the stack (the operands) and replace these words by a single word at the top of the stack. The keywords are:

AND — Logically ANDs the operands on a bit-for-bit basis, ie:

$$0 \text{ and } 0 = 0$$
$$0 \text{ and } 1 = 0$$
$$1 \text{ and } 0 = 0$$
$$1 \text{ and } 1 = 1$$

OR — Logically ORs the operands on a bit-for-bit basis, ie:

$$0 \text{ or } 0 = 0$$
$$0 \text{ or } 1 = 1$$
$$1 \text{ or } 0 = 1$$
$$1 \text{ or } 1 = 1$$

XOR — Logically Exclusive ORs the operands on a bit-for-bit basis, ie:

$$0 \text{ xor } 0 = 0$$
$$0 \text{ xor } 1 = 1$$
$$1 \text{ xor } 0 = 1$$
$$1 \text{ xor } 1 = 0$$

NOT — Inverts the logical state of the flag at the top of the stack.

The logical operator can be used to operate on flag data types as well as any logical data types defined for a specific application.

4.3.6 Relational Operators

The relational operators are unary or binary operators which return a flag, where True is a 16-bit word with an integer value of 1 and False is a 16-bit word with an integer value of 0. The operators follow:

= — Pops the top two stack entries and pushes a True if the entries are equal. It otherwise pushes a False.

> — Pops the top two stack values and pushes a True if the second stack entry is greater than the top entry. It otherwise pushes a False. It assumes signed integers on the stack.

< — Pops the top two stack values and pushes a True if the second stack entry is less than the top entry. It otherwise pushes a False. It assumes signed integers on the stack.

0= — Pops the top stack value and returns a True if the top stack entry is zero. It otherwise pushes a False.

0< — Pops the top stack value and returns a True if the top stack entry is a negative two's complement number. It otherwise pushes a zero.

A comment is in order about the use of = as a relational operator only. Some languages use = as both a relational operator and an equivalence (or replacement) operator. The use of RPN (reverse Polish notation) eliminates the use of = in arithmetic operations. The replacement operator becomes the "!" (store) operator and its usage is only required to free stack space or simplify stack management.

4.3.7 Input/Output Operators

The I/O operators considered here will be the most basic I/O operations. Fundamentally, the TIL can be interfaced to the keyboard and video display via the system-monitor utility subroutines or separate drivers can be included in the TIL. It is very dependent on the type of operating system your particular machine has. Systems that have disks and stand-alone serial terminals are different from systems that use cassette mass storage and memory-mapped video refresh.

I have probably vacillated more over I/O routines than any other aspect of program design. This is one area I would most like to ignore. Unfortunately, it is not an area that can be easily ignored in the hope that it will disappear. Thus, the following operators are presented:

KEY — This keyword will push to the stack the next character entered from the keyboard. In my current system this keyword routine contains the software timing loop that controls the blinking underscore cursor. It also recognizes a non-ASCII keyboard-generated code that causes the system monitor to be entered, thus exiting any program currently in control. In any routine of this type, the keyboard should be reset on entry and before exit.

ECHO — This keyword pops the top stack entry and outputs the low-order byte to the display driver. This displays a *printing* character at the cursor point and moves the cursor right one character position.

CLEAR — This keyword outputs the control code to the video display that will clear the display screen and leave the cursor at the upper left (home the cursor).

CRET — This keyword outputs the *carriage return-line feed* code sequence to the video display. This holdover from the teletypewriter convention simply leaves the cursor at the start of the next display line (which is blank).

SPACE — This keyword outputs an ASCII space code to the display screen.

TYPE — This keyword expects an address at the top of the stack that points to a memory location. This location will contain a byte count and is followed by a list of ASCII code characters of this length in the following memory locations. The keyword pops this address, extracts the count, and outputs that many characters to the display from the subsequent memory locations.

DISPLAY — This keyword expects a sequence of ASCII code characters on the stack in the low-order byte positions. The last character in the sequence will have the high-order bit in the code set to one. This keyword will pop successive entries from the stack, output the low-order byte, and repeat until the character with the high-order bit set has been output.

<# — This keyword prepares the stack for number conversion by pushing to the stack an ASCII space code with the high-order bit set (A0 hex) in the low-order byte of the word. It also copies the top stack entry to the return stack. (Note that both <# and #> must occur within a single definition.)

— This keyword pops the top stack entry, divides the unsigned number by the system variable BASE, converts the residual to an equivalent ASCII code in the set (0 thru 9, A thru Z), pushes the result to the stack, and then pushes the quotient to the stack.

#S — This keyword executes successive # routines until a zero is at the top stack entry. It always executes at least one # routine.

SIGN — The keyword pushes an ASCII minus sign to the stack if the top return stack entry is negative.

#> — This keyword pops the top return stack entry, discards it, and displays the character string on the stack using the DISPLAY format. (Note that both <# and #> must occur within a single definition.)

ASCII — The keyword expects a positive binary integer between zero and 36 as the top stack entry. The number is converted to the equivalent ASCII number code 0 thru 9, A thru Z, and left in the low-order byte position of the top stack entry.

. — This keyword pops the top stack entry, converts the signed value to a sequence of ASCII characters representing the number, and displays the result to the operator followed by a space.

.R — This keyword expects a print field width as the top stack entry and a signed number as the second entry. It converts the number just as with the "." keyword, but if fewer characters than are in the top stack entry number result (including the terminating space), additional ASCII spaces are output before the converted number is displayed.

? — **(C?)** — This keyword pops the top stack entry, extracts the word (byte) addressed by this entry, and displays the value to the operator using the "." keyword sequence.

4.3.8 System Operators ————————————————————————

There is a class of operators which have a more system-oriented flavor. Some of the operators are used to implement the outer interpreter, the defining words, and the compiling words. However, they are so useful and necessary that they are directly available to the operator. Others are simply required for system operation.

The system keywords include the following:

, — Pops the top stack entry word and stores it at the DP (dictionary pointer) address. It then increments DP by two (ie: encloses the top stack entry word in the dictionary).

C, — Pops the top stack entry word and stores the low-order byte at the DP address. It then increments DP by 1 (ie: encloses the top stack entry byte in the dictionary).

HERE — This keyword pushes the address stored at the system variable DP to the stack. This is the address of the next available location in the free dictionary space.

?SP — This keyword pushes to the stack the address which was the top stack entry address prior to its execution. A test for stack underflow is made and the stack is reinitialized before the address is pushed if an underflow condition exists.

?RS — This keyword pushes the address of the return stack to the stack. No validity test is made on the return stack address since the system usually goes bananas when the return stack is blown.

TOKEN — TOKEN pops the top stack entry byte as the separator and moves the next token in the line buffer to the free dictionary space in extended header format (length plus all characters). It does not enclose the token in the dictionary.

' — The tick keyword scans the next token in the input buffer following its occurence and searches the CONTEXT and CURRENT vocabularies for the keyword corresponding to the token. If the keyword is found, the word address of the keyword is pushed to the stack. If it is not found, the token is echoed to the operator followed by ■?.

ABORT — This keyword causes an unconditional jump to the START/RESTART routine, which reinitializes the system, displays the restart message, and reverts to the operator in the input submode.

ASPACE — This keyword pushes an ASCII space code to the stack. It is usually used to set the separator for a TOKEN call.

ENTRY — ENTRY pushes to the stack the address of the first byte in the header of the latest keyword defined in the CURRENT vocabulary. This will usually become the link address of a keyword being defined.

CA! — This keyword pops an address from the stack and stores it at the word address of the latest keyword in the CURRENT vocabulary. It is used by defining words to change the code address of a keyword to the address necessary to implement the new defining action.

SINGLE — If the top stack entry number is a valid byte-length number, this keyword will push a False flag to the stack. Otherwise, it will push a True flag to the stack.

SEARCH — This keyword expects the address of a given vocabulary on the stack (a pointer to the first keyword header location of the vocabulary). The vocabulary is searched in an attempt to match a keyword with the length and characters of the token which is located in the free dictionary space. If found, the word address of the keyword is returned as the second stack entry and a False flag is returned as the top entry. Otherwise, a single True flag is returned on the stack.

4.3.9 Utility Operators

There exists a class of operators with great utility and no real home among the previous groups. These orphans are collected together here as follows:

FILL — This keyword expects three keywords on the stack. The second stack entry is a starting address, the top stack entry is an ending address, and the low-order byte of the third entry is the entry number. The routine fills all memory between the address boundaries with the entry number. It removes all three entries from the stack.

ERASE — Similar to FILL except only the memory boundaries are on the stack. The entry number is an ASCII space (20 hexadecimal).

DUMP — This keyword expects two numbers on the stack. The second stack entry is a starting address and the top entry is the ending address of a memory area. The contents of this block of memory are displayed in hexadecimal. The format is: an address as four hexadecimal characters; a sequence of a space plus two hexadecimal characters for the proceeding eight memory locations, a space, a sequence of a space plus two hexadecimal characters for the next eight memory locations. Thus an address plus up to sixteen memory location contents are displayed per line with an extra space between the first and last eight memory location contents. DUMP removes the two numbers from the stack.

ADUMP — Similar to DUMP but the characters are displayed as the ASCII equivalent character corresponding to the lower 7 bits of each location rather than as two hexadecimal characters. To prevent collisions between the memory contents and display control characters, there are several alternatives. Offhand, I can think of at least three.

WAIT — WAIT is an operative keyword that expects nothing on the stack. On evocation, WAIT scans the keyboard to see if any key has been depressed.

If it has, the keyboard port is reset and the system enters a loop that scans the keyboard for its next entry. If the next entry from the keyboard is an escape code (either an existing non-ASCII key or a control-[, the ASCII escape code) the system enters the START/RESTART sequence to return to operator control. If the next entry is not the escape code, or if a key was not depressed, WAIT simply terminates. WAIT is used, for example, after every DUMP or ADUMP line is output to allow the operator to stop and examine the display by pressing any key blindly. I usually need the blindly part as what I am looking for goes zipping past.

MOVE — This keyword presumes three addresses on the stack. The third and second stack entries are the starting and ending addresses of a block of memory. The top address is the starting address of a second block of memory. The first memory block is moved to the second memory block. There are no restrictions on block overlaps.

4.4 Loop and Branch Keywords

The loop and branch keywords are system directives that are applicable only in the compile mode. These keywords are all immediate keywords that exist in the COMPILER vocabulary. Most of the keywords load the word addresses of program control directives and relative branch constant to the threaded list of instruction being compiled.

The loop and branch keywords are designed to yield a fully-structured language. There are no constructs such as the BASIC command GOTO XX where XX is some program line number. The threaded interpretive language does not support this type of construct. I have used a command of this type in a TIL system monitor but it simply transfers control out of the TIL. That's right folks, I actually run BASIC using a TIL-based system monitor with subroutined utility programs.

All of the loop and branch program control directive are primitives to insure fast execution. All of the loop and branch keywords are secondaries for compactness. (The actual compilation process is so fast that the operator is rarely conscious of the delay between entering ";" and the occurrence of the ■OK response.)

4.4.1 BEGIN . . . END

The simplest and most primitive loop construct is the BEGIN . . . END loop. It is also usually the fastest loop. The syntax for the construct is:

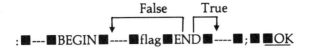

The keyword BEGIN marks the beginning of the loop and END marks the loop end. The flag just before END is an indication that a test value (a flag) must be on the stack. All code between BEGIN and END will be repeated until the flag goes True ($\neq 0$) during execution. Endless loops are created by a 0■END variation.

There are two levels to consider: the actions that occur when the loop is compiled and the actions that occur when the definition is evoked. First consider the actions during the compile mode.

BEGIN — This immediate keyword pushes the address of the next free dictionary location to the stack. This is the address where the word address of the next token that follows BEGIN in the definition will be stored in the dictionary.

END — This immediate keyword adds the word address of the program control directive *END to the threaded list and encloses it in the dictionary. It then pops the top stack entry (the address stored by BEGIN), subtracts it from the current address of the next free dictionary location and encloses the low-order byte of the result in the dictionary as the relative jump constant.

Note that any immediate keywords between BEGIN and END must not leave values on the stack or END will not compute a valid relative jump constant. The relative jump constant is an unsigned byte constant with a range of $2 \leq n \leq 256$.

When the definition which contains the BEGIN . . . END loop is executed, the threaded code will be executed until the *END word address is encountered. When *END is executed, it pops the top stack value (the flag) and tests it for zero. If the flag is zero, the routine extracts the byte at the address contained in the *instruction register* (the relative jump byte), subtracts it from the instruction register and exits to the inner interpreter routine NEXT. The instruction register will then contain the address of the word address of the token that followed BEGIN in the original definition. This is the next instruction that will be executed. This sequence will be repeated until *END encounters a nonzero flag. In this case, it increments the instruction register by one and exits to NEXT. The instruction register then contains the address of the word address of the token following END in the original definition. This terminates the loop.

BEGIN . . . END loops can occur within BEGIN . . . END loops several levels deep. The only restriction is the 256-byte relative jump limit in the outermost loop. Caution is advised in stack management using loops. If n items plus the flag are placed on the stack within the loop and the loop is repeated m times, a stack depth of n*m items results. The stack space had best be capable of handling the data.

The routine *END is an example of a dictionary entry with no header. The routine END must know the word address of *END, but the operator cares less. The loop is available to the operator through the BEGIN and END keywords (but only in the compile mode).

The keyword BEGIN requires no bytes within the definition. The keyword END requires 3 bytes within the definition compiled, 2 for the word address of *END and 1 for the relative jump constant.

4.4.2 IF . . . ELSE . . . THEN

The IF . . . ELSE . . . THEN constructs provide for conditional execution of code. The syntax for the constructs are:

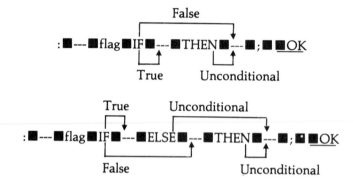

The flag just before IF indicates that a test value must be left on the stack (by the code preceding IF) during execution. If the flag is True (± 0), the code following the IF will be executed. This code may end with either an ELSE or a THEN. In either event an unconditional transfer to the code following the construct occurs. If the flag is False ($=0$), the code following the termination keyword for the true code (an ELSE or THEN) will be executed.

During compilation, the following actions occur:

IF — This immediate keyword adds the word address of the program control directive *IF to the threaded code list being defined and encloses it in the dictionary. It then pushes the address of the next free dictionary location to the stack and advances the address by one to reserve 1 byte in the dictionary for a relative jump constant. This constant will be filled in by either the ELSE or the THEN keyword.

ELSE — This immediate keyword adds the word address of the program control directive *ELSE to the threaded code list being defined and encloses it in the dictionary. Then, it pushes the address of the next free dictionary location to the stack and advances the pointer by one to reserve 1 byte in the dictionary for a relative jump constant. Finally, it pops the top two stack entries, pushes the top entry back on the stack, subtracts the previous second entry from the address of the next free dictionary location and stores the low-order byte of the result at the address of the previous second entry. This rather complex procedure leaves the address of the reserved byte following *ELSE on the stack and fills the reserved byte following *IF with the relative jump value necessary to reach the address following the *ELSE reserved byte. This is the address of the word address of the token following ELSE in the definition. The relative jump may be up to 255 bytes.

THEN — This immediate keyword will load the relative jump byte reserved by either an IF or an ELSE. It pops the address at the top of the stack, subtracts this address from the address of the next free dictionary location and stores the low-order byte of the result at the address of the previous top stack entry. This relative jump may be up to 256 bytes.

During execution of a definition containing the IF . . . ELSE . . . THEN construct, consider that *IF is to be executed next. The *IF routine pops the flag from the stack. If the flag is true, the routine increments the instruction register, which initially points to the relative jump byte following *IF and returns to the inner interpreter routine NEXT. The increment causes the instruction register to point to the address of the word address of the token following IF in the original definition. If the flag is false, *IF jumps to the code body of *ELSE. The routine *ELSE is always entered with the instruction register pointing to a relative branch constant. *ELSE extracts this constant, adds its value to the instruction register and exits to NEXT. This causes a forward jump to the code following THEN in the original definition.

Both IF and ELSE take 3 bytes in the definition being compiled. THEN requires no bytes in the definition.

4.4.3 WHILE

The basic loop and branch constructs may be combined using the operator keyword WHILE. The syntax for these constructs are:

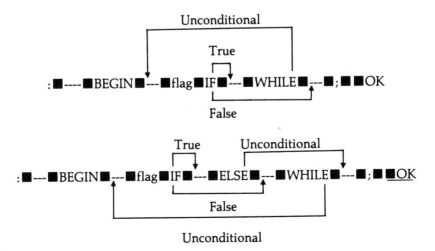

Unconditional

The only new keyword in these constructs is WHILE. All of the other keywords are exactly as previously explained.

During compilation, the action of WHILE is:

WHILE — This immediate keyword expects two addresses on the stack. First the word address of the program control directive *WHILE is added to the threaded list being compiled and enclosed in the dictionary. The second stack entry (the address stored by BEGIN) is removed from the stack, the value is subtracted from the address of the next free dictionary location and the low-order byte is enclosed in the dictionary. This is the relative jump byte required to jump back to the word address of the token following BEGIN. It next removes the top entry, subtracts the address of the next free dictionary location from this value and stores the low-order byte at the address which previously was the top entry. This is the relative jump byte required by either an IF or an ELSE to jump forward to the word address of the token following WHILE.

During execution of a definition that contains this construct, the *WHILE routine is entered with an instruction register content that points to the relative branch constant. *WHILE extracts this constant, subtracts this value from the instruction register and exits to the inner interpreter routine NEXT. This causes a backward jump to the code following BEGIN in the original definition.

WHILE takes 3 bytes in the definition being compiled.

4.4.4 DO . . . LOOP

The DO . . . LOOP construct allows a code sequence to be executed a specific number of times. This type of loop can be implemented using the basic BEGIN . . . END loop but it is not as efficient as using the DO . . . LOOP form. There are four basic DO . . . LOOP constructs as follows:

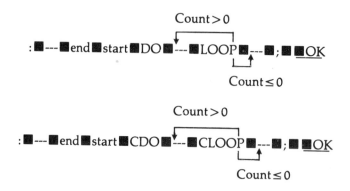

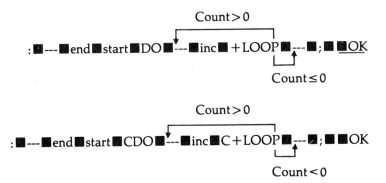

The only difference between DO and CDO forms is that the latter forms use byte-length indices rather than word-length indices.

The end and start preceding the DO indicates that DO expects two values on the stack at execution time: the ending argument and the starting index argument for the loop. Each execution of the loop causes the index argument to be incremented by one after the loop code is executed. The loop code will be executed as long as the difference between the ending argument and the index argument (the count) is *greater than zero*. The +LOOP forms are very similar except they expect an increment on the stack to be used to increment the index.

The compilation events are as follows:

DO — (CDO) — This immediate keyword causes the word address of the program control directive *DO (*CDO) to be added to the threaded list being compiled and enclosed in the dictionary. The address of the next free dictionary location is then pushed to the stack.

LOOP — (CLOOP) — (+LOOP) — (C+LOOP) — This immediate keyword causes the word address of the program control directive *LOOP (*CLOOP, *+LOOP,*C+LOOP) to be added to the threaded list being defined and enclosed in the dictionary. The top stack value is popped, subtracted from the address of the next free dictionary location and the low-order byte of the result enclosed in the dictionary. This is the relative jump constant back to the token following DO (CDO) in the original definition.

When executed, the *DO (*CDO) routine expects two 16-bit words on the stack. The top two stack entries are moved to the return stack as 16-(8) bit numbers with the second entry as the second return stack entry. The top return stack entry is the index value which initially is the start value. The *LOOP (*CLOOP) routine increments the loop index value by one. The *+LOOP (*C+LOOP) routine expects a value on the stack and pops this value to increment the index. The index (the top return stack value) is subtracted from the end argument (the second return stack entry). If this count value is greater than zero, the relative jump value pointed to by the instruction register is added to the instruction register and the routine exits to the inner interpreter routine NEXT. This causes the word address of the token following DO (CDO) in the original definition to be executed next. If the count value is less than or equal to zero, the instruction register is incremented by one, the top two return stack entries are popped and an exit to NEXT occurs. This causes the code following *LOOP (*CLOOP,*+LOOP,*C+LOOP) to be executed.

The rather strange ordering of the loop arguments is purposeful. In variable length loops, it is more common to want to change the ending argument than the starting value. This ordering allows for definition of keywords that contain a starting argument plus the loop construct. The variable ending argument is then pushed to the stack before this keyword is evoked.

The index is incremented in these constructs before being compared to the ending argument, thus:

: ■2FOURS■3■1■DO■4■.■LOOP■;■ ■OK

2FOURS■4■4■ ■OK

Only two fours are printed, not three. Further, the loop test occurs after the loop code so that the loop code must be executed at least once. The main purpose for providing the byte forms of the loop constructs is execution speed. If the loop arguments are in the range $-128 \leq n \leq 127$, the byte forms can be used to achieve a faster loop.

If the basic loop formats disturb you, redesign them. The order of the inputs can be reversed, the test can be done before the code rather than after, or the end value may be incremented once by the DO construct to yield a more familiar loop. The choice is yours.

The DO . . . LOOP constructs may be nested many levels deep. The constraints are the 256-byte relative jump limitation in the outermost loop and sufficient return stack depth to hold the loop arguments.

Several other words are available within the loop constructs. The keyword I> (CI>) pushes the loop index of the innermost loop to the data stack. The keyword J> (CJ>) pushes the loop index of the second level loop and K> (CK>) the third level. These constructs do not change the return stack but they presume only loop arguments of the same type are on the stack.

Sometimes it would be nice to be able to leave a loop prematurely if some specific event occurs. A keyword is provided to do this in a controlled manner.

LEAVE — (CLEAVE) — This immediate keyword causes the word address of the program control directive *LEAVE (*CLEAVE) to be added to the threaded list being compiled and encloses it in the dictionary.

When *LEAVE (*CLEAVE) is executed, it changes the innermost loop index value to the end argument value. This will cause the loop to terminate on the next argument test. The keyword LEAVE (CLEAVE) is generally used within an IF construct to be conditionally executed if some specific event occurs within the loop.

4.4.5 Case Constructs

There is no directly available ON . . . GOSUB construct in the TIL language as there exists in BASIC. The language will allow this type of alternate action to be defined for some specific application. It is best illustrated by example.

Suppose that a function index (an integer) between zero and three is on the stack as the result of a computation, an operator input, or from some peripheral device. Depending on the value of the integer, one of four distinct functions (subprograms) is to be executed. The four functions are first defined as keywords: say, 0CASE, 1CASE, 2CASE and 3CASE. A table (array) named NCASE of the word addresses of these functions is first generated as follows:

'■0CASE■VARIABLE■NCASE■'■1CASE■,■'■
2CASE■,■'■3CASE■,■■__OK__

Each " ' " keyword returns the word address of token following its occurrence, so that an array of the word addresses has been compiled as the variable array keyword NCASE. A keyword CASE is then defined as:

:■CASE■2*■NCASE■+■@■EXECUTE■;■■__OK__

The keyword CASE expects an integer between zero and three on the stack when it is evoked. It first doubles this value to achieve a word (2-byte) offset pointer. This pointer is added to the base address retrieved by NCASE and the contents of this address are fetched using @. This leaves the word address of the function corresponding to the integer on the stack. EXECUTE simply executes this function, achieving the desired goal.

The vectored case construct is easy to define and very flexible. It also contains the seeds of disaster. In our example, an integer not in the set (zero thru three) can be executed by CASE, leading to unknown results. Protective code is advised.

4.5 Compiling and Defining Keywords

Compiling new operators and defining new parameters is central to the threaded language concept of extensibility. Even more important is the ability to define new defining keywords. This is a feature that lends more utility to a TIL. A detailed look at the compiling and defining keywords should fill in the details of the process.

4.5.1 CREATE

This keyword is central to all defining words: words that create dictionary headers for both active and passive keywords. All defining words use CREATE either directly or indirectly to form the dictionary header. CREATE forms the dictionary header and puts the address of the first byte of the code body in the word address location. This forms the header and code address for a primitive.

CREATE — This keyword scans the token following the CREATE location in the input buffer and moves the next token length plus all of the token characters to the free dictionary space. It extracts the address of the last dictionary header in the CURRENT vocabulary and pushes it to the stack. It then replaces this address with the address of the next free dictionary location (which points to the length parameter of the header being formed). It advances the dictionary pointer by four to enclose the length plus the next three characters in the dictionary space in the dictionary. (If the header has less than three characters, the unused places can contain anything.) The top stack entry is popped and enclosed in the dictionary as the link address. Finally, the address of the next free dictionary location is accessed, incremented by two and enclosed in the dictionary at the next free dictionary location address. (This places a primitive code address in the word address.)

4.5.2 Compiling Directives

The compiling directives are central to the extensibility theme. The directives are as follows:

: — This defining keyword first sets the CONTEXT vocabulary to the CURRENT vocabulary. This allows new definitions added to the CURRENT vocabulary to be found during keyword searches. The token following ":" in the input buffer is scanned and a primitive dictionary header is formed using CREATE. The code address of this keyword is then changed to form a secondary keyword by placing the address of the inner interpreter COLON routine at the word address. Finally, the system MODE variable is set to True to establish the compile mode.

; — This immediate keyword encloses the word address of the inner interpreter routine SEMI in the dictionary. It then sets the system MODE variable to False to establish the execution mode.

;CODE — This immediate keyword encloses the word address of the SCODE routine in the dictionary. It then sets the system MODE variable to False to establish the execution mode.

The difference between ";" and ;CODE is important. The ;CODE ending is used in compiling new defining words and is always followed by machine code which specifies the generic action of the defining word.

4.5.3 Parameter Defining Words

The parameter defining words always create named parameters of a particular data type. Three distinct levels must be considered: one when the defining word is compiled (defined), one when the defining word is evoked, and one when the parameter name is evoked.

When a defining word is defined, the sequence is always of the form:

:■defining name■defining code■;CODE■generic code

The *defining name* is the name of the keyword that will evoke creation of a particular data type. The *defining code* will always contain CREATE, either directly or indirectly, to create a dictionary header when the defining name is evoked, and to create optional code to initialize the code body of this passive keyword. The keyword ;CODE is executed, which stores SCODE in the definition and establishes the execute mode. The *generic code* is then entered into the dictionary directly in machine code (using a sequence of numbers and "," or C,) or in assembly language (by evoking an assembler). The generic code is not executed; it is added to the dictionary. The generic code always ends with a call to the inner interpreter routine NEXT.

When used to define a parameter of type defining name, the sequence is:

data■defining name■parameter name

This sequence is always evoked in the execute mode. The *data* is optional but is always stored on the stack. The defining name evokes the defining code, which creates the dictionary header for *parameter name* and initializes the code body with the data as appropriate. All data is removed from the stack. The *secondary keyword* SCODE is then evoked. This keyword pops the return stack and replaces the code address of the passive keyword being defined with this address. Since the return address of a secondary always points to the instruction following its call in the threaded list of code, this address is the address of the generic code following SCODE in the definition of the parameter type. When SCODE completes, its original return address is no longer there. What is there is the return address stored when the *secondary defining name* was executed by the outer interpreter. Thus, when SCODE completes, return to the outer interpreter occurs. The generic code is not executed.

When parameter name is evoked, its word address contains the code address stored by SCODE. This causes the generic code to be executed to manipulate the data contained in the code body of the passive keyword as appropriate to the data type.

The defining word CONSTANT is thus defined as:

: ■CONSTANT■CREATE■,■;CODE■constant generic code

When evoked to define the constant name the sequence is:

n■CONSTANT■name

This creates a constant called name with a value of n. When name is evoked, the constant n will be pushed to the stack by the constant machine code. An equivalent byte form exists as CCONSTANT.

Since a variable places an initial value in its code body, the defining word VARIABLE is defined as:

: ■VARIABLE■CONSTANT■;CODE■variable generic code

This sequence actually results in the creation of the dictionary header first as a primitive, then as a replacement of its code address by that of a constant, and then as a second replacement of its code address by that of a variable, the address of the *variable code*.

When evoked to define the variable name the sequence is:

n■VARIABLE■name

This creates a variable called name with an initial value of n. When name is evoked, the address of the variable is pushed to the stack. An equivalent byte form is available as CVARIABLE.

4.5.4 Defining USER Blocks ───────────────────

The USER block defining word is more literal-like than defining-like. Fundamentally, the procedure leads to almost an indexed variable form except that blocks are available in 256-byte blocks and any byte within the block is available. The basic concept is relatively simple.

USER — An immediate keyword that first adds the word address of the primitive *USER literal handler to the threaded list being compiled and encloses it in the dictionary. The next token following USER is scanned from the input buffer and converted to a number using the system base valid *at the time it is executed*. If valid, the low-order byte of the number is enclosed in the dictionary as the offset. If invalid, the definition being compiled is terminated.

When *USER is evoked, the contents addressed by the instruction register are accessed (the offset) and added to a fixed number established when *USER was defined. The result is pushed to the stack. The instruction register is then incremented by one. It exits to the inner interpreter NEXT routine.

The base of the USER block is established by the *USER definition. The offset is fixed at compile time and is cast in concrete. It does not matter what the system number base is when *USER is executed, only what the number base is when USER is executed.

By adroit use of the definition of USER and *USER, a more index-like variable scheme is possible. For example, if data is known to exist as 4-byte units, USER can be defined to include a multiply by four following number extraction and before offset enclosure. The allowable offset numbers in a definition are then 0 thru 63 and the system automatically computes the address of the first byte of each block of data. (Forcing the multiply at compile time is more time efficient than doing it at execution time in *USER.)

Another method leads to an almost BASIC-like variable structure. In this scheme, *USER does not use a fixed number as the base, but uses a number stored in some variable, say *U. Keywords can be defined to set the *U variable when they are evoked. This is the old base address plus offset trick.

Remember there are no fixed rules about "rightness" in a TIL. The right definition of the names of keywords and the right definition of their action is strictly applications and/or personal preference dependent. A TIL will support your idiosyncrasies, whereas most other languages demand that you support theirs.

4.5.5 High-Level Defining Words

The defining words considered to this point create single definitions of keywords. Generic classes of defining words can also be built with a TIL. Since the concept is more than passingly complex, a careful look at the details will be undertaken.

Suppose I have decided to add an assembler to the basic TIL. I know there is a group of 1-byte machine code instructions that exists for my central processing unit, all of which have no parameters. There are fourteen or so of these instructions for the Z80. I could straightforwardly define each of these instructions as:

HEX ■ : ■ name ■ number ■ C, ■ ; ■ ■ <u>OK</u>

Here name is the assembler mnemonic, number is the machine code instruction in hexadecimal, and C, stores the number in the dictionary. This requires 6 bytes for the header, 2 for COLON, 3 or 4 for the literal handler and the number, and 2 each for C, and SEMI. At best this requires 15 bytes per definition. A primitive definition requires even more memory per keyword.

Two keywords, < BUILDS and DOES >, allow a more memory-conservative approach to the problem by allowing definition of a generic defining keyword which can be used to define the 1-byte assembler mnemonics. First a keyword 1BYTE will be defined as:

: ■1BYTE■ < BUILDS ■DOES > ■C@ ■C, ■; ■ ■OK

Each mnemonic is then defined using:

HEX ■1BYTE ■name ■number ■C, ■ ■OK

Note that name was not compiled. The keyword 1BYTE is a defining word that creates a header named name. As with all defining words (except ":"), the execution mode is in effect. Obviously, the ■number ■C, ■ sequence stored the number in the code body of the keyword called name.

In fact, the code body of the keyword contains the address of the C@ keyword in the 1BYTE definition followed by the single number stored when name was defined. This definition form requires a 6-byte header for each mnemonic, a 2-byte code address and a 3-byte code body, or a total of 11 bytes per mnemonic. The definition of 1BYTE requires 18 bytes. Since the 1BYTE form gains at the rate of 4 bytes per mnemonic, the break-even point in terms of memory usage is 5 mnemonics.

All of this sounds neat, but you ask "How does it work?" Carefully! When the assembler mnemonic is evoked, the code address of the keyword points to code which will first push the instruction register to the return stack. This is similar to the start of the COLON nesting operation. The word address register points to the code body of the keyword where the address of the C@ following DOES > is stored. This address is placed in the instruction register. The word address register is then incremented twice so that it points to the third byte in the code body of the mnemonic, and then it is pushed to the stack. This is the address of the instruction hexadecimal code in our mnemonic definition. The code ends with a jump to the inner interpreter NEXT routine.

Since the instruction register contains the address of the C@ following DOES >, this is the next instruction that will be executed. The C@ instruction replaces the address at the top of the stack with the contents of the address as the lower 8 bits of the top stack entry. The C, pops the stack and encloses the low-order byte in the dictionary. The SEMI routine stored by ";" then de-nests one level to get the next instruction following the occurrence of the mnemonic.

If this still does not satisfy you, I'll tell you how the mnemonic keyword was built. The keyword < BUILDS, when evoked, scans the next token from the input buffer, creates a dictionary header, reserves a code address and 2 bytes in the code body of the keyword, and completes. Note that < BUILDS is evoked when 1BYTE is executed so that it builds a keyword using the mnemonic name. The secondary DOES > pops the return stack or the address of the word following DOES > and stores it in the code body of the keyword in the location reserved by < BUILDS. It then executes a SCODE, which replaces the code address of the word being defined just as explained previously. Since the SCODE has popped the return stack, the return address points to the outer interpreter return. The C@ and C, following DOES > is not executed when 1BYTE is evoked.

Formal definitions of <BUILDS and DOES> are:

: ■ < BUILDS ■0■CONSTANT ■ ; ■OK
: ■DOES> ■R> ■ENTRY ■8■ + ■!■ ; ■---

Here the "---" is machine code entered in the dictionary when DOES> is defined. It is this code that is executed to do the nesting operation when the mnemonic is evoked. For the Z80 the code for a return from a subroutine is hexadecimal C9. Thus:

HEX■1BYTE■RET■C9■C,■ ■OK

A memory map of the results of this definition is given in figure 4.1.

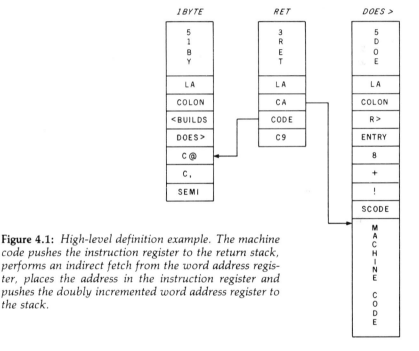

Figure 4.1: *High-level definition example. The machine code pushes the instruction register to the return stack, performs an indirect fetch from the word address register, places the address in the instruction register and pushes the doubly incremented word address register to the stack.*

The general form of these high-level defining words is:

: ■defining name ■ < BUILDS ■defining time code ■
DOES> ■run time secondary code■ ; ■ ■OK

Here *defining time code* is executed at definition time of the defining name. The run-time code is executed when a keyword defined using the defining word is evoked. When this code is executed, the stack contains the address of the third byte of the code body of the keyword on the first byte available for data storage.

To illustrate the defining time code utility, an alternate definition of 1BYTE is:

: ■1BYTE■ < BUILDS ■C, ■DOES > ■C@ ■C, ■; ■ ■OK

With this definition, RET is then defined as:

HEX ■C9 ■1BYTE ■RET ■ ■OK

After < BUILDS constructs the constant header RET, the C, between < BUILDS and DOES > adds the C9 hex number to the dictionary following the 2 bytes reserved by the constant header form: that is, the third byte in the code of RET. DOES > then does its thing.

4.5.6 Vocabulary Defining Word

The vocabulary defining word is an example of a defining word that uses a high-level definition. The definition of VOCABULARY is:

: ■VOCABULARY ■ < BUILDS ■ENTRY ■, ■DOES > ■
CONTEXT ■! ■; ■ ■OK

A new vocabulary called name is created by:

VOCABULARY ■name ■ ■OK

This evokes < BUILDS to create the dictionary entry for name and link it to the current vocabulary. The ENTRY ■, actually retrieves the address of the first header byte of name and enters this address as the third and fourth byte of the code body of name. DOES > then does its thing.

When name is evoked the address of the third and fourth byte is stored in CONTEXT as the pointer to the last header in vocabulary name. Note that the keyword name exists in the vocabulary that was current when name is defined and the vocabulary name is linked where it is defined. Any extensions added to this vocabulary after name is defined are not linked to (included in) name.

4.6 Vocabulary Keywords

The vocabulary keywords are the system directives that allow management (or mismanagement) of the vocabularies defined in your TIL. Most of the keywords have been mentioned at one point or another. Just for drill, they will be repeated here.

VOCABULARY — A defining keyword used to define new vocabularies. See Section 4.5.6.

IMMEDIATE — This keyword delinks the latest keyword entered in the CURRENT vocabulary from the CURRENT vocabulary and links it to the COMPILER vocabulary. What was previously the second entry in the CURRENT vocabulary becomes the latest entry.

DEFINITIONS — This keyword sets the system variable CURRENT to the value at the system variable CONTEXT so that new definitions will enter the correct vocabulary.

FORGET — This keyword sets CONTEXT to CURRENT and searches the CONTEXT vocabulary for the token following FORGET in the input buffer. If the keyword is located, the keyword is delinked from the CURRENT vocabulary and the DP is reset to the first header byte of the located keyword. If not found, the keyword is echoed to the operator followed by "?".

CORE — The core language vocabulary.

COMPILER — The compiler vocabulary.

4.7 Babblings

Not all of the language elements have been presented here. I promise to pull some off-the-wall keywords out of my magic hat at some unexpected moments during the course of the remaining text. There are two reasons for this: forgetfulness and a desire to see if anyone is paying attention. What good is a magic hat if it can't be used occasionally?

5 | Routines, Routines, Routines

*There are not a large number of routines needed to imple-
ment a TIL. However, the number of routines that can be
created with a machine as simple as a computer is absolutely
amazing. There are routine routines, obscure routines,
clever routines, etc, etc, etc. I personally prefer lucid TIL
routines, but these are very rare creatures indeed.*

5.1 Core TIL Design Notes

The core of any threaded interpretive language is that set of code and
routines necessary to achieve a self-generating language. Fundamental to
designing the core is assessing the resources available to generate and support
the proposed language. The available memory, peripherals and operating
system have a tremendous impact on the design process. Similarly, the
available support software can materially affect the generation process.

To bring the problem down to earth, a certain level of software must exist in
order to generate the TIL. A system monitor/software support system is
presumed and must support program generation, display, debug, execution
and storage on some mass media. It is impossible to bootstrap a language
without some resources. The more sophisticated the support system, the easier
the task.

The very first step in the design process is to segment the available memory.
Memory area is required for stacks, the input buffer, system variables and the
language itself. Remember that the system variables must be initialized, either
by loading them in conjunction with the TIL language load from the mass
media or by an initialization routine. The 1 K-byte stack and input buffer
area presented in figure 3.2 is more than generous. Actually, a 64-byte line
buffer, a variable area, and the stacks could all be contained in a 256-byte area
with few potential problems. But if you can afford the memory, use a
1 K-byte configuration.

The next step is to assess the I/O subroutines available in the system
monitor/software support system. Usually these routines can be "borrowed,"

either by accessing them as subroutines or simply by relocating the routines to the TIL area. Special care must be exercised to clearly identify the protocol used to pass data to and receive data from the I/O.

The actual allocation of processor registers and the design of the inner interpreter is the next step. This design must consider the interfacing of the primitives and secondaries to the inner interpreter. I urge you to spend sufficient time on this design process to convince yourself that a more time efficient design is not possible. Chapter 3 is the design guide for this activity.

The next step in the design process is consideration of a machine code subroutine calling convention. Almost always there will be "functions" that are called by several primitives and may be exactly the same function performed by a keyword. All subroutines must preserve all registers except those used to return parameters and must always preserve the instruction register. A subroutine may use the stack as a means of saving registers for restoration when it completes. It may even return a value on the stack. The calling code must always expect the parameter in a specific return location.

An example of a subroutine that may be called by a primitive and exists as a keyword is the display carriage return-line feed sequence. Suppose a subroutine called $CRLF that performs this function is written. This subroutine may be directly called by primitive machine code. The keyword CRET is then defined as a primitive which simply calls $CRLF and then returns to the inner interpreter NEXT routine.

All subroutines are generally preceded by the symbol $ in this text. This is simply a personal holdover from some forgotten project. Choose a convention to suit yourself and then stick with it.

Given the inner interpreter design, the subroutine calling convention and the register allocations, the input/output routines must be re-examined to verify that conflicts do not exist vis-a-vis the instruction register. Conflicts are resolved in favor of the inner interpreter. The minimum set of I/O routines that must exist is:

$KEY — An input subroutine in machine code that first resets the keyboard and then awaits the next keyboard input. The next input is returned in a known register or address and the keyboard is reset again before exit. This routine must preserve the instruction register. Additional possible functions were discussed in Section 4.3.7.

$ECHO — An output subroutine in machine code that controls the display interface. The routine must recognize ASCII codes and implement display routines for carriage return, line feed, and backspace, and a control code to clear the screen and home the cursor. (Control of the cursor by this routine is assumed.) Printing ASCII codes are displayed and the cursor is moved right one character. This routine must preserve the instruction register.

There are other functions that $ECHO could perform. One that I highly recommend is a variable, time delay loop following a carriage return. This allows routines such as DUMP and ADUMP to be slowed down sufficiently to allow leisurely viewing. Full cursor control (up, down, right, left, and home) is also useful as is a reverse video function. Note that a line feed results in the next display line being cleared, whereas a cursor down command merely moves the cursor down one line with automatic last-to-first line wraparound.

Since the display usually recognizes a subset of the control codes, protection from a function such as ADUMP (which could output characters that are within the display control set) is an excellent idea. One possible way to achieve this end is to set the high-order bit in general display output bytes passed to the $ECHO routine. Then $ECHO would automatically assume that any byte with a high-order bit set is to be displayed and take appropriate action to assure displayability. This latter function is display specific.

If the I/O routines exist as subroutines within the system software, the interface task is generally easy. If not, these routines must be written before the actual TIL design can proceed. This is also true for any software needed to support the development of the TIL code.

One note must be directed toward the line buffer, token separators, and the carriage return function of the input submode. There are several ways to handle the problem of deciding when all the tokens in the line buffer have been extracted and the line buffer is empty. Obviously one way to handle the problem is to store a carriage return ASCII code in the line buffer at the point where it occurs. There are several reasons why this is not a good idea.

Fundamentally, the token scan routine must be able to recognize any character as a token separator, not just the ASCII space code. This allows keywords such as the literal handler "[" to use characters other than the space as a separator since the literal may contain embedded space codes. Secondly, the token scan routine resets the line buffer pointer to point to the first character past the separator after extracting the token. This allows changing the separator for a single call but prevents the next call from returning the previous calls separator as the next token. Finally, there must be a way to recognize that the end of the line has been reached.

The easiest way to handle the problem is to place a termination sequence at the end of the line buffer area. I usually use two terminator characters with their high-order bits 1 set. This implies that they are two's complement negative (easy to test) and not in the ASCII code set (no conflicts). Two characters insure that failure to properly enter an expected separator will not allow skipping over a single terminator.

The input submode always fills the line buffer with ASCII space codes when it is entered. The carriage return simply outputs an ASCII space code to the display to move the cursor right one place before terminating the input submode.

The token scan routine TOKEN takes its separator from the stack. If it is the ASCII space code, leading spaces are ignored in extracting a token. The last character of any token is the character before either the separator or the terminator. In either case, the line buffer pointer is reset to point to the first character past the terminator character before the routine completes.

The terminator character is not in the dictionary and cannot be a number. The invalid keyword handling routine can easily distinguish between an invalid keyword and the terminator. Remember, though, that the terminator characters must be set by the initializing sequence.

Alternates to this technique are possible. I have used different ones. This particular approach, however, leaves the full display line available for input.

Once the preliminary designs and the design decisions have been made, the task of actually designing the outer interpreter can proceed.

5.2 Outer Interpreter Design

A standard approach I use to design a TIL program is the old, inscrutable, top-down structured programming method. I don't know anything about it, but I do like the divide and conquer words. After pursuing this attack to a certain level, I then chuck the top-down and get on with the bottom-up coding. When the top-down meets the bottom-up, I have a checked program.

To design the outer interpreter, I always start with a flow diagram. Figure 5.1 is the example we will pursue. Each subprogram block in the diagram except for START/RESTART and $PATCH will be a dictionary entry. The only reason for this segmentation is that it allows easier checkout of the loop. Each decision block in the diagram implies that the preceding subprogram block has left a flag on the stack to allow the decision to be made.

The general specification of what each routine is to do is *written down*. This includes a specification of its stack input and output along with its interaction with and control over system variables. The type of routine will also be determined — primitive or secondary.

A general specification for the START/RESTART routine is:

START/RESTART — A machine code routine that initializes the system. If the system START flag is True, the address of the start message is placed in the word address register, the system number BASE is set to hexadecimal, and the START flag is set False. If the START flag is initially False, the restart message address is placed in the word address register. (An unconditional jump from the $PATCH routine or other error routines occurs to the code at this point and the address of the error message is expected in the word address register.) The data stack and return stack pointers are initialized and the word address register is pushed to the data stack as the parameter for TYPE. The system MODE and STATE flags are set False. The line buffer termination characters are set as appropriate. Other system registers are initialized as appropriate (design dependent), and a jump to the inner interpreter routine occurs to begin execution of the outer interpreter.

Examples of the start and restart messages are:

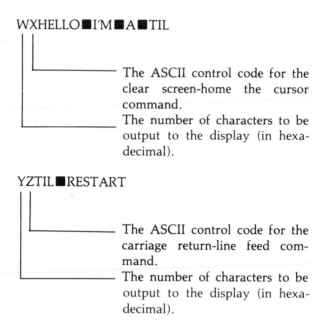

WXHELLO■I'M■A■TIL

The ASCII control code for the clear screen-home the cursor command.

The number of characters to be output to the display (in hexadecimal).

YZTIL■RESTART

The ASCII control code for the carriage return-line feed command.

The number of characters to be output to the display (in hexadecimal).

Personalizing these messages is half the fun of the design of your own language.

There are several methods to jump to the inner interpreter such that the outer interpreter begins execution. They all depend on initializing the instruction register to correctly point to the threaded code for the outer interpreter. From the flow diagram the preliminary outer interpreter threaded code list is designed. For the diagram of figure 5.1, the threaded code list for the outer interpreter is shown in figure 5.2. For this example, the address of TYPE in this threaded list is put in the instruction register, and an unconditional jump to the inner interpreter routine NEXT is executed.

The threaded code list of figure 5.2 was taken directly from the flow diagram of figure 5.1. Each YES in figure 5.1 corresponds to a True (T) in the control flow of figure 5.2; each NO to a False (F). The outer interpreter code does not show the jumps out of inner interpreter control (the dashed lines of figure 5.1). The keyword names are really the word address of the keywords when the actual threaded list of the outer interpreter is coded.

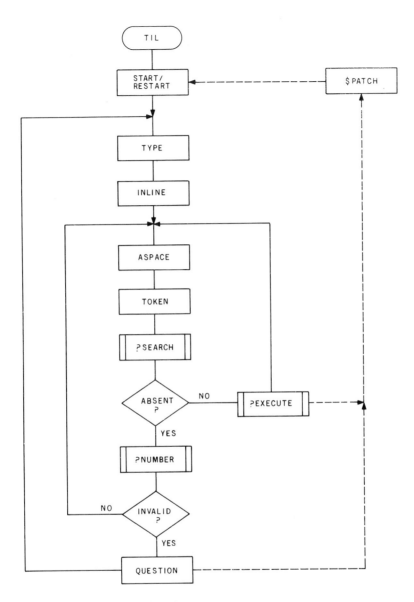

Figure 5.1: *Outer interpreter flowchart.*

The outer interpreter threaded code list is somewhat deceptive. Buried in this list are several secondaries and large primitives needed to do the outer interpreter tasks. Few outer interpreter designs require very many bytes of code. Fundamentally this is because using complex secondaries in the outer interpreter seldom leads to observable time penalties. The outer interpreter is interacting with the operator, who is orders of magnitude slower than the outer interpreter.

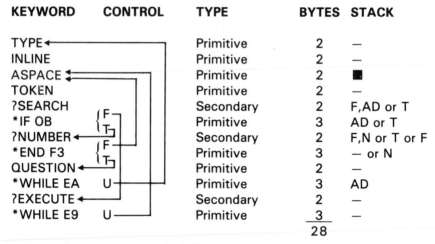

KEYWORD	CONTROL	TYPE	BYTES	STACK
TYPE		Primitive	2	—
INLINE		Primitive	2	—
ASPACE		Primitive	2	■
TOKEN		Primitive	2	—
?SEARCH	F	Secondary	2	F,AD or T
*IF OB	T	Primitive	3	AD or T
?NUMBER	F	Secondary	2	F,N or T or F
*END F3	T	Primitive	3	— or N
QUESTION		Primitive	2	—
*WHILE EA	U	Primitive	3	AD
?EXECUTE		Secondary	2	—
*WHILE E9	U	Primitive	3	—
			28	

Figure 5.2: *Outer interpreter code design.*

TYPE — A primitive with a header. This routine pops the address of a message in TYPE format on the stack (ie: a pointer to the message length followed by that many ASCII characters) and outputs the message to the display. These messages may contain embedded ASCII control codes to control the format of the display. The start message should contain a control code to clear the screen and home the cursor before the message. The restart message should contain control code to issue a "carriage-return line-feed" sequence to the display line. The entrance from $EXECUTE via $PATCH will leave a stack pointer error message address on the address. This message will also contain the "carriage return-line feed" sequence. The entrance from QUESTION via $PATCH will only leave the address of the ■? message on the stack. The "carriage return-line feed" sequence and unrecognized token must be issued by QUESTION before the restart is executed. The direct QUESTION entrance will leave the address of the ■OK message on the stack. It does not contain any control codes. TYPE does not alter any system variables or leave anything on the stack.

INLINE — A primitive without a header that implements the input submode. It expects no stack inputs and returns none. This routine first executes a "carriage return-line feed" sequence to leave the cursor at the first character position of the next display line, and clears the line buffer. It recognizes a backspace command from the keyboard that outputs a space to the current cursor location and moves the cursor left one place, unless the cursor is at the first buffer position location. It recognizes a line-delete command from the keyboard that outputs a line-delete character to the current cursor location and then returns to the start of the INLINE routine. It recognizes a carriage return key and outputs a space to the current cursor location, moves the cursor right one place, sets the system *line buffer pointer* to the first address of the line buffer and exits this routine via a jump to the inner interpreter. All other keyboard input characters are echo displayed and moved to the line buffer (unless the last buffer place has been filled) with lowercase alphabetic characters changed to uppercase. When the last buffer location has been filled, the cursor is no longer advanced. Further entries simply replace the last character on the display line and in the line buffer.

ASPACE — A CCONSTANT with value hexadecimal 20. This routine simply pushes an ASCII space to the low-order byte of the stack. This is the token separator for TOKEN's use in scanning the input line. No system variables are manipulated.

TOKEN — A primitive with a header. This routine expects a token separator on the stack in the low-order byte location. It pops this terminator and also retrieves the *line buffer pointer* from the system variable area. If the separator is an ASCII space, all leading spaces are ignored (ie: the line buffer pointer is advanced to point to the first non-space character). This pointer value is saved and a byte count to the next occurrence of the separator or terminator is generated. This count is placed in the first location of the free dictionary space followed by all the token characters. The system dictionary pointer variable points to the start of the free dictionary area but is not advanced by TOKEN. The line buffer pointer is advanced to point to the character following the terminating separator. The routine leaves no parameters on the stack.

?SEARCH — A secondary with no header. This routine will first search the context vocabulary — trying to locate a keyword whose header matches the token length and descriptor characters of the string moved to the dictionary space by TOKEN. The system variable CONTEXT contains the address of the appropriate context vocabulary. If the search is successful, the keyword word address is returned to the stack as the second stack entry, and a False flag is returned as the top stack entry. If the context vocabulary search is unsuccessful, the system MODE flag is tested. If the MODE flag is False (execute mode), a single True flag is returned at the top of the stack. If the MODE flag is True (compile mode), the COMPILER vocabulary is searched. If the search is successful, the word address of the located keyword is returned to the stack as the second stack entry, a False flag is returned as the top stack entry and the system flag STATE is set True. If the compiler vocabulary search is unsuccessful, a single True flag is returned as the top stack entry. The threaded code for ?SEARCH is shown in figure 5.3. A flag is always the top stack entry when ?SEARCH completes. If this flag is False, the word address of a located keyword is the second stack entry as a parameter for ?EXECUTE.

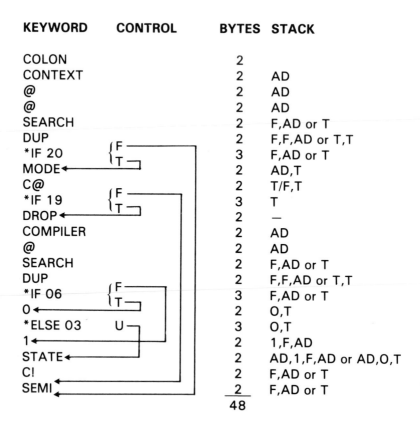

KEYWORD	CONTROL	BYTES	STACK
COLON		2	
CONTEXT		2	AD
@		2	AD
@		2	AD
SEARCH		2	F,AD or T
DUP		2	F,F,AD or T,T
*IF 20	F / T	3	F,AD or T
MODE		2	AD,T
C@		2	T/F,T
*IF 19	F / T	3	T
DROP		2	—
COMPILER		2	AD
@		2	AD
SEARCH		2	F,AD or T
DUP		2	F,F,AD or T,T
*IF 06	F / T	3	F,AD or T
0		2	O,T
*ELSE 03	U	3	O,T
1		2	1,F,AD
STATE		2	AD,1,F,AD or AD,O,T
C!		2	F,AD or T
SEMI		2	F,AD or T
		48	

Figure 5.3: *Code design for ?SEARCH.*

?EXECUTE — A secondary with no header. This routine tests the states of the system MODE flag and the system STATE flag. If the flag states are equal, the word address of the top stack entry is executed. If not, the word address at the top stack entry is enclosed in the dictionary. The system STATE flag is always set False before the possible execution of a keyword can occur. After each keyword execution, a test for stack underflow is made. If underflow occurs, the address of the stack underflow message must be loaded into the word address register and an unconditional jump to the $PATCH routine occurs. The threaded code for the ?EXECUTE routine is shown in figure 5.4.

KEYWORD	CONTROL	BYTES	STACK
COLON		2	AD
STATE		2	AD,AD
C@		2	FG,AD
STATE		2	AD,FG,AD
COSET		2	FG,AD
MODE		2	AD,FG,AD
C@		2	FG,FG,AD
=		2	T/F,AD
*IF 08	F T	3	AD
EXECUTE ←		2	—
*STACK		2	—
*ELSE 03	U	3	—
, ←		2	—
SEMI ←		2	—
		30	

Figure 5.4: *Code design for ?EXECUTE.*

?NUMBER — A secondary with no header. This routine attempts to convert the token located at the free dictionary space to a binary number using the current system number base. If the conversion is unsuccessful, a True flag is pushed to the stack. This will occur if the token is the terminator or if the token is unidentifiable. If a successful conversion occurs, the system MODE flag is checked. If the MODE flag is True, a literal handler plus a number must be added to the dictionary. If the number is within the byte number range, the word address of the byte number literal handler *C# is added to the dictionary followed by the byte number. If the number is not within a byte range, the word address of the word number literal handler *# is added to the dictionary followed by the number. After the literal handler and number entry to the dictionary, a False flag is pushed to the stack. If the conversion is successful and if the system MODE flag is False, the number is pushed to the stack and a False flag is pushed to the stack. This can leave an excess number on the stack which is exactly the right answer in the execute mode. The thread code design for ?NUMBER is shown in figure 5.5

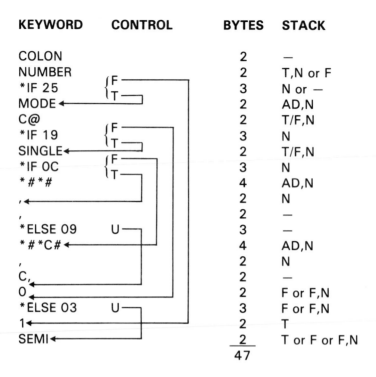

KEYWORD	CONTROL	BYTES	STACK
COLON		2	—
NUMBER		2	T,N or F
*IF 25	F	3	N or —
MODE	T	2	AD,N
C@		2	T/F,N
*IF 19	F	3	N
SINGLE	T	2	T/F,N
*IF 0C	F	3	N
##	T	4	AD,N
,		2	N
,		2	—
*ELSE 09	U	3	—
*#*C#		4	AD,N
,		2	N
C,		2	—
0		2	F or F,N
*ELSE 03	U	3	F or F,N
1		2	T
SEMI		2	T or F or F,N
		47	

Figure 5.5: *Code design for ?NUMBER.*

(A fundamentally circular definition is encountered in the design of ?NUMBER. It fields literals but contains the word number literal handler as a literal number, which is itself the word address of the literal handler followed by its own word address. Thus, if the literal handler word address were XXYY hex, the *#*# of figure 5.5 is YYXX YYXX given the reversed address order of a microcomputer.)

QUESTION — A primitive with a header. This routine tests the high-order bit of the second byte in the free dictionary space. If this bit is 1 set, all of the input buffer tokens have been scanned and a terminator is in the free dictionary space. The address of the ■OK message is pushed to the stack and exit occurs to the inner interpreter NEXT routine. If the bit is zero set, an unidentifiable token has been scanned. In this event, a carriage return-line feed is issued to the display, the token in the free dictionary space is displayed, the address of the ■? message is placed in the word address register and an unconditional jump to the $PATCH routine occurs.

$PATCH — A machine code routine that patches several system variables in the event a system error occurs during the compile mode. $PATCH resets the dictionary pointer and the current vocabulary link to the values that existed prior to the attempt to compile the aborted definition. This also allows a convenient way to abort a semi-completed definition. Simply entering a token which you know the system won't recognize does the trick. I usually use a sequence of Xs to accomplish an abort. A line delete will do the same unless the definition extends over one line or has been partially entered via carriage return. A definition may extend over as many input lines as your mind can support, but remember that the TIL will do exactly what you ask. It doesn't forget unless you type FORGET.

All of the outer interpreter secondaries have been detailed. They are composed of primitives only. The major reason for defining routines as headerless secondaries is simply to make testing easier. The total code count for the outer interpreter and all of its subroutine secondaries is:

Outer Interpreter	28
?SEARCH	48
?EXECUTE	30
?NUMBER	47
	153 bytes

An 18-byte penalty is paid for defining the three headerless secondaries. This is a price well worth paying at checkout time.

A complete list of the keywords needed to directly implement the outer interpreter is given in table 5.1. The rough size of each keyword (including headers) is given in this list. A byte count to this point yields:

Inner Interpreter	≈	50
Start/Restart	≈	50
Secondaries	≈	150
Primitives	≈	825
		1075

This list of code is still deceptively small. It does not consider the I/O subroutines needed to support table 5.1 primitives, several system variables, and the defining and compiling keywords required both in support of the table 5.1 keywords and in allowing a self-generating language. There are between 400 and 700 bytes involved in these routines.

KEYWORD TYPE	KEYWORD NAME	≈ BYTES
OPERATORS	TYPE	25
	INLINE	95
	SEARCH	70
	TOKEN	60
	NUMBER	90
	@	15
	C@	20
	,	20
	C,	20
	DUP	15
	DROP	10
	C1SET	15
	COSET	15
	=	25
	SINGLE	20
	*STACK	20
	QUESTION	35
CONSTANTS	ASPACE	10
	0	10
	1	10
VARIABLES	CONTEXT	15
	COMPILER	15
	STATE	15
	MODE	15
PROGRAM CONTROL DIRECTIVES	*IF	10
	*END	10
	*WHILE	10
	*ELSE	10
LITERAL HANDLERS	*#	15
	*C#	15
SUBROUTINES	$PATCH	35
	$CRLF	15
SYSTEM MESSAGES		40

Table 5.1: *Outer interpreter keyword sizes.*

At this point I will abandon the pursuit of the exact keywords needed to complete the TIL design. After all, this is only one example of an outer interpreter. There is no "right" design and no "right" choice of a keyword as a primitive or a secondary.

The design procedure to this point is really nothing more than identifying the functions to be performed and associating a keyword name with the function. I highly recommend "headerless" secondaries as a method of segmenting larger code blocks as long as timing consideration allows. In the outer interpreter for a terminal-directed TIL, the slower secondary nesting is acceptable.

This slower approach may not be feasible in a high-speed widget sorting program.

5.3 Routine Routines

There are obviously a number of routines, both primitive and subroutine, needed to mechanize the outer interpreter. These routines are really the heart of the system design. To present the designs both flowcharts and Z80 specific listings will be used.

5.3.1 START/RESTART

The start/restart routine really has two entrances: one that initializes the entire system and calls up either the start or restart message, and one that does a partial system initialization and presumes an error message has already been set up.

A listing of equivalent Z80 assembly code is given in listing 5.1. This particular mechanization presumes that the system variables MODE and STATE share adjacent memory cells, and the system variable BASE is initially stored as zero during system loading. The variable BASE may thus be used to distinguish a start from a restart. The abort entrance, like a restart, does not change the system base but performs all other initializations.

```
START:  LD    DE,RSTMSG    ;RESTART MESSAGE ADDRESS TO WA
        LD    A,{BASE}     ;GET SYSTEM BASE
        AND   A            ;TEST IT FOR ZERO
        JR    NZ,ABORT     ;IF IT'S ZERO, IT'S A START
        LD    A,10         ;ELSE GET HEX BASE
        LD    {BASE},A     ;AND STORE IT AT BASE
        LD    DE,SRTMSG    ;START MESSAGE ADDRESS TO WA
ABORT:  LD    SP,STACK     ;SET SYSTEM DATA STACK
        PUSH  DE           ;PUSH MESSAGE ADDRESS
        LD    HL,0
        LD    {MODE},HL    ;SET MODE=0, STATE=0
        LD    IY,NEXT      ;SET I² NEXT ADDRESS TO IY
        LD    IX,RETURN    ;SET RETURN STACK
        LD    HL,8080      ;GET TWO TERMINATORS
        LD    {LBEND},HL   ;STORE TO END OF LINE BUFFER
        LD    BC,OUTER     ;START OF OUTER INTERPRETER
        JP    NEXT         ;JUMP TO I² NEXT CODE
```

Listing 5.1: *Assembly code for START/RESTART. Note that OUTER is the address of TYPE in the threaded list for the outer interpreter.*

5.3.2 INLINE

The input submode is mechanized by the INLINE routine. Although INLINE could be implemented as either a primitive or a secondary, a primitive form will be presumed.

A flowchart of the INLINE function is shown in figure 5.6. One point is worth stressing in this design. The routine controls the cursor location by issuing carriage return, line feed and backspace commands to the display device. The buffer pointer BP points to the line buffer position where the next character will be stored. An equivalent Z80 assembly code listing is given in listing 5.2.

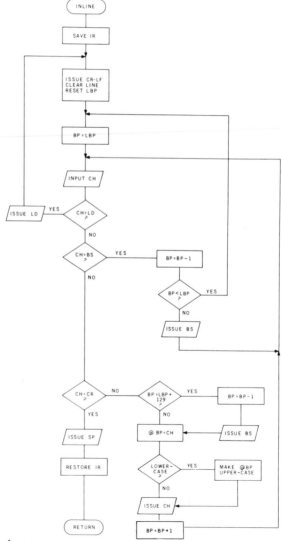

Figure 5.6: *INLINE flowchart.*

```
INLINE:    * + 2                ;PRIMITIVE CODE ADDRESS
           PUSH   BC            ;SAVE THE IR
START:     CALL   $CRLF         ;ISSUE CR-LF
           LD     HL,LBADD      ;GET START OF LINE BUFFER
           LD     {LBP},HL      ;RESET LBP
           LD     B,LENGTH      ;SET BUFFER LENGTH
CLEAR:     LD     {HL},20       ;LOAD SPACE TO BUFFER
           INC    HL            ;BUMP BUFFER POINTER
           DJNZ   CLEAR         ;LOOP TO CLEAR BUFFER
ZERO:      LD     L,0           ;BACK TO FIRST BUFFER LOCATION
INKEY:     CALL   $KEY          ;INPUT A CHARACTER
           CP     "LD"          ;IS IT A LINE DELETE?
           JR     NZ,TSTBS      :IF NOT SKIP LD CODE
           CALL   $ECHO         ;ELSE ISSUE LINE DELETE
           JR     START         ;AND START OVER
TSTBS:     CP     "BS"          ;IS IT A BACK SPACE?
           JR     NZ,TSTCR      ;IF NOT SKIP BS CODE
           DEC    L             ;DECREMENT BUFFER POINTER
           JP     M,ZERO        ;RESET TO ZERO IF NEGATIVE
           LD     {HL},20       ;LOAD SPACE TO THE BUFFER
ISSUE:     CALL   $ECHO         ;DISPLAY THE CHARACTER
           JR     INKEY         ;AND RETURN FOR NEXT
TSTCR:     CP     "CR"          ;IS IT A CARRIAGE RETURN ?
           JR     Z,LAST1       ;IF SO, GO TO EXIT INLINE
           BIT    7,L           ;IF BIT SET, AT 129TH PLACE
           JR     NZ,END        ;DO BUFFER END TASK AT 129
SAVEIT:    LD     {HL},A        ;SAVE CHARACTERS IN BUFFER
           CP     61            ;IS IT LESS THAN LC A?
           JR     C,NOTLC       ;IF SO, SKIP LC CODE
           CP     7B            ;IS IT MORE THAN LC Z ?
           JR     NC,NOTLC      ;IF SO, SKIP LC CODE
           RES    5,{HL}        ;ELSE MAKE LC UC IN BUFFER
NOTLC:     INC    L             ;BUMP POINTER
           JR     ISSUE         ;GO ISSUE CHARACTER
END:       DEC    L             ;BACK UP TO 128TH PLACE
           LD     C,A           ;SAVE THE INPUT CHARACTER
           LD     A,"BS"        ;GET BACK SPACE CHARACTER
           CALL   $ECHO         ;MOVE CURSOR LEFT
           LD     A,C           ;RESTORE ORIGINAL CHARACTER
           JR     SAVEIT        ;GO PUT IT AT 128TH PLACE
LAST1:     LD     A,20          ;REPLACE CR BY A SPACE
           CALL   $ECHO         ;AND ISSUE IT
           POP    BC            ;RESTORE IR
           JP     {IY}          ;RETURN TO I² NEXT ROUTINE
```

Listing 5.2: *INLINE Z80 primitive. This routine presumes a 128 byte line buffer which starts on a page boundary.*

5.3.3 Token Extracting

The token-extracting routine is mechanized as the keyword TOKEN in the design presented. The TOKEN keyword can be either a primitive or a secondary, although I usually design it as a primitive. This routine moves the next token in the line buffer to the free dictionary space in extended header format.

A flowchart of the TOKEN routine is shown in figure 5.7. Note that LBP

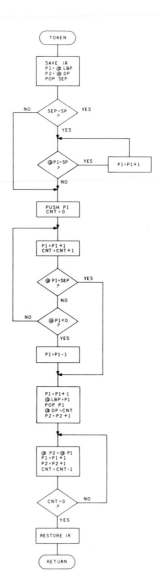

Figure 5.7: *TOKEN flowchart. P1 points to the line buffer; P2 points to the dictionary space; SEP is the separator.*

and DP are system variables whose contents point to the line buffer and dictionary free space respectively. The LBP variable will point to the start of the line buffer the first time TOKEN is used to scan a token after a line entry. TOKEN will reset LBP to point to the first line buffer address following the token separator each time it is called. This particular design presumes that two terminators are stored immediately following the line buffer. These terminators act as permanent separators. Two terminators are required to allow the first to terminate the last token on the line and to insure that the next call to TOKEN will return a terminator. A listing of the Z80 assembly code to implement TOKEN is given in listing 5.3.

```
                DATA   #5,T,O,K    ;TOKEN'S IDENTIFIER
                DATA   "LINK"      ;LINK ADDRESS
TOKEN:   *+2                       ;PRIMITIVE CODE ADDRESS
                EXX                ;SAVES IR
                LD     HL,{LBP}    ;GET POINTER TO TOKEN
                LD     DE,{DP}     ;GET POINTER TO DICTIONARY
                POP    BC          ;SEPARATOR IN C, B IS ZERO
                LD     A,20        ;SPACE CODE TO A REG
                CP     C           ;IS SEPARATOR A SPACE ?
                JR     NZ,TOK      ;IF NOT, TOKEN START
IGNLB:   CP     {HL}              ;IS IT A SPACE ?
                JR     NZ,TOK      ;IF NOT, TOKEN START
                INC    L           ;BUMP THE POINTER
                JR     IGNLB       ;TRY NEXT CHARACTER
TOK:     PUSH   HL                 ;SAVE TOKEN START ADDRESS
COUNT:   INC    B                  ;INCREMENT COUNT
                INC    L           ;BUMP THE POINTER
                LD     A,{HL}      ;GET THE NEXT CHARACTER
                CP     C           ;IS IT A SEPARATOR ?
                JR     Z,ENDTOK    ;IF SO, TOKEN END
                RLA                ;BIT 7 TO CY
                JR     NC,COUNT    ;IF CY=0, NOT AT END
                DEC    L           ;BACK UP 1 IF A TERMINATOR
ENDTOK:  INC    L                  ;STEP PAST SEPARATOR
                LD     {LBP},HL    ;UPDATE LBP FOR NEXT CALL
                LD     A,B         ;MOVE COUNT TO A REG
                LD     {DE},A      ;LENGTH TO DICTIONARY
                INC    DE          ;BUMP DICTIONARY ADDRESS
                POP    HL          ;GET TOKEN START ADDRESS
                LD     C,B         ;GET COUNT TO BC
                LD     B,0         ;
                LDIR               ;MOVE TOKEN TO DICTIONARY
                EXX                ;RESTORE IR
                JP     {IY}        ;RETURN TO I² NEXT ROUTINE
```

Listing 5.3: *TOKEN: Z80 primitive.*

5.3.4. SEARCH

SEARCH is the routine within ?SEARCH which actually searches the vocabularies for a given keyword. It has a header since it will be compiled into other keywords after a self-generating language is achieved. I generally code this routine as a primitive to insure that keywords can be located as rapidly as possible.

SEARCH is called with the address of the first keyword header in the linked list to be searched as the top stack entry (ie: the address of the three in the DUP header in the example of figure 2.1). The token being searched for is located in the free dictionary space in extended header format. The search routine will test the length and up to three characters of the keyword name. The first detected mismatch causes the next header in the linked list to become the next candidate for a match. This procedure will continue until either a match occurs or the bottom of the list is reached (a zero link address). If a match occurs, the word address of the located keyword is pushed to the stack followed by a False flag. If the bottom of the list is reached, a True flag is pushed to the stack.

A flow diagram of the SEARCH routine is given in figure 5.8 and a Z80 assembly code listing is given in listing 5.4.

```
         DATA  #6,S,E,A   ;SEARCH'S IDENTIFIER
         DATA  "LINK"     ;LINK ADDRESS
SEARCH:  *+2              ;PRIMITIVE CODE ADDRESS
         EXX              ;SAVES IR
         POP   HL         ;GET 1ST HEADER ADDRESS
TESTIT:  PUSH  HL         ;SAVE START OF HEADER
         LD    DE,{DP}    ;GET DICTIONARY POINTER
         LD    C,0        ;USED WITH B AS A FALSE FLAG
         LD    A,{DE}     ;GET DICTIONARY TOKEN LENGTH
         CP    {HL}       ;SAME AS KEYWORD LENGTH ?
         JR    NZ,NXTHDR  ;IF NOT, GO TO NEXT HEADER
         CP    4          ;IS LENGTH OVER 3 ?
         JR    C,BELO4    ;IF NOT, SKIP 3 SET CODE
         LD    A,3        ;SET LENGTH TO 3
BELO4:   LD    B,A        ;SAVE LENGTH AS COUNT
NXTCH:   INC   HL         ;BUMP HEADER POINTER
         INC   DE         ;BUMP DICTIONARY POINTER
         LD    A,{DE}     ;GET NEXT DICTIONARY CHARACTER
         CP    {HL}       ;MATCH KEYWORD CHARACTER ?
         JR    NZ,NXTHDR  ;IF NOT, GO TO NEXT HEADER
         DJNZ  NXTCH      ;ELSE GO TEST NEXT CHARACTER
         POP   HL         ;START OF FOUND HEADER
         LD    DE,6       ;START OF HEADER PLUS 6
         ADD   HL,DE      ;EQUALS WORD ADDRESS
         PUSH  HL         ;PUSH WA; BC=0 FOR FLAG
         JR    FLAG       ;DONE AND KEYWORD FOUND
```

```
NXTHDR: POP   HL         ;GET START OF CURRENT HEADER
        LD    DE,4       ;PLUS 4 EQUALS LINK ADDRESS
        ADD   HL,DE      ;TO NEXT KEYWORD
        LD    E,{HL}     ;GET LINK ADDRESS OR THE
        INC   HL         ;START OF THE NEXT
        LD    D,{HL}     ;HEADER
        EX    DE,HL      ;
        LD    A,H        ;TEST LINK ADDRESS FOR ZERO
        OR    L          ;OR LAST KEYWORD
        JR    NZ,TESTIT  ;IF NOT 0, TEST NEXT HEADER
        LD    C,1        ;FLAG = 1, IF NOT FOUND
FLAG:   PUSH  BC         ;PUSH FLAG
        EXX              ;RESTORE IR
        JP    {IY}       ;RETURN TO I² NEXT ROUTINE
```

Listing 5.4: *SEARCH: Z80 primitive.*

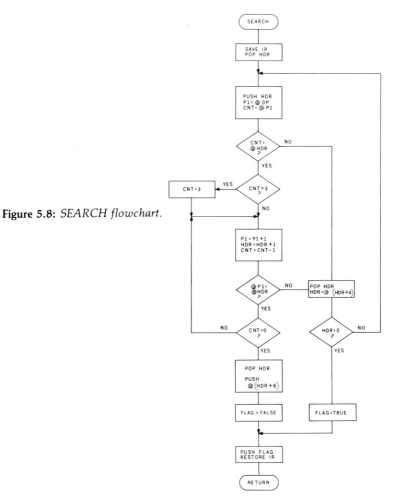

Figure 5.8: *SEARCH flowchart.*

5.3.5. NUMBER ───────────────────────────

The NUMBER routine is a headerless primitive called by ?NUMBER to convert tokens to binary numbers. It is the single most complex routine in the design. On entrance there is a token, in extended header form at the free dictionary space, a length character followed by that number of ASCII characters. NUMBER will convert this token to a binary number if it is a valid number and push the number and a True flag to the stack. If NUMBER determines that the token is not a valid number, it pushes only a False flag (zero) to the stack.

The first character in a valid number token may be an ASCII minus sign (hexadecimal 2D). With this exception, all token characters are first tested to determine that they are in the set hexadecimal 30 thru 39 by subtracting hexadecimal 30 from the character (remember that hexadecimal 30 is an ASCII 0 and hexadecimal 39 is an ASCII 9) and testing to see that the result is between 0 and 9. If the result is negative the character cannot be in the valid number set. If the result is more than hexadecimal 9 but less than hexadecimal 11, it is not in the valid character set since an ASCII A less hexadecimal 30 is 11 hexadecimal. If the result is more than hexadecimal 10, an additional hexadecimal 7 is subtracted which converts ASCII A,B,...F,G,... to 0A, 0B,...,0F, 10,... hexadecimals. The procedure to this point simply converts ASCII characters to binary numbers. The number is then tested to verify that it is in the set {0 thru (BASE−1)}. If all goes well the token is still in the acceptable number token set.

The overall procedure is a sequential conversion process. The result is first set to zero. The process then tests to see if a leading minus sign is present. A flag is set to indicate this event. As each token character is scanned and converted to a number, the results are updated as:

$$Result = Result * BASE + Number$$

When all token characters have been input, the sign flag is tested. If the original token had a leading minus sign, the two's complement of the number is saved as the result.

The procedure is depicted in the flowchart of figure 5.9 and a Z80 listing is given in listing 5.5.

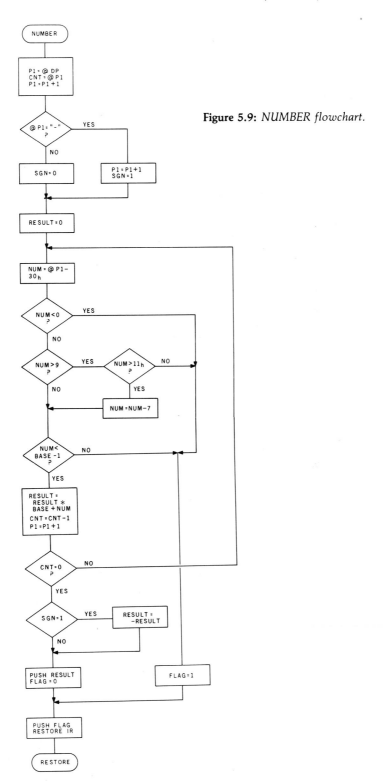

Figure 5.9: *NUMBER flowchart.*

```
NUMBER:   * +2                      ;NUMBER'S CODE ADDRESS
          EXX                       ;SAVES IR
          LD     HL,{DP}            ;GET POINTER TO DICTIONARY
          LD     B,{HL}             ;GET LENGTH OF TOKEN {COUNT}
          INC    HL                 ;BUMP POINTER
          LD     A,{HL}             ;GET FIRST CHARACTER
          CP     2D                 ;IS IT A MINUS SIGN ?
          LD     A,0                ;SET SIGN FLAG TO FALSE
          JR     NZ,SKIPSAV         ;IF POSITIVE, SKIP TO FLAG SAVE
          DEC    A                  ;MAKE SIGN FLAG TRUE
          DEC    B                  ;DECREASE COUNT BY 1
          INC    HL                 ;BUMP PAST MINUS SIGN
SKIPSAV:  EX     AF,AF'             ;SAVE SIGN FLAG IN AF'
          LD     DE,0               ;ZERO DE REG PAIR
          PUSH   DE                 ;SAVE AS FLAG
          PUSH   DE                 ;SAVE AS RESULT
NLOOP:    LD     A,{HL}             ;GET NEXT CHARACTER
          SUB    30                 ;SUBTRACT NUMBERS BIAS
          JR     C,NOTNO            ;IF·CY = 1, NOT A NUMBER {<0}
          CP     0A                 ;LESS THAN 10 {A DIGIT} ?
          JR     C,NUMB             ;IF CY = 1, IT'S A DIGIT
          CP     11                 ;IF A UC LETTER, IT'S OVER 17
          JR     C,NOTNO            ;ELSE IT'S NOT A NUMBER
          SUB    7                  ;SUBTRACT ADDITIONAL LETTERS BIAS
NUMB:     LD     E,A                ;SAVE BINARY NUMBER IN E REG
          LD     A,{BASE}           ;GET SYSTEM NUMBER BASE
          DEC    A                  ;VALID SET IS {0,BASE − 1}
          CP     E                  ;IS THE BINARY NUMBER VALID ?
          JR     NC,ANUMB           ;CHEERS, IT'S A VALID NUMBER
NOTNO:    POP    HL                 ;POP RESULT, LEAVING FALSE ON
          EXX                       ;THE STACK; RESTORE IR
          JP     {IY}               ;RETURN TO I² NEXT ROUTINE
ANUMB:    EX     {SP},HL            ;GET RESULT & SAVE POINTER
          EX     DE,HL              ;RESULT TO DE AS MULTIPLICAND
          PUSH   BC                 ;SAVE COUNT
          PUSH   HL                 ;SAVE NEW BINARY NUMBER
          LD     BC,0800            ;GET MULTIPLY COUNT
          INC    A                  ;RESTORE BASE IN A REG {MULTIPLIER}
          LD     L,C                ;ZERO HL AS THE PRODUCT AREA
          LD     H,C
MLOOP:    ADD    HL,HL              ;SHIFT PRODUCT AND MULTIPLIER
          ADC    A                  ;LEFT 1 BIT
          JR     NC,SKPADD          ;IF CY = 0, SKIP ADD
          ADD    HL,DE              ;ELSE ADD MULTIPLICAND
SKPADD:   DJNZ   MLOOP              ;LOOP TO COMPLETE MULTIPLY
          POP    DE                 ;GET BINARY NUMBER BACK
          ADD    HL,DE              ;RESULT = PRODUCT + NUMBER
```

```
          POP   BC          ;RESTORE COUNT
          EX    {SP},HL     ;GET POINTER & SAVE RESULT
          INC   HL          ;BUMP THE POINTER
          DJNZ  NLOOP       ;LOOP FOR ALL CHARACTERS
          POP   DE          ;GET FINAL RESULT
          POP   HL          ;THE FALSE FLAG {A ZERO}
          EX    AF,AF'      ;GET SIGN FLAG FROM AF'
          AND   A           ;IS IT ZERO ? {ALSO CY=0}
          JR    Z,DONE      ;SKIP COMPLEMENT IF POSITIVE
          SBC   HL,DE       ;COMPLEMENT RESULT
          EX    DE,HL       ;FINAL FINAL RESULT TO DE
DONE:     PUSH  DE          ;FINAL RESULT TO THE STACK
          SCF               ;MAKE AF TRUE {≠0}
          PUSH  AF          ;PUSH TRUE FLAG
          EXX               ;RESTORE IR
          JP    {IY}        ;RETURN TO I² NEXT ROUTINE
```

Listing 5.5: *NUMBER: Z80 primitive.*

5.3.6 QUESTION ──────────────────────────────────

The QUESTION keyword is a non-structured primitive. It has a single entrance but may return to the inner interpreter or may exit to START/RESTART via $PATCH. The first character in the token at the free dictionary space determines which action will occur. If the high-order bit of this character is set, the token is a terminator. This implies that all operator requested actions are complete and the line buffer is empty. In this event the address of the ■OK message is pushed to the stack and the routine exits to NEXT. The outer interpreter will then jump into TYPE to display this message.

If the token is not a terminator, it must be an unknown token since it could not be found in the dictionary or converted to a valid number. In this event, a carriage return-line feed is issued to the display and the unknown token is echo displayed to the operator. The address of the ■? message is then loaded to the WA register and the routine exits to $PATCH. The $PATCH routine will patch the system if the unknown token was discovered while the compile mode was in effect.

A listing of the Z80 assembly code for this routine is given in listing 5.6. In this listing, note that the primitive TYPE is called as an in-line subroutine by changing the IY register to force a return to QUESTION.

```
QUESTION:  *+2              ;QUESTION'S CODE ADDRESS
           LD    HL,{DP}    ;GET POINTER TO DICTIONARY
           INC   HL         ;STEP OVER TOKEN LENGTH
```

```
              BIT    7,{HL}          ;IF BIT SET, A TERMINATOR
              JR     Z,ERROR         ;IF NOT SET, AN ERROR
              LD     DE,OK           ;PUT OK MESSAGE ADDRESS IN WA
              PUSH   DE              ;SAVE OK MESSAGE
              JP     {IY}            ;RETURN TO I² NEXT ROUTINE
ERROR:        CALL   $CRLF           :ISSUE CR−LF BEFORE UNKNOWN TOKEN
              LD     IY,RETURN       ;SET IY TO RETURN TO THIS ROUTINE
              DEC    HL              ;BACK-UP TO TOKEN LENGTH
              JP     $TYPE           ;GO ECHO UNKNOWN TOKEN
RETURN:       LD     DE,MSG?         ;? MESSAGE ADDRESS TO WA
              JP     $PATCH          ;GO PATCH SYSTEM BEFORE RESTART
```

Listing 5.6: *QUESTION: Z80 primitive.*

5.3.7 *STACK

The *STACK routine is a primitive without a header. Like QUESTION, *STACK is a nonstructured routine in that it has a single entrance but a dual exit. *STACK tests for stack underflow. If an underflow condition does not exist, a normal exit to NEXT occurs. If underflow is detected, the stack pointer is reset to point to the correct top of stack address, the stack error message address is loaded to the WA register and a jump to $PATCH is executed. This will patch the system and reinitialize the system before displaying the stack error message and reverting to the input submode. A Z80 assembly code listing for this routine is given in listing 5.7.

```
*STACK:   *+2                  ;*STACK'S CODE ADDRESS
          LD     HL,STACK      ;GET TOP OF STACK ADDRESS
          AND    A             ;RESET THE CARRY FLAG
          SBC    HL,SP         ;SUBTRACT CURRENT SP
          JR     NC,OK         ;IF CY=0, NO UNDERFLOW
          ADD    HL,SP         ;ELSE RESTORE TOP ADDRESS
          LD     SP,HL         ;AND RESET STACK POINTER
          LD     DE,STKMSG     ;STACK ERROR MESSAGE ADDRESS TO WA
          JP     $PATCH        ;GO PATCH SYSTEM BEFORE RESTART
OK:       JP     {IY}          ;RETURN TO I² IF NO UNDERFLOW
```

Listing 5.7: *STACK: Z80 primitive.*

5.3.8 $PATCH

The routine $PATCH is a machine language routine that is used to patch system variables in the event a system-detected error occurs during the compile mode. Any system-detected error that could occur during the compile mode should enter START/RESTART via $PATCH. System-detected errors that can occur only in the execute mode may jump unconditionally to START/RESTART.

$PATCH resets the dictionary pointer DP and the CURRENT vocabulary link to the values that existed prior to the start of the aborted compile mode definition. If the MODE of the system is the compile mode on entry, $PATCH resets DP to the address that is the header address of the latest keyword in the CURRENT vocabulary. The link address in this header is then stored as the pointer to the latest entry in the CURRENT vocabulary. This delinks the partially entered keyword from the system and re-establishes the dictionary free space to its previous value. A Z80 assembly code listing for this routine is given as listing 5.8.

```
$PATCH: LD    A,{MODE}       ;GET MODE VARIABLE
        AND   A              ;IS IT ZERO {EXECUTE} ?
        JP    Z,ABORT        ;IF SO, GO TO RESTART
        PUSH  DE             ;ELSE SAVE MESSAGE ADDRESS
        LD    HL,{CURRENT}   ;GET VOCABULARY ADDRESS
        LD    E,{HL}         ;IT POINTS TO THE LATEST
        INC   HL             ;ENTRY,WHICH WAS ABORTED
        LD    D,{HL}         ;THIS IS WHERE DP SHOULD
        EX    DE,HL          ;POINT
        LD    {DP},HL        ;RESTORE DP
        LD    A,5            ;BUMP POINTER TO THE
        ADD   A,L            ;LINK ADDRESS OF THE ABORTED
        LD    L,A            ;KEYWORD BY ADDING 5
        JR    NC,SKIP        ;
        INC   H              ;
SKIP:   LD    A,{HL}         ;MOVE LINK ADDRESS TO THE
        LD    {DE},A         ;CURRENT VOCABULARY AS
        DEC   HL             ;THE POINTER TO ITS
        DEC   DE             ;LATEST ENTRY
        LD    A,{HL}         ;
        LD    {DE},A         ;
        POP   DE             ;RESTORE MESSAGE ADDRESS
        JP    ABORT          ;AND EXIT TO RESTART
```

Listing 5.8: *$PATCH code.*

5.4 Doing It

Given the design, the actual coding can begin. There are as many ways to program a TIL as there are computer/software combinations. My favorite way involves hand-assembling and machine-coding the language until the self-generating phase is reached, but there are other methods. Almost all coding methods involve keeping track of the header addresses and word addresses of the individual keywords as well as their vocabulary linkage. One assembly listing of the entire TIL can be generated. This will keep track of all the addresses using a symbol table.

One neat trick for testing a TIL involves a register trapping scheme. My systems always support a trap routine that will display all registers and several levels of the stack. Defining a primitive that calls this trap routine results in an easy way to debug the TIL. I almost always start the TIL code by coding the system variables and their access routines: the start/restart routine, the inner interpreter, the system messages, and the TYPE keyword. The outer interpreter is initially defined as just the TYPE word address followed by the trap primitive word address. Within half an hour of starting the actual code generation, the system is happily saying:

HELLO, I'M A TIL

followed by the trap register and stack display. The registers, the stack, and the initialization of the systems variables can then be verified.

As each new keyword in the outer interpreter is coded, its word address is added to the outer interpreter threaded list and the trap routine is moved to the next following location (or the next relative jump location). When the first secondary is called, it is first defined as just the trap primitive. The build and test then follows down this secondary. As each new keyword is added, the build and test extends, until a return to the outer interpreter occurs.

A gentle build process allows a fairly thorough testing of the routines as they are added. A top-down testing approach has as many advantages as the top-down design approach.

5.5 Arithmetic Subroutines

Most microcomputers are noted for their lack of arithmetic machine-code instructions. Almost all have 8-bit addition and subtraction instructions; some even have 16-bit addition and subtraction instructions, but few have multiply and divide instructions. The multiply and divide keywords of Section 4.3.4 must be implemented using algorithms, based on the addition and subtraction instructions. The keywords selected for inclusion in the TIL are based partially on constraints arising from the need to emulate multiplication and division.

Multiplication of unsigned integers is fairly easy to emulate on most microcomputers. Division is usually more difficult and slower. The multiply- and divide-based keywords depend somewhat on how easy it is to define reasonably efficient algorithms. Execution speed is the primary design goal, but memory utilization cannot be neglected. Depending on the instruction set available to the designer, a subroutine approach is usually most efficient.

To emulate signed multiply and divide keywords, there are four steps (or subroutines) that can be isolated. The input numbers from the stack are first converted to positive integers after having computed and saved the sign of the result. The multiply or divide of the positive integers is then done resulting in a positive integer. The sign of the result is changed if the sign of the result computed during the input step calls for a negative result. Finally, the results are formatted and returned to the stack. The subroutines associated with these four steps need to be identified and designed.

Table 5.2 lists the keywords of interest and associates each keyword with the appropriate root unsigned multiply and/or divide algorithm(s). The root algorithms are subroutined as follows:

$US* — An 8 by 8 bit multiply with a 16-bit product.
$UD* — A 16 by 8 bit multiply with a 24-bit product.
$US/ — A 16 by 8 bit divide with a 8-bit quotient and 8-bit remainder.
$UD/ — A 24 by 8 bit divide with a 16-bit quotient and 8-bit remainder.

These subroutines expect positive input integers in pre-defined registers (or memory locations) and return result in pre-defined locations.

INPUT	KEYWORD	OUTPUT	SUBROUTINE
N1(8)*NO(8)	S*	NO(16)	$US*
N1(16)*NO(8)	*	NO(16)	$UD*
N1(16)*NO(8)	D*	NO(8)$_h$,N1(16)$_l$	$UD*
N1(16)/NO(8)	/MOD	NO(8)$_r$,N1(8)$_q$	$US/
N1(16)/NO(8)	/	NO(8)$_q$	$US/
N1(16)/NO(8)	MODU/	NO(8)$_q$,N1(8)$_r$	$US/
N1(16)/NO(8)	MOD	NO(8)$_r$	$US/
N2(16)$_l$,N1(8)$_h$/NO(8)	D/MOD	NO(8)$_r$,N1(16)$_q$	$UD*
N2(16)*N1(8)/NO(8)	*/	NO(16)$_q$	$UD*,$UD/
N2(16)*N$(8)/NO(8)	*/MOD	NO(8)$_r$,N1(16)$_q$	$UD*,$UD/

Table 5.2: *Multiply and divide operations.*

All of the keywords, except D/MOD, "*/" and */MOD, expect two stack numbers on entry. Even in the case of an expected 8-bit number, the inputs are on the stack as 16-bit signed numbers. Except for the three keywords noted, a common routine can be defined to compute and save the sign of the result and convert any negative input integer to positive. The products or quotients returned are always pushed to the stack as signed 16-bit numbers except for the results of D*. Note that remainders are always positive. A common routine can be used to correct the results if they are negative for all of the keywords except D*. Two subroutines can then be defined as:

$ISIGN— The signs of the input numbers are exclusive-OR'ed and the result is saved as the result sign bit. Both input members are converted to positive integers as required.

$OSIGN — Retrieves the result sign bit and two's complements the result if the bit is 1 set.

It should be realized that $ISIGN also expects the input numbers in a known location and not on the stack, otherwise the input numbers are below the subroutine return which is pushed to the stack when $ISIGN is called.

These six subroutines are then used to implement the ten keywords associated with the multiply and divide keywords. The decision to use subroutines results in slower keywords than if in-line code routines had been defined. However, subroutines are very memory-efficient and the speed penalty is slight. The definition of the root algorithms as subroutines also allows them to be used to define other keywords. For example, a 16 by 16-bit multiply that returns a 32-bit product can be easily designed based on two calls to $UD*. In point of fact this results in the fastest 16 by 16-bit multiply for the Z80.

Exactly how you define your number crunching routines depends on your application. The extremes run the gamut from a secondary definition to multiply by successive addition (using add and loop primitives) to a straight non-looping algorithm in machine code with in-line sign fielding. Number crunching may not even be required for some applications and may be omitted entirely. The subroutined approach given here along with fast looping root algorithms is a compromise that achieves fair execution efficiency along with reasonable memory needs.

6 | Words, Words, and More Words

If you think that I'm merely going to bandy words with you, you're right. Ignore walruses and other figments of mathematical minds; the time is here and now. After all, CABBAGES and KINGS are both viable TIL keyword names.

6.1 The Word

Following a few, brief introductory remarks, here are page upon page of keyword descriptions. With any sort of luck at all, they will be arranged in ASCII alphabetic order. The composite collection is not quite a language specification nor is it really intended to be. The code descriptions are Z80 specific in many cases, which limits their universal applicability. Most of the descriptions are simple enough to allow recoding for an alternate central processing unit.

The general format of the descriptions is as follows:

Name — My arbitrary name for the keyword which may be changed to your favorite flavor.
Class — A vague attempt to classify the keywords into groups of like usage.
Function — A description of what the keyword is to accomplish.
Usage — Given you have got it, why you want it.
Z80 Code — A semi Z80 assembly language description of the code body of primitives, including explanatory comments. These listings do not include the header or the code address, but include the return address if and only if a label precedes the return.
Code — A list of the primitive and secondary keywords that constitute the code body of a secondary. They include relative jump bytes in hexadecimal. Sans headers, COLON addresses and SEMI addresses.
Bytes — The total byte count for the keyword including the header, the code address and the return address where applicable. Specific to the Z80 for Z80

code listings but generally indicative of keyword sizes.

Notes — A list of the funnies and restrictions associated with some keywords.

Formal Definition — The formal definition of the secondary keywords given that the entire language existed. These keywords cannot usually be defined by the formal definition. For example, the formal definition of ":" presumes the existence of ":".

On with the show.

!

Class:	Memory Reference
Function:	Stores second stack entry at the address at the top stack entry, removing both entries.
Input/Output:	Two stack entries/None
Usage:	Storage of word length data in programmable memory.
Z80 Code:	

```
          POP   HL      ;GET ADDRESS
          POP   DE      ;GET DATA
          LD    {HL},E  ;STORE BYTE
          INC   HL      ;BUMP ADDRESS
          LD    {HL},D  ;STORE BYTE
```

BYTES: 15

#

Class:	I/O
Function:	Pops the top stack entry, computes the quotient and remainder relative to the system number base, converts the remainder to an ASCII character (0 thru 9, A thru Z), pushes the character, then pushes the quotient.
Input/Output:	One stack entry/Two stack entries.
Usage:	Does one conversion in the process of generating formatted display outputs.
Code:	

```
          0        ;24 BIT NUMBER EXTENSION
          BASE     ;NUMBER BASE ADDRESS
          C@       ;NUMBER BASE
          D/MOD    ;REMAINDER THEN QUOTIENT
          ASCII    ;REMAINDER TO ASCII CHARACTER
          SWAP     ;REMAINDER TO NUMBER STRING
```

BYTES: 22

Formal Definition:

```
    :■#■0■BASE■C@■D/MOD■ASCII■SWAP■;
```

#>

Class:	I/O
Function:	Pops the the sign byte left on the return stack by <#, discards it and then displays the string on the stack using the DISPLAY format convention.
Input/Output:	One return stack entry and a variable length stack string/None.
Usage:	Display formatted strings built onto the stack.
Z80 Code:	INC IX ;DROP RETURN
	JP $DISPLAY ;GO ECHO STRING
BYTES:	13
Notes:	This routine jumps to the code body of DISPLAY and thus has no return address.

#S

Class:	I/O
Function:	Converts the top stack entry to a sequence of ASCII characters equivalent to the entry given the current system number base. Sequentially pushes the number characters with the most significant character to the top stack entry.
Input/Output:	One stack entry/One to sixteen stack entries.
Usage:	Converting numbers to a display string.
Code:	# ;CONVERT 1 CHARACTER
	DUP ;DUP QUOTIENT
	0= ;IS IT ZERO?
	*END F8 ;IF NOT LOOP
	DROP ;DROP 0 QUOTIENT
Bytes:	21
Notes:	Always does at least one conversion producing an ASCII 0 if the top entry was 0.

Formal Definition:
        : ■#S ■BEGIN ■# ■DUP ■0= ■END ■DROP ■;

$CRLF

Class:	Subroutine
Function:	Issue a carriage return-line feed sequence to the display to scroll the display if required, clear the next display line and leave the cursor at the left end of the blank line.

Input/Output:	None/None.		
Usage:	Formatting the display.		
Z80 Code:	LD	A,0D	;GET A CR
	CALL	$ECHO	;ISSUE IT
	LD	A,0A	;GET A LF
	CALL	$ECHO	;ISSUE IT
	RET		;RETURN
Bytes:	11		

$ECHO

Class:	Subroutine
Function:	Interfaces the system to the display
Input/Output:	None/None.
Usage:	Available only to the system.
Code:	Not applicable.
Notes:	Usually called via a transfer vector. $ECHO must interface to existing system software or may be specifically written to field the display function for the TIL.

$ISIGN

Class:	Subroutine			
Function:	Computes and saves the sign of an arithmetic result and converts negative integers to positive integers.			
Input/Output:	None/None.			
Usage:	Available only to the system. See Section 5.5.			
Z80 Code:	$ISIGN:	LD	A,D	;SIGN OF 1ST
		XOR	B	;XOR SIGN OF 2ND
		EX	AF,AF'	;RESULT SIGN TO AF'
		LD	A,D	;SIGN OF 1ST
		AND	A	;TEST SIGN, CY=0
		JP	P,TST2	;IF +, IT'S OK
		LD	HL,0	;ELSE GET ZERO
		SBC	HL,DE	;MAKE 1ST POSITIVE
		EX	DE,HL	;RESTORE 1ST
	TST2:	LD	H,B	;MOVE 2ND HIGH BYTE
		LD	L,C	;MOVE 2ND LOW BYTE
		LD	A,B	;SIGN OF 2ND
		AND	A	;TEST SIGN, CY=0
		RET	P	;IF +, RETURN
		LD	HL,0	;ELSE GET ZERO
		SBC	HL,BC	;MAKE 2ND POSITIVE
		RET		;RETURN

Bytes:	25
Notes:	Numbers in DE and BC on entrance and DE and HL on exit. Result sign in AF′ on exit.

$KEY

Class:	Subroutine
Function:	Interfaces the keyboard to the system.
Input/Output:	None/None.
Usage:	Available only to the system.
Code:	Not applicable.
Notes:	Usually called via a transfer vector. $KEY must interface to existing system software or may be specifically written to field keyboard data for the TIL.

$OSIGN

Class:	Subroutine
Function:	Negates a positive integer arithmetic result if the result sign bit is 1 set.
Input/Output:	None/None.
Usage:	Available only to the system. See Section 5.5.

Z80 Code:

```
$OSIGN: EX    AF,AF'    ;RETRIEVE SIGN FLAGS
        RET   P         ;IF +, SIGN IS OK
        EX    DE,HL     ;ELSE, RESULT TO DE
        LD    HL,0      ;ZERO HL
        SBC   HL,DE     ;MINUS RESULT TO HL
        RET             ;RETURN
```

Bytes:	9
Notes:	Result in HL on entrance and exit. Result sign bit in AF′ on entrance.

$UD*

Class:	Subroutine
Function:	Multiplies a 16-bit unsigned integer by an 8-bit unsigned integer and returns a 24-bit product.
Input/Output:	None/None.
Usage:	Available only to the system. See Section 5.5.

Z80 Code:	$UD*:	LD	A,L	;MULTIPLICAND TO A

```
Z80 Code:    $UD*:    LD    A,L          ;MULTIPLICAND TO A
                      LD    BC,0800      ;COUNT=8, DUMMY=0
                      LD    H,C          ;ZERO HIGH RESULT
                      LD    L,C          ;ZERO LOW RESULT
             D*LOOP:  ADD   HL,HL        ;SHIFT RESULT AND
                      ADC   A            ;MULTIPLICAND LEFT 1
                      JR    NC,SKADD     ;IF CY=0, SKIP ADD
                      ADD   HL,DE        ;ADD MULTIPLIER
                      ADC   C            ;PROPOGATE CARRY
             SKADD:   DJNZ  D*LOOP       ;LOOP 8 TIMES
                      LD    C,A          ;+ HIGH 8 BITS IN C
                      RET                ;LOW 16 IN HL
```

Bytes: 16

Notes: On entrance, L contains an 8-bit multiplicand and DE contains a 16-bit multiplier. On exit BC contains the most significant 8 bits and HL the 16 least significant bits. No test is made to verify a valid 8-bit number in L on entrance.

$US*

Class:	Subroutine
Function:	Multiplies an 8-bit unsigned integer by an 8-bit unsigned integer and returns a 16-bit product.
Input/Output:	None/None.
Usage:	Available only to the system. See Section 5.5.

```
Z80 Code:    $US:     LD    H,L          ;MULTIPLICAND TO H
                      LD    L,0          ;ZERO RESULT LOW
                      LD    D,L          ;MULTIPLIER HIGH=0
                      LD    B,8          ;SET MULTIPLY COUNT
             S*LOOP:  ADD   HL,HL        ;SHIFT RESULT AND XCAN
                      JR    NC,SKPAD     ;IF CY=0, SKIP ADD
                      ADD   HL,DE        ;ADD MULTIPLIER
             SKPAD:   DJNZ  S*LOOP       ;LOOP 8 TIMES
                      RET                ;RESULT IN HL
```

Bytes: 13

Notes: On entrance, L and E contain 8-bit unsigned integers and H and D are presumed 0 (assumes valid 8-bit numbers). On exit, HL contains the 16-bit product.

$UD/

Class:	Subroutine
Function:	Divides a positive 24-bit integer by a positive 8-bit integer and returns a positive 8-bit remainder and 16-bit quotient.

Input/Output:	None/None.			
Usage:	Available only to the system. See Section 5.5.			
Z80 Code:	$UD/:	LD	B,10	;DIVIDE COUNT=16
	D/LOOP:	ADD	HL,HL	;SHIFT LOW 16
		LD	A,D	;GET HIGH 8
		ADC	A,D	;SHIFT HIGH 8
		LD	D,A	;RESTORE HIGH
		SUB	E	;SUBTRACT DIVISOR
		JP	M,SKIP	;TOO MUCH, IT'S OK
		INC	L	;SET RESULT LOW BIT=1
		LD	D,A	;DECREASE DIVIDEND
	SKIP:	DJNZ	D/LOOP	;LOOP 16 TIMES
		LD	C,D	;REMAINDER TO C
		RET		;QUOTIENT IN HL

Bytes: 16

Notes: On entrance, D,HL contains a 24-bit positive dividend and E contains an 8-bit positive divisor. On exit, C contains an 8-bit remainder and HL contains a 16-bit quotient. No test is made to verify a correct 16-bit quotient.

$US/

Class:	Subroutine			
Function:	Divides a positive 16-bit dividend by a positive 8-bit divisor and returns a positive 8-bit remainder and 8-bit quotient.			
Input/Output:	None/None.			
Usage:	Available only to the system. See Section 5.5.			
Z80 Code:	$US/:	LD	B,8	DIVIDE COUNT=8
	S/LOOP:	ADD	HL,HL	;SHIFT DIVIDEND
		LD	A,H	;GET HIGH BYTE
		SUB	E	;SUBTRACT DIVISOR
		JP	M,SKP	;TOO MUCH, IT'S OK
		INC	L	;SET RESULT LOW BIT=1
		LD	H,A	;DECREASE DIVIDEND
	SKP:	DJNZ	S/LOOP	;LOOP 8 TIMES
		LD	C,H	;REMAINDER IN C
		LD	H,B	;RESULT HIGH=0
		RET		;RESULT IN HL

Bytes: 15

Notes: On entrance, HL contains a positive 16-bit dividend and E contains a positive 8-bit divisor. On exit, C contains an 8-bit remainder and L contains an 8-bit quotient. No test is made to verify a correct 8-bit quotient.

' (tick)

Class:	System
Function:	Scans the token following the ' (tick) in the input buffer and searches the CURRENT and CONTEXT vocabularies for the keyword corresponding to the token. Returns the word address of the keyword as the top stack entry if it is located. If not found, the token is echoed to the operator and followed by a "?".
Input/Output:	None/One stack entry or none.
Usage:	Operator location of keywords.
Code:	

```
ASPACE     ;GET THE SEPARATOR
TOKEN      ;SCAN THE NEXT TOKEN
CONTEXT    ;CONTEXT ADDRESS
@          ;CONTAINS VOCABULARY ADDRESS
@          ;CONTAINS THE LATEST ENTRY
SEARCH     ;SEARCH THE VOCABULARY
*IF 0A     ;IF FALSE, FOUND; OTHERWISE
ENTRY      ;GET LATEST CURRENT
SEARCH     ;SEARCH CURRENT
*IF 03     ;IF FALSE, FOUND; OTHERWISE
QUESTION   ;ECHO TOKEN AND ?
SEMI       ;WA ON THE STACK
```

Bytes:	34

Formal Definition:
: ■'■ASPACE■TOKEN■CONTEXT■@■@■SEARCH■IF■ENTRY■
SEARCH■IF■QUESTION■THEN■THEN■;

*(asterisk)

Class:	Arithmetic
Function:	Does a signed multiply of the second stack word by the low-order byte of the top stack entry and replaces both entries by the 16-bit (word) product.
Input/Output:	Two stack entries/One stack entry.
Usage:	Signed integer arithmetic.
Z80 Code:	

```
EXX                  ;SAVE IR
POP    BC            ;GET FIRST
POP    DE            ;GET SECOND
CALL   $ISIGN        ;FIELD INPUT SIGNS
CALL   $UD*          ;MULTILY 16X8
CALL   $OSIGN        ;JUSTIFY RESULT
PUSH   HL            ;RESULT TO STACK
EXX                  ;RESTORE IR
```

Bytes:	24
Notes:	Does not test the top stack entry to insure it is a valid 8-bit number. No test is made to insure a valid 16-bit product.

*#

Class:	Literal Handler (Headerless)
Function:	Pushes to the stack the word whose address is in the instruction register and increments the instruction register twice (past the word literal).
Input/Output:	None/One stack entry.
Usage:	Available only to the system.
Z80 Code:	

```
            LD      A,{BC}      ;GET BYTE AT IR
            LD      E,A         ;MOVE IT TO DE
            INC     BC          ;BUMP IR
            LD      A,{BC}      ;GET BYTE AT IR
            LD      D,A         ;MOVE IT TO DE
            INC     BC          ;BUMP IR
            PUSH    DE          ;PUSH WORD AT DE
```

Bytes:	11

*+LOOP

Class:	Program Control Directive (Headerless)
Function:	Gets the return stack pointer, pops the index byte from the stack, and then transfers to the *LOOP code to mechanize a non-unity indexed loop.
Input/Output:	One stack entry/None.
Usage:	Available only to the system.
Z80 Code:	

```
            PUSH    IX          ;GET RETURN STACK
            POP     HL          ;TO THE REGISTERS
            POP     DE          ;GET INC BYTE
            LD      A,E         ;TO THE A REGISTER
            JP      $LOOP       ;JUMP TO *LOOP CODE
```

Bytes:	10
Notes:	*+LOOP has a code address but not a return address. Increments must be in the set $-128 \leq I \leq 127$.

*/

Class:	Arithmetic
Function:	Does a signed multiply of the third stack word by the low-order byte of the second stack word and a signed divide of the 24-bit product by the low-order byte of the top stack entry. Replaces the three entries with the 16-bit quotient.
Input/Output:	Three stack entries/One stack entry.
Usage:	Signed integer arithmetic.

Z80 Code:		LD	IY,RETTO	;CHANGE NEXT RETURN
		JP	$*/MOD	;DO */MOD CODE
	RETTO:	POP	HL	;DROP REMAINDER
		LD	IY,NEXT	;SET NEXT RETURN

Bytes: 22

Notes: This illustrates a sneaky way to use a primitive as a subroutine. The */MOD code is executed as normal but the JP {IY} return jumps back to the */ code rather than NEXT. This code then restores the normal return to NEXT.

*/MOD

Class: Arithmetic

Function: Does a signed multiply of the third stack word by the low-order byte of the second stack entry and a signed divide of the 24-bit product by the low-order byte of the top stack entry. Replaces the three entries with the 16-bit quotient as the second and the 8-bit residual as the top stack entry.

Input/Output: Three stack entries/Two stack entries.

Z80 Code:

```
$*/MOD: POP   HL            ;DIVISOR TO L
        EXX                 ;SAVE IR AND DIVISOR
        POP   BC            ;MULTIPLICAND {8}
        POP   DE            ;MULTIPLIER {16}
        CALL  $ISIGN        ;FIELD * SIGN
        CALL  $UD*          ;DO 16X8 MULTIPLY
        EXX                 ;GET DIVISOR AND IR
        EX    AF,AF'        ;GET / SIGN FLAG
        XOR   L             ;XOR IN DIVISOR SIGN
        EX    AF,AF'        ;SAVE RESULT SIGN
        LD    A,L           ;GET DIVISOR
        EXX                 ;SAVE IR AGAIN
        AND   A             ;TEST DIVISOR SIGN
        JP    P,SKIPN       ;IF +, IT'S OK
        NEG                 ;MAKE DIVISOR +
SKIPN:  LD    D,C           ;MOVE HIGH 8 BITS OF 24
        LD    E,A           ;MOVE DIVISOR
        CALL  $UD/          ;DO 24X8 DIVIDE
        CALL  $OSIGN        ;JUSTIFY RESULT
        PUSH  HL            ;QUOTIENT TO STACK
        PUSH  BC            ;REMAINDER TO STACK
        EXX                 ;RESTORE IR
```

Bytes: 43

Notes: The $*/MOD entrance is used by */. No tests are performed to insure valid number lengths.

*C#

Class:	Literal Handler (Headerless)
Function:	Pushes to the stack the byte whose address is in the instruction register and increments the instruction register once (past the literal).
Input/Output:	None/One stack entry.
Usage:	Available only to the system.
Z80 Code:	

```
LD    A,{BC}    ;GET BYTE AT IR
LD    E,A       ;MOVE IT TO DE
INC   BC        ;BUMP IR
RLA             ;SIGN TO CY
SBC   A,A       ;FF IF NEG ELSE 00
LD    D,A       ;SET SIGN EXTENSION
PUSH  DE        ;PUSH 16-BIT WORD
```

Bytes: 10

*C+LOOP

Class:	Program Control Directive (Headerless)
Function:	Pops the top stack entry and increments the top return stack byte by the low-order byte from the stack. Control is then transferred to the *CLOOP code to mechanize a non-unity byte indexed loop.
Input/Output:	One stack entry and one return stack byte/One return stack byte.
Usage:	Available only to the system.
Z80 Code:	

```
PUSH  IX        ;GET RETURN STACK
POP   HL        ;POINTER
POP   DE        ;GET INC BYTE
LD    A,{HL}    ;GET LOOP COUNT
ADD   E         ;ADD INCREMENT
LD    {HL}A     ;RESTORE LOOP COUNT
JP    $CLOOP    ;JUMP TO *CLOOP CODE
```

Bytes: 12
Notes: *C+LOOP has a code address but not a return address. Increments must be in the set $-128 \le I \le 127$.

*CDO

Class:	Program Control Directive (Headerless)
Function:	Moves the low-order byte of the top stack entry (the loop start index) and the low-order byte of the second stack en-

try (the loop termination argument) to the return stack with the start index as the top return stack entry and the terminator as the second entry. This initializes the byte indexed loop.

Input/Output: Two stack entries/Two return stack byte entries.

Usage: Available only to the system.

Z80 Code:

```
POP   HL              ;GET START INDEX
LD    {IX−2},L        ;TO RETURN TOP
POP   HL              ;GET TERMINATOR
LD    {IX−1},L        ;TO RETURN SECOND
DEC   IX              ;RESET RETURN
DEC   IX              ;STACK POINTER
```

Bytes: 16

*CLEAVE

Class: Program Control Directive (Headerless)

Function: Replaces the top return stack byte (the byte loop index) with the second return stack byte (the terminating argument) to force loop exit on the next byte loop test.

Input/Output: Two return stack bytes/Two return stack bytes.

Usage: Availabe only to the system.

Z80 Code:

```
LD    A,{IX+1}    ;GET TERMINATOR
LD    {IX+0},A    ;TO INDEX
```

Bytes: 10

*CLOOP

Class: Program Control Directive (Headerless)

Function: Increments the top return stack byte by 1 and compares it to the second return stack byte entry. If the second byte is larger than the first, a jump to the *WHILE code occurs to implement a relative backwards jump. Otherwise the top two return stack entries are dropped and the instruction register is incremented by 1 to step past the relative jump byte. Controls byte loop termination.

Input/Output: Two return stack bytes/Two return stack bytes except on completion.

Usage:	Available only to the system.		
Z80 Code:		PUSH IX	;GET RETURN
		POP HL	;STACK POINTER
		INC {HL}	;INCREMENT INDEX
	$CLOOP:	LD A,{HL}	;GET INDEX
		INC HL	;POINT TO TERMINATOR
		SUB {HL}	;INDEX − TERMINATOR
		JP C,$WHILE	;IF CY=1, JUMP BACK
		INC IX	;ELSE DROP INDEX
		INC IX	;AND TERMINATOR
		INC BC	;INCREMENT IR

Bytes: 19
Notes: *C+LOOP uses the $CLOOP entrance.

*DO

Class: Program Control Directive (Headerless)
Function: Moves the top stack entry word (the loop start index) and the second stack entry word (the loop terminating argument) to the return stack with the start index as the top return stack entry and the terminator as the second entry. This initializes a word indexed loop.
Input/Output: Two stack entries/Two return stack word entries.
Usage: Available only to the system.

Z80 Code:	POP HL	;GET START INDEX
	LD {IX−4},L	;MOVE TO THE RETURN
	LD {IX−3},H	;STACK AS TOP ENTRY
	POP HL	;GET TERMINATOR
	LD {IX−2},L	;MOVE TO THE RETURN
	LD {IX−1},H	;STACK AS 2ND ENTRY
	LD DE, −4	;RESET RETURN
	ADD IX, DE	;STACK POINTER

Bytes: 23

*ELSE

Class: Program Control Directive (Headerless)
Function: Increments the instruction register by the value whose address is in the instruction register to effect a relative forward jump.
Input/Output: None/None.
Usage: Available only to the system.

Z80 Code:	$ELSE:	LD	A,{BC}	;GET JUMP BYTE
		ADD	C	;ADD IT TO IR
		LD	C,A	;RESET IR
		JR	NC,OUT	;PAST PAGE?
		INC	B	;YES
	OUT:	JP	{IY}	;RETURN
Bytes:	10			
Notes:	The $ELSE entrance is used by *IF.			

*END

Class:	Program Control Directive (Headerless)
Function:	If the top stack entry is 0, the instruction register is incremented by the value whose address is in the instruction register to implement a relative backwards jump. Otherwise the instruction register is incremented by 1 to step past the relative jump byte.
Input/Output:	One stack entry/None.
Usage:	Available only to the system.

Z80 Code:	POP	HL	;GET THE FLAG
	LD	A,L	;ARE ALL BITS 0
	OR	H	;OR FALSE
	JP	Z,$WHILE	;IF 0, JUMP
	INC	BC	;ELSE BUMP IR

Bytes:	11
Notes:	The jump to $WHILE evokes the backwards jump.

*IF

Class:	Program Control Directive (Headerless)
Function:	If the top stack entry is 0, the instruction register is incremented by the value whose address is in the instruction register to implement a relative forward jump. Otherwise the instruction register is incremented by 1 to step past the relative jump byte.
Input/Output:	One stack entry/None.
Usage:	Available only to the system.

Z80 Code:	POP	HL	;GET THE FLAG
	LD	A,L	;ARE ALL BITS 0
	OR	H	;OR FALSE
	JP	Z,$ELSE	;IF 0, JUMP
	INC	BC	;ELSE BUMP IR

Bytes:	11
Notes:	The jump to $ELSE evokes the relative forward jump.

*LEAVE

Class:	Program Control Directive (Headerless)
Function:	Replaces the top return stack word (the word loop index) with the second return stack word (the terminating argument) to force loop exit on the next word loop test.
Input/Output:	Two return stack words/Two return stack words.
Usage:	Available only to the system.

Z80 Code:

```
        LD   A,{IX+3}   ;GET TERM LOW BYTE
        LD   {IX+1},A   ;TO INDEX LOW BYTE
        LD   A,{IX+2}   ;GET TERM HIGH BYTE
        LD   {IX+0},A   ;TO INDEX HIGH BYTE
```

Bytes: 16

*LOOP

Class:	Program Control Directive (Headerless)
Function:	Increments the top return stack word by 1 and compares it to the second return stack word entry. If the second word is larger than the first, a jump to the $WHILE code occurs to implement a relative backwards jump. Otherwise the top return stack entries are dropped and the instruction register is incremented by 1 to step past the relative jump byte. Controls word loop termination.
Input/Output:	Two return stack words/Two return stack words except on completion.
Usage:	Available only to the system.

Z80 Code:

```
          PUSH  IX            ;GET RETURN
          POP   HL            ;STACK POINTER
          LD    A,1           ;GET INCREMENT
$LOOP:    ADD   {HL}          ;INC INDEX LOW
          LD    {HL},A        ;RESTORE LOW INDEX
          INC   HL            ;BUMP TO INDEX HIGH
          JR    NC,PAGE       ;PAST PAGE?
          INC   {HL}          ;BUMP PAGE
PAGE:     LD    D,{HL}        ;GET INDEX HIGH
          INC   HL            ;BUMP TO TERM LOW
          SUB   {HL}          ;INDEX-TERM {LOW}
          LD    A,D           ;INDEX HIGH TO A
          INC   HL            ;BUMP TO TERM HIGH
          SBC   {HL}          ;INDEX-TERM-CY {HIGH}
          JP    C,$WHILE      ;IF CY=1, JUMP BACK
          LD    DE,4          ;ELSE DROP INDEX
          ADD   IX,DE         ;AND TERMINATOR
          INC   BC            ;INCREMENT IR
```

Bytes: 30

Notes: *+LOOP uses the $LOOP entrance.

*SYS

Class:	System (Incomplete)
Function:	Used by the system to recover the addresses of system variables.
Input/Output:	See notes.
Usage:	Available only to the system.

Z80 Code:

```
$SYS:   LD    A,{DE}      ;DE=WA, @WA=OFFSET
        LD    HL,#SYS     ;START OF SYS BLOCK
        ADD   A,L         ;ADD OFFSET
        LD    L,A         ;VARIABLE ADDRESS LOW
        PUSH  HL          ;ADDRESS TO STACK
        JP    {IY}        ;JUMP TO NEXT
```

Bytes: 9

Notes: This code is the generic code for a user block type defined keyword without the header-creating code.

All system variables defined in the system block contain $SYS as their code address followed by a 1-byte offset as their code body. The offset points to the system variable, relative to the start of the block. A full 256-byte block is not reserved for system variables (only 20 thru 30 bytes are used), which is why there is no defining code. A possibility exists for overwriting system code if this were allowed. All system variables are predefined.

*WHILE

Class:	Program Control Directive (Headerless)
Function:	Increments the instruction register by the value whose address is in the current instruction register to implement a relative backwards jump.
Input/Output:	None/None.
Usage:	Available only to the system.

Z80 Code:

```
$WHILE: LD    A,{BC}      ;GET JUMP BYTE
        ADD   A,C         ;ADD IT TO IR
        LD    C,A         ;RESET IR
        JR    C,OUT       ;PAST PAGE?
        DEC   B           ;YES
OUT:    JP    {IY}        ;RETURN
```

Bytes: 10

Notes: The $WHILE entrance is used by *END, *LOOP, and *CLOOP to execute the backward jump.

*[

Class:	Literal Handler (Headerless)
Function:	Uses the Instruction Register (IR) as a pointer to a string embedded in the threaded code. Extracts the string length from the first byte pointed to by the IR and outputs that many characters to the display. Leaves the IR pointing to the first byte past the embedded string.
Input/Output:	None/None.
Usage:	Available only to the system.

Z80 Code:

```
           LD    A,{BC}        ;BC=IR, @IR=LENGTH
           LD    D,A           ;SAVE LENGTH
SLOOP:     INC   BC            ;BUMP IR
           LD    A,{BC}        ;GET AT IR
           CALL  $ECHO         ;ECHO CHARACTER
           DEC   D             ;DECREMENT LENGTH
           JR    NZ,SLOOP      ;LOOP UNTIL LENGTH=0
           INC   BC            ;ADJUST IR
```

Bytes: 15

+

Class:	Arithmetic
Function:	Adds the second stack entry and the top stack entry and replaces both with the single two's complement sum as the top stack entry.
Input/Output:	Two stack entries/One stack entry.
Usage:	Signed arithmetic.

Z80 Code:

```
           POP   HL            ;GET 1ST WORD
           POP   DE            ;GET 2ND WORD
           ADD   HL,DE         ;ADD THEM
           PUSH  HL            ;PUSH SUM
```

Bytes: 14
Notes: No check of carry or overflow is done.

+!

Class:	Memory Reference
Function:	Pops two stack entries and adds the word at the second entry to the word whose address is the top entry.
Input/Output:	Two stack entries/None.
Usage:	Incrementing and decrementing word length data stored in programmable memory.

Z80 Code:

```
POP   HL          ;GET ADDRESS
POP   DE          ;GET INC/DEC
LD    A,{HL}      ;GET LOW BYTE
ADD   A,E         ;INC/DEC LOW BYTE
LD    {HL},A      ;STORE IT BACK
INC   HL          ;STEP TO HIGH BYTE
LD    A,{HL}      ;GET HIGH BYTE
ADC   A,D         ;INC/DEC HIGH BYTE
LD    {HL},A      ;STORE IT BACK
```

Bytes: 19
Notes: Overflow and carry in high-byte add are ignored.

+LOOP

Class: Compiler Directive (Immediate)
Function: Adds the word address of the program control directive *+LOOP to the dictionary, then computes the difference between the current free dictionary address and the address at the top of the stack and encloses the low-order byte in the dictionary as the relative jump byte.
Input/Output: One stack entry/None.
Usage: Used to terminate a DO . . . +LOOP construct in the compile mode.
Code:
```
*# XX        ;WORD ADDRESS OF *+LOOP {LITERAL}
END,         ;ENCLOSE RELATIVE JUMP BYTE
```
Bytes: 16
Formal Definition:
: ■ +LOOP ■ XX ■ END, ■ ; ■ IMMEDIATE

+SP

Class: System
Function: Adds the current stack pointer to the number at the top of the stack.
Input/Output: One stack entry/One stack entry.
Usage: Direct addressing of data on the stack.
Z80 Code:
```
POP   HL          ;GET NUMBER
ADD   HL,SP       ;ADD STACK POINTER
PUSH  HL          ;RESTORE POINTER
```
Bytes: 13

, (comma)

Class:	System
Function:	Pops the top stack entry word and encloses it in the free dictionary space.
Input/Output:	One stack entry/None.
Usage:	Used to build dictionary keywords.
Z80 Code:	

```
POP   DE          ;GET WORD
LD    HL,{DP}     ;GET @DP
LD    {HL},E      ;STORE LOW BYTE
INC   HL          ;BUMP @DP
LD    {HL},D      ;STORE HIGH BYTE
INC   HL          ;BUMP @DP
LD    {DP},HL     ;UPDATE @DP
```

Bytes:	21

— (minus)

Class:	Arithmetic
Function:	Pops the top two stack entries and two's complement subtracts the top entry from the second entry and pushes the result.
Input/Output:	Two stack entries/One stack entry.
Z80 Code:	

```
POP    DE        ;GET B
POP    HL        ;GET A
AND    A         ;RESET CARRY
SBC    HL,DE     ;FORM A−B
PUSH   HL        ;PUSH RESULT
```

Bytes:	16
Notes:	No tests of overflow or carry are made.

−SP

Class:	System
Function:	Subtracts the current stack pointer from the number at the top of the stack.
Input/Output:	One stack entry/One stack entry.
Usage:	Direct addressing of stack data.
Z80 Code:	

```
POP    HL        ;GET THE NUMBER
AND    A         ;RESET CARRY
SBC    HL,SP     ;SUBTRACT STACK POINTER
PUSH   HL        ;PUSH POINTER
```

Bytes:	15

. (period)

Class:	I/O
Function:	Displays the top stack entry number to the operator (given the current number base) and follows by a space. Destroys the top stack entry in the process.
Input/Output:	One stack entry/None.
Usage:	Displaying signed numbers to the operator.
Code:	

```
<#        ;INITIALIZE CONVERSION
ABS       ;TAKE THE ABSOLUTE VALUE
#S        ;CONVERT ABSOLUTE VALUE
SIGN      ;ADD − SIGN IF REQUIRED
#>        ;DISPLAY RESULT
```

Bytes: 20

Formal Definition:

    : ■. ■ < # ■ABS ■#S ■SIGN ■# > ■;

.R

Class:	I/O
Function:	Displays the second stack number to the operator (given the current system number base) in a field width determined by the top stack entry. The number is right adjusted in the field and followed by a space. The field width is the minimum field width.
Input/Output:	Two stack entries/None.
Usage:	Formatting display number output.
Code:	

```
2*        ;DOUBLE CHARACTER COUNT
−SP       ;SUBTRACT CURRENT STACK POINTER
<R        ;SAVE AS TEMPORARY
<#        ;INITIALIZE CONVERSION {SAVE SIGN}
ABS       ;CONVERT NUMBER TO POSITIVE VALUE
#S        ;CONVERT TO A STRING
SIGN      ;ADD SIGN IF NEGATIVE
CR>       ;GET SIGN FROM TEMPORARY
DROP      ;DROP IT
R>        ;GET TEMPORARY
+SP       ;ADD CURRENT STACK POINTER
PAD       ;ADD SPACES IF REQUIRED
DISPLAY   ;DISPLAY RESULT
```

Bytes: 36

Formal Definition:

    : ■.R ■2* ■ −SP ■ < R ■ < # ■ABS ■#S ■SIGN ■CR > ■DROP ■
    R > ■ +SP ■PAD ■DISPLAY ■;

/ (divide)

Class:	Arithmetic
Function:	Does a signed divide of the second stack word by the low-order byte of the top stack entry. Replaces both entries with an 8-bit quotient expanded to 16 bits.
Input/Output:	Two stack entries/One stack entry.
Usage:	Signed integer arithmetic.

Z80 Code:

```
EXX                ;SAVE IR
POP   DE           ;GET DIVISOR {8 BITS}
POP   BC           ;GET DIVIDEND {16 BITS}
CALL  $ISIGN       ;FIELD INPUT SIGNS
CALL  $US/         ;DIVIDE 16X8
CALL  $OSIGN       ;JUSTIFY RESULT
PUSH  HL           ;QUOTIENT TO STACK
EXX                ;RESTORE IR
```

Bytes:	24
Notes:	Does not test the top stack entry to insure it is a valid 8-bit number. No test is made to insure a valid 8-bit quotient.

/MOD

Class:	Arithmetic
Function:	Does a signed divide of the second stack entry by the low-order byte of the top stack entry. Replaces these entries with the 8-bit quotient expanded to 16 bits as the second entry and the positive 8-bit remainder expanded to 16 bits as the top entry.
Input/Output:	Two stack entries/Two stack entries.
Usage:	Signed integer arithmetic.

Z80 Code:

```
EXX                ;SAVE IR
POP   DE           ;GET DIVISOR {8 BITS}
POP   BC           ;GET DIVIDEND {16 BITS}
CALL  $ISIGN       ;FIELD INPUT SIGNS
CALL  $US/         ;DIVIDE 16X8
CALL  $OSIGN       ;JUSTIFY RESULT
PUSH  HL           ;QUOTIENT TO STACK
PUSH  BC           ;REMAINDER TO STACK
EXX                ;RESTORE IR
```

Bytes:	25
Notes:	Does not test the top stack entry to insure it is a valid 8-bit number. No test is made to insure a valid 8-bit quotient.

0<

Class:	Relational	
Function:	If the top stack entry is two's complement negative, it is replaced by a True flag. Otherwise it is replaced by a False flag.	
Input/Output:	One stack entry/One stack entry.	
Usage:	Test conditioning prior to branching.	
Z80 Code:		

```
            POP     AF              ;GET NUMBER
            LD      DE,0            ;SET FLAG FALSE
            RLA                     ;SIGN TO CY
            JR      NC,PUSHIT       ;IF CY=0, PUSH FALSE
            INC     E               ;ELSE FLAG TRUE
PUSHIT:     PUSH    DE              FLAG TO STACK
```

Bytes: 19

0=

Class:	Relational
Function:	If the top stack value is 0, it is replaced by a True flag. Otherwise it is replaced by a False flag.
Input/Output:	One stack entry/One stack entry.
Usage:	Test conditioning prior to branching.
Z80 Code:	

```
            POP     HL              ;GET WORD
            LD      A,L             ;MOVE LOW BYTE
            OR      H               ;OR IN HIGH BYTE
            LD      DE,0            ;GET FALSE
            JR      NZ,OUT          ;NOT ZERO PUSHES FALSE
            INC     DE              ;ELSE MAKE FLAG TRUE
OUT:        PUSH    DE              ;PUSH FLAG
```

Bytes: 20

0SET

Class:	Memory Reference
Function:	Pops the top stack entry and sets the word whose address was the top entry to 0.
Input/Output:	One stack entry/None.
Usage:	Initializing word length data in programmable memory to 0 or setting word length flags in programmable memory to False.

Z80 Code:		POP	HL	;GET ADDRESS
		XOR	A	;ZEROS A REGISTER
		LD	{HL},A	;ZERO LOW BYTE
		INC	HL	;BUMP ADDRESS POINTER
		LD	{HL},A	;ZERO HIGH BYTE
Bytes:	15			

1+

Class:	Arithmetic
Function:	Increments the top stack entry by 1.
Input/Output:	One stack entry/One stack entry.
Usage:	Signed arithmetic, byte addressing and index incrementing.

Z80 Code:		POP	HL	;GET WORD
		INC	HL	;BUMP IT 1
		PUSH	HL	;RESTORE IT
Bytes:	13			
Notes:	No tests of overflow or carry are made.			

1−

Class:	Arithmetic
Function:	Decrements the top stack entry by 1.
Input/Output:	One stack entry/One stack entry.
Usage:	Signed arithmetic, byte addressing and index decrementing.

Z80 Code:		POP	HL	;GET WORD
		DEC	HL	;DECREMENT IT
		PUSH	HL	;RESTORE IT
Bytes:	13			
Notes:	No tests of overflow or carry are made.			

1SET

Class:	Memory Reference
Function:	Pops the top stack entry and sets the word whose address was the top entry to one.
Input/Output:	One stack entry/None.
Usage:	Initializing word length data in programmable memory to one or setting word-length flags in programmable memory to True.

Z80 Code:	POP	HL	;GET ADDRESS
	LD	{HL},1	;1 SET LOW BYTE
	INC	HL	;BUMP ADDRESS POINTER
	LD	{HL},0	;0 SET HIGH BYTE
Bytes:	16		

2*

Class:	Arithmetic
Function:	Multiplies the top stack entry by 2.
Input/Output:	One stack entry/One stack entry.
Usage:	Signed integer arithmetic.

Z80 Code:	POP	HL	;GET WORD
	ADD	HL,HL	;DOUBLE IT
	PUSH	HL	;RESTORE IT
Bytes:	13		
Notes:	No tests of overflow or carry are made.		

2+

Class:	Arithmetic.
Function:	Increments the word at the top of the stack by 2.
Input/Output:	One stack entry/One stack entry.
Usage:	Word addressing and incrementing.

Z80 Code:	POP	HL	;GET WORD
	INC	HL	;WORD + 1
	INC	HL	;WORD + 2
	PUSH	HL	;PUSH WORD + 2
Bytes:	14		
Notes:	No test for overflow or carry is made.		

2−

Class:	Arithmetic
Function:	Decrements the word at the top of the stack by 2.
Input/Output:	One stack entry/One stack entry.
Usage:	Word addressing and decrementing.

Z80 Code:	POP	HL	;GET WORD
	DEC	HL	;WORD −1
	DEC	HL	;WORD −2
	PUSH	HL	;PUSH WORD −2
Bytes:	14		
Notes:	No tests of overflow or carry are made.		

2/

Class:	Arithmetic
Function:	Divides (signed) the top stack word by 2.
Input/Output:	One stack entry/One stack entry.
Usage:	Signed integer arithmetic.
Z80 Code:	

```
POP   HL      ;GET WORD
SRA   H       ;ARITHMETIC SHIFT
RR    L       ;PROPAGATE CY
PUSH  HL      ;PUSH WORD/2
```

Bytes: 16

2DUP

Class:	Stack
Function:	Duplicates the top stack entry twice.
Input/Output:	One stack entry/Three stack entries.
Usage:	Duplication of data on the stack.
Z80 Code:	

```
POP   HL      ;GET WORD
PUSH  HL      ;RESTORE IT
PUSH  HL      ;DUP IT
PUSH  HL      ;DUP IT AGAIN
```

Bytes: 14

2OVER

Class:	Stack
Function:	Duplicates the third stack entry over the top two and pushes the word to the stack.
Input/Output:	Three stack entries/Four stack entries.
Usage:	Stack data management.
Z80 Code:	

```
EXX           ;SAVE IR
POP   HL      ;GET TOP
POP   DE      ;GET 2ND
POP   BC      ;GET 3RD
PUSH  BC      ;PUSH 3RD
PUSH  DE      ;PUSH 2ND
PUSH  HL      ;PUSH TOP
PUSH  BC      ;PUSH 3RD TO TOP
EXX           ;RESTORE IR
```

Bytes: 19

2SWAP

Class:	Stack
Function:	Interchanges the top and third stack words.
Input/Output:	Three stack entries/Three stack entries.
Usage:	Stack management.
Z80 Code:	

```
POP    HL          ;GET TOP
POP    DE          ;GET 2ND
EX     {SP},HL     ;TOP TO STACK
PUSH   DE          ;RESTORE 2ND
PUSH   HL          ;3RD TO TOP
```

Bytes: 15

:

Class:	Defining Word
Function:	Sets the CONTEXT vocabulary equal to the CURRENT vocabulary, creates a secondary header for the token following ":" in the input buffer and links it to the CURRENT vocabulary and sets the system mode to the compile mode.
Input/Output:	None/None.
Usage:	Initiate compilation of secondary keywords.
Code:	

```
CURRENT    ;CURRENT ADDRESS
@          ;CONTAINS VOCABULARY ADDRESS
CONTEXT    ;CONTEXT ADDRESS
!          ;CURRENT INTO CONTEXT
CREATE     ;CREATE PRIMITIVE HEADER
*# XX      ;ADDRESS OF COLON ROUTINE
CA!        ;REPLACE CODE ADDRESS
MODE       ;MODE ADDRESS
C1SET      ;SET COMPILE MODE {MODE=1}
```

Bytes: 30

Formal Definition:

: ■ : ■CURRENT■ @ ■CONTEXT■!■XX■CA!■MODE■C1SET■;

;

Class:	Compile Mode Termination Directive (Immediate)
Function:	Encloses the word address of the inner interpreter SEMI routine in the dictionary and sets the system mode to the execute mode.
Input/Output:	None/None.
Usage:	Terminates the definition of a secondary and re-establishes the execute mode.

Code:	*# XX ;ADDRESS OF SEMI ROUTINE
	, ;ENCLOSE IT IN THE DICTIONARY
	MODE ;MODE ADDRESS
	C0SET ;SET EXECUTE MODE {MODE=0}
Bytes:	20

Formal Definition:
: ■ ; ■XX ■ , ■MODE ■C0SET ■ ; ■IMMEDIATE

;CODE

Class:	Compile Mode Termination Directive (Immediate)
Function:	Encloses the word address of the keyword SCODE in the dictionary and sets the system mode to execute.
Input/Output:	None/None.
Usage:	Terminates a defining keyword definition. Always followed by generic machine code that defines the execution time action of the defined class.
Code:	*# XX ;WORD ADDRESS OF SCODE
	, ;ENCLOSE IT IN THE DICTIONARY
	MODE ;MODE ADDRESS
	C0SET ;SET EXECUTE MODE {MODE=0}
Bytes:	20

Formal Definition:
: ■ ;CODE ■XX ■ , ■MODE ■C0SET ■ ; ■IMMEDIATE

<

Class:	Relational
Function:	If the second stack entry is less than the top entry, both entries are replaced by a True flag. Otherwise both are replaced by a False flag.
Input/Output:	Two stack entries/One stack entry.
Usage:	Test conditioning prior to branching.

Z80 Code:

```
        POP   DE           ;GET TOP
        POP   HL           ;GET 2ND
        AND   A            ;RESET CARRY
        SBC   HL,DE        ;2ND-TOP
        LD    DE,0         ;SET FLAG FALSE
        JP    P,PUSHIT     ;IF POSITIVE, FALSE
        INC   E            ;SET FLAG TRUE
PUSHIT; PUSH  DE           ;FLAG TO STACK
```

Bytes:	23

<

Class:	I/O
Function:	Pops the top stack entry, pushes an ASCII space code with its high-order bit set to the stack, restores the top stack entry and copies the high-order byte to the return stack.
Input/Output:	One stack entry/Two stack entries and one return stack byte entry.
Usage:	Prepares for number conversion and display by saving the number sign on the return stack, pushing the string termination character to the stack and leaving the original top stack entry on the top.

Z80 Code:

```
POP   HL          ;GET THE NUMBER
LD    E,A0        ;SPACE WITH B7=1
PUSH  DE          ;PUSH STRING STOP
PUSH  HL          ;RESTORE NUMBER
DEC   IX          ;DEC RSP
LD    {IX+0},H    ;SIGN TO RETURN
```

Bytes:	20
Notes:	Must be followed by a #> or CR> within a definition to clean up the return stack and leave a valid return address on the stack.

< BUILDS

Class:	Defining Word
Function:	Creates a CONSTANT keyword definition with an initial value of 0. The keyword name is the next available token in the input buffer when < BUILDS is executed.
Input/Output:	None/None.
Usage:	Used to initiate a high-level defining word which must later be terminated with a DOES> .

Code:

```
0                 ;INITIAL VALUE
CONSTANT ;CREATES A CONSTANT KEYWORD
```

Bytes:	14
Notes:	See Section 4.5.5.

Formal Definition:

: ■ < BUILDS ■0■CONSTANT ■;

< R

Class:	Interstack
Function:	Pops the top stack word and pushes it to the return stack.
Input/Output:	One stack entry/One return stack word entry.

Usage:	Temporary storage of data within a definition or direct return stack control.

Z80 Code:

```
            POP   HL          ;GET WORD
            DEC   IX          ;PUSH IT TO THE
            LD    {IX+0},H    ;RETURN STACK
            DEC   IX          ;
            LD    {IX+0},L    ;
```

Bytes: 21

Notes: Temporary data stored on the return stack must be removed before exit to prevent incorrect return.

=

Class:	Relational
Function:	If the top two stack entries are equal, both are replaced by a True flag. Otherwise both are replaced by a False flag.
Input/Output:	Two stack entries/One stack entry.
Usage:	Test conditioning prior to branching.

Z80 Code:

```
            POP     HL          ;GET TOP
            POP     DE          ;GET 2ND
            AND     A           ;RESET CARRY
            SBC     HL,DE       ;TOP-2ND
            LD      DE,0        ;SET FLAG FALSE
            JR      NZ,PUSHIT   ;IF=, PUSH FALSE
            INC     E           ;SET FLAG TRUE
    PUSHIT: PUSH    DE          ;FLAG TO STACK
```

Bytes: 22

>

Class:	Relational
Function:	If the second stack entry is greater than the top entry, both entries are replaced by a True flag. Otherwise both are replaced by a False flag.
Input/Output:	Two stack entries/One stack entry.
Usage:	Test conditioning prior to branching.

Z80 Code:

```
            POP     HL          ;GET TOP
            POP     DE          ;GET 2ND
            AND     A           ;RESET CARRY
            SBC     HL,DE       ;TOP-2ND
            LD      DE,0        ;SET FLAG FALSE
            JP      P,PUSHIT    ;IF POSITIVE, FALSE
            INC     E           ;SET FLAG TRUE
    PUSHIT: PUSH    DE          ;FLAG TO STACK
```

Bytes: 23

?

Class:	I/O
Function:	Displays to the operator (using the current system number base) the word whose address is the top stack entry. Number display is always followed by a space.
Input/Output:	One stack entry/None.
Usage:	Displaying signed numbers to the operator, generally the contents of variables.
Code:	@ ;GET THE NUMBER
	. ;DISPLAY IT
Bytes:	14

?RS

Class:	System
Function:	Pushes to the stack the current return stack pointer.
Input/Output:	None/One stack entry.
Usage:	Return stack display and control.
Z80 Code:	PUSH IX ;PUSH RETURN POINTER
Bytes:	12

?SP

Class:	System
Function:	Pushes to the stack the address of the top stack entry prior to the execution of ?SP. If underflow occurs, the stack is reset prior to the push.
Input/Output:	None/One stack entry.
Usage:	Data stack display and control.
Z80 Code:	

```
            LD    HL,0       ;GET STACK
            ADD   HL,SP      ;POINTER
            EX    DE,HL      ;
            LD    HL,STACK   ;GET END OF STACK
            AND   A          ;RESET CARRY
            SBC   HL,DE      ;END-SP
            JR    NC,SKIP    ;NC IS OK STACK
            LD    SP,STACK   ;ELSE INIT STACK
    SKIP:   PUSH  DE         ;PUSH PRIOR SP
```

| Bytes: | 27 |

@

Class:	Memory Reference
Function:	Replaces the address at the top of the stack with the word at that address.
Input/Output:	One stack entry/One stack entry.
Usage:	Returns word length data stored in memory.
Z80 Code:	

```
POP   HL          ;GET THE ADDRESS
LD    E,{HL}      ;LOW BYTE AT ADDRESS
INC   HL          ;BUMP ADDRESS
LD    D,{HL}      ;HIGH BYTE AT ADDRESS
PUSH  DE          ;PUSH CONTENTS
```

Bytes:	15
Notes:	Low-byte, high-byte order is central processing unit dependent.

ABORT

Class:	System
Function:	Does an unconditional jump to the START/RESTART routine to re-initialize the system and the stacks.
Input/Output:	None/None.
Usage:	Used when the operator is totally at sea. (The system knows exactly what's going on.)
Z80 Code:	JP START ;TO START/RESTART
Bytes:	11
Notes:	ABORT has no return address. See Section 5.3.1 and listing 5.1.

ABS

Class:	Arithmetic
Function:	If the top stack entry is two's complement negative, its two's complement (a positive integer) is returned to the stack. Otherwise the original positive integer is returned to the stack.
Input/Output:	One stack entry/One stack entry.
Usage:	Signed integer arithmetic.

Z80 Code:

```
              POP   DE        ;GET NUMBER
              BIT   7,D       ;IF POSITIVE, Z=1
              JR    Z,OUT     ;IF Z=1, IT'S OK
              LD    HL,0      ;ELSE GET A ZERO
              AND   A         ;RESET CARRY
              SBC   HL,DE     ;ZERO-NUMBER
              EX    DE,HL     ;IS POSITIVE
       OUT:   PUSH  DE        ;POSITIVE NUMBER
```

Bytes: 23

ADUMP

Class:	I/O
Function:	Does a memory dump taking the second stack entry as the starting address and the top entry as the ending address. Displays a line consisting of the address, eight characters of ASCII, a space, and eight more characters of ASCII. Control ASCII codes are not displayed. Removes both entries.
Input/Output:	Two stack entries/None.
Usage:	Examining memory to locate or display string data.

Code:

```
    OVER          ;PREPARE FOR LOOP START INDEX
    *DO           ;INITIALIZE DO LOOP
    CRET          ;ISSUE CR-LF
    DUP           ;DUPLICATE LINE ADDRESS
    *C# 4         ;FOUR CHARACTER LINE ADDRESS
    .R            ;PRINT LINE ADDRESS
    APART         ;ISSUE FIRST 8 CHARACTERS
    APART         ;ISSUE SECOND 8 CHARACTERS
    WAIT          ;TIME TO STOP AND WAIT?
    *C# 10        ;NUMBER OF CHARACTERS AS INDEX
    *+LOOP EC     ;LOOP UNTIL DONE
    DROP          ;DROP ADDRESS POINTER
```

Bytes: 37

Formal Definition:
: ■ADUMP■OVER■DO■CRET■DUP■4■.R■APART■APART■
WAIT■10■+LOOP■DROP■;

AND

Class:	Logical
Function:	Pops the top two stack words, does a logical AND of all bits on a bit-by-bit basis and pushes the result to the stack.

Input/Output:	Two stack entries/One stack entry.		
Usage:	Logical operations.		
Z80 Code:	POP	HL	;GET TOP
	POP	DE	;GET 2ND
	LD	A,L	;AND LOW BYTES
	AND	E	;
	LD	L,A	;BACK TO L
	LD	A,H	;AND HIGH BYTES
	AND	D	;
	LD	H,A	;BACK TO H
	PUSH	HL	;RESULT TO STACK
Bytes:	19		

APART

Class: I/O

Function: Displays eight characters of ASCII using the top stack entry as a pointer. The pointer is incremented with each character access. ASCII control code is converted to a displayable form before being echoed.

Input/Output: One stack entry/One stack entry.

Usage: Displaying memory.

Code:

SPACE	;FORMAT CONTROL
*C# 8	;LOOP ENDING INDEX
0	;LOOP STARTING INDEX
*CDO	;INITIATE DISPLAY LOOP
DUP	;DUPLICATE POINTER
C@	;GET MEMORY BYTE
*C# 80	;TO SET MSB TO 1
OR	;MAKE CONTROL CODE DISPLAYABLE
ECHO	;DISPLAY BYTE AS ASCII
SPACE	;SPACE BETWEEN CHARACTERS
1+	;INCREMENT POINTER
*CLOOP EF	;LOOP UNTIL DONE

Bytes: 37

Formal Definition:
: ■APART■SPACE■8■0■CDO■DUP■C@■80■OR■ECHO■
SPACE■1+■CLOOP■;

ASCII

Class: I/O

Function: Converts the low-order byte of the top stack entry from a binary number to an ASCII code in the set 0 thru 9, A thru Z.

Input/Output:	One stack entry/One stack entry.		
Usage:	Converts binary numbers to their equivalent ASCII code for conversion to displayable formats.		
Z80 Code:		POP HL	;GET BINARY
		LD A,30	;ASCII 0 CODE
		ADD A,L	;ADD BINARY
		CP 3A	;LETTER?
		JR C,OUT	;IF CY=1, A DIGIT
		ADD A,7	;ADD LETTERS BIAS
	OUT:	LD L,A	;BACK TO L
		PUSH HL	;CODE TO STACK
Bytes:	22		

ASPACE

Class: System

Function: Pushes an ASCII space code to the low-order byte of the stack.

Input/Output: None/One stack entry.

Usage: The normal token separator and to insert blanks in formatted displays.

Code: Not applicable.

Bytes: 9

Formal Definition:

HEX■20■CCONSTANT■ASPACE

BASE

Class: System Variable

Function: Pushes to the stack the address of the number base variable.

Input/Output: None/One stack entry.

Usage: Used to access the system variable which contains the radix for system I/O.

Code: Not applicable.

Bytes: 9

Notes: In the SYS user block. The code body contains an offset number and there is no return address. See *SYS. BASE is a CVARIABLE and must be referenced using byte-length addressing keywords..

BEGIN

Class: Compiler Directive (Immediate)

Function:	Pushes to the stack the address of the next available free dictionary location.
Input/Output:	None/One stack entry.
Usage:	Initiates a BEGIN . . . END loop in the compile mode.
Code:	HERE ;GET AT DP
Bytes:	12
Notes:	The immediate form of HERE.

Formal Definition:
   : ■BEGIN ■HERE ■; ■IMMEDIATE

BINARY

Class:	System
Function:	Sets the system number base to 2 decimal or the binary radix.
Input/Output:	None/None.
Usage:	Sets I/O to the binary radix notation.
Z80 Code:	LD A,2 ;GET 2 DECIMAL
	LD {BASE},A ;SET BASE TO 2
Bytes:	15

C!

Class:	Memory Reference
Function:	Stores the low-order byte of the second stack entry at the address at the top stack entry, removing both entries.
Input/Output:	Two stack entries/None.
Usage:	Storage of byte length data in programmable memory.
Z80 Code:	POP HL ;GET ADDRESS
	POP DE ;GET BYTE
	LD {HL},E ;STORE BYTE
Bytes:	13

C+!

Class:	Memory Reference
Function:	Pops two stack entries and adds the byte in the low-order byte of the second stack entry to the byte whose address is the top stack entry.
Input/Output:	Two stack entries/None.
Usage:	Incrementing/decrementing byte-length data stored in programmable memory.

Z80 Code:	POP	HL	;GET ADDRESS
	POP	DE	;GET BYTE
	LD	A,{HL}	;GET AT ADDRESS
	ADD	E	;ADD BYTE
	LD	{HL},A	;STORE AT ADDRESS

Bytes: 15

Notes: No tests for overflow or carry are made.

C+LOOP

Class: Compiler Directive (Immediate)

Function: Adds the word address of the program control directive *C+LOOP to the dictionary, then computes the difference between the current free dictionary address and the address at the top of the stack and encloses the low-order byte in the dictionary as the relative jump byte.

Input/Output: One stack entry/None.

Usage: Used to terminate a CDO . . . C+LOOP construct in the compile mode.

Code:
```
*# XX       ;WORD ADDRESS OR C+LOOP {LITERAL}
END,        ;ENCLOSE RELATIVE JUMP BYTE
```

Bytes: 16

Formal Definition:
```
: ■C+LOOP■XX■END, ■; ■IMMEDIATE
```

C,

Class: System

Function: Pops the top stack word and encloses the low-order byte in the dictionary

Input/Output: One stack entry/None.

Usage: Used to build dictionary keywords.

Z80 Code:	POP	DE	;GET BYTE
	LD	HL,{DP}	;GET @DP
	LD	{HL},E	;STORE BYTE
	INC	HL	;BUMP @DP
	LD	{DP},HL	;UPDATE @DP

Bytes: 19

C0SET

Class:	Memory Reference
Function:	Pops the top stack entry and sets the byte whose address was the top entry to 0.
Input/Output:	One stack entry/None.
Usage:	Initializing byte-length data in programmable memory to 0 or setting byte-length flags in programmable memory to False.

Z80 Code:
```
POP   HL          ;GET ADDRESS
LD    {HL},0      ;ZERO @ADDRESS
```

Bytes: 13

C1SET

Class:	Memory Reference
Function:	Pops the top stack word and sets the byte whose address was the top entry to 1.
Input/Output:	One stack entry/None.
Usage:	Initializing byte-length data in programmable memory to 1 or setting byte-length flags in programmable memory to True.

Z80 Code:
```
POP   HL          ;GET ADDRESS
LD    {HL},1      ;ONE SET @ADDRESS
```

Bytes: 13

C<R

Class:	Interstack
Function:	Pops the top stack entry and pushes the low-order byte to the return stack.
Input/Output:	One stack entry/One return stack byte entry.
Usage:	Temporary storage of byte data within a definition. or direct return stack control.

Z80 Code:
```
POP   HL          ;GET TOP BYTE
DEC   IX          ;PUSH IT TO THE
LD    {IX+0},L    ;RETURN STACK
```

Bytes: 16

Notes: Temporary data stored on the return stack must be removed before the end of a definition to prevent incorrect return.

C?

Class:	I/O
Function:	Displays to the operator (using the current system number base) the byte whose address is popped from the stack. The number is always followed by a space.
Input/Output:	One stack entry/None.
Usage:	Displaying signed numbers to the operator; generally the contents of byte variables or constants.
Code:	C@ ;GET THE BYTE
	. ;DISPLAY IT
Bytes:	14

C@

Class:	Memory Reference
Function:	Replaces the address at the top of the stack with the byte at that address (in sign extended format).
Input/Output:	One stack entry/One stack entry.
Usage:	Returns byte-length data stored in memory in a format compatible with 16-bit signed arithmetic.

Z80 Code:

```
POP   HL          ;GET ADDRESS
LD    E,{HL}      ;GET BYTE @ADDRESS
LD    A,E         ;GET THE BYTE
RLA               ;SIGN TO CY
SBC   A,A         ;FF IF NEG ELSE 00
LD    D,A         ;SET SIGN EXTENSION
PUSH  DE          ;PUSH 16-BIT WORD
```

Bytes: 17

CA!

Class:	System
Function:	Stores the address at the top of the stack in the word address location of the latest entry in the CURRENT vocabulary, ie: the top stack entry is the code address of the keyword currently in the process of being defined.
Input/Output:	One stack entry/None.
Usage:	Used to define defining keywords.

Code:

```
ENTRY       ;ADDRESS OF LATEST HEADER
*C# 6       ;LITERAL 6
+           ;HEADER PLUS 6 EQUAL WORD ADDRESS
!           ;STORE CODE ADDRESS
```

Bytes: 19

Formal Definition:

: ■CA!■ENTRY■6■ + ■!■;

CCONSTANT

Class:	Defining Word
Function:	Creates a byte constant keyword dictionary entry whose name is the token following CCONSTANT and whose value equals the low-order byte of the top stack entry.
Input/Output:	One stack entry/None.
Usage:	Defining byte-length named constants.

Z80 Code:

```
CREATE                          ;CREATE PRIMITIVE
C,                              ;STORE BYTE TO BODY
SCODE                          ;REPLACE CODE ADDRESS
          LD      A,{DE}        ;GET BYTE IN CODE BODY
          LD      L,A           ;TO L REGISTER
          RLA                   ;SIGN TO CY
          SBC     A,A           ;FF IF NEG ELSE 00
          LD      H,A           ;SET SIGN EXTENSION
          PUSH    HL            ;PUSH 16-BIT WORD
          JP      {IY}          ;JUMP TO NEXT
```

Bytes: 22

Formal Definition:
: ■CCONSTANT■CREATE■C,■;CODE■ .....

Notes: The ". . . ." is the assembly or machine code.

CDO

Class:	Compiler Directive (Immediate)
Function:	Encloses the word address of the program control directive *CDO in the dictionary and then pushes the address of the next free dictionary location to the stack.
Input/Output:	Used to initiate a CDO...CLOOP or CDO...C+LOOP construct in the compile mode.

Code:

```
*# XX        ;WORD ADDRESS OF *CDO {LITERAL}
DO,          ;STORE AND PUSH
```

Bytes: 16

Formal Definition:
: ■CDO■XX■DO,■;■IMMEDIATE

CI>

Class:	Interstack
Function:	Pushes to the stack the loop index for the innermost byte-length loop which is the top return stack byte.

Input/Output:	One return stack byte/One stack entry and one return stack byte entry.		
Usage:	Retrieval of the current byte loop index.		
Z80 Code:	LD	L,{IX+0}	;GET RETURN TOP
	LD	A,L	;GET THE BYTE
	RLA	A	;SIGN TO CY
	SBC	A,A	;FF IF NEG ELSE 00
	LD	H,A	;SET SIGN EXTENSION
	PUSH	HL	;PUSH 16-BIT INDEX
Bytes:	18		
Notes:	Assumes the byte loop index is at the top of the return stack.		

CJ>

Class:	Interstack		
Function:	Pushes to the stack the loop index for the second innermost byte-length loop.		
Input/Output:	Three return stack byte entries/Three return stack entries and one stack entry.		
Usage:	Retrieval of the next level byte index.		
Z80 Code:	LD	L,{IX+2}	;GET 2ND INDEX
	LD	A,L	;GET THE BYTE
	RLA	A	;SIGN TO CY
	SBC	A,A	;FF IF NEG ELSE 00
	LD	H,A	;SET SIGN EXTENSION
	PUSH	HL	;PUSH 16-BIT INDEX
Bytes:	18		
Notes:	Assumes only byte loop parameters are on the return stack.		

CJOIN

Class:	Stack		
Function:	Pops the top two stack entries and combines them to a single word by moving the low-order byte of the top entry into the high-order byte of the second entry and pushes the resulting 16-bit word to the stack.		
Input/Output:	Two stack entries/One stack entry.		
Usage:	Stack manipulation for multi-byte signed integers.		
Z80 Code:	POP	HL	;GET LOW BYTE
	POP	DE	;GET HIGH BYTE
	LD	D,L	;COMBINE
	PUSH	DE	;PUSH RESULT
Bytes:	14		

CK >

Class:	Interstack
Function:	Pushes to the stack the loop index for the third innermost byte-length loop.
Input/Output:	Five return stack byte entries/Five return stack byte entries and one stack entry.
Usage:	Retrieval of the second next level byte loop index.
Z80 Code:	

```
        LD    L,{IX+4}    ;GET 3RD INDEX
        LD    A,L         ;GET THE BYTE
        RLA   A           ;SIGN TO CY
        SBC   A,A         ;FF IF NEG ELSE 00
        LD    H,A         ;SET SIGN EXTENSION
        PUSH  HL          ;PUSH 16-BIT INDEX
```

Bytes:	18
Notes:	Assumes only byte loop parameters are on the return stack.

CLEAR

Class:	I/O
Function:	Clears the CRT display and homes the cursor.
Input/Output:	None/None.
Usage:	Control of display formatting.
Z80 Code:	

```
        LD    A,CLEAR     ;LOAD CLEAR CODE
        CALL  $ECHO       ;ISSUE TO DISPLAY
```

Bytes:	15
Notes:	Presumes that the display driver recognizes a command to clear the screen and homes the cursor.

CLEAVE

Class:	Compiler Directive (Immediate)
Function:	Encloses the word address of the program control directive *CLEAVE in the dictionary
Input/Output:	None/None.
Usage:	Compiles a command to cause an immediate exit from a byte loop construct at execution time. Used within a conditional branch structure.
Code:	

```
        *# XX       ;WORD ADDRESS OF *CLEAVE
                    {LITERAL}
              ,     ;ENCLOSE IT IN THE DICTIONARY
```

Bytes:	16
Formal Definition:	

: ■CLEAVE■XX■,■;■IMMEDIATE

CLOOP

Class:	Compiler Directive (Immediate)
Function:	Adds the word address of the program control directive *CLOOP to the dictionary, then computes the difference between the current free dictionary address and the address at the top of the stack and encloses the low-order byte in the dictionary.
Input/Output:	One stack entry/None.
Usage:	Used to terminate a CDO . . . CLOOP construct in the compile mode.
Code:	*# XX ;WORD ADDRESS OF *CLOOP
	{LITERAL}
	END, ;ENCLOSE RELATIVE JUMP BYTE
Bytes:	16

Formal Definition:
: ■CLOOP■XX■END, ■; ■IMMEDIATE

COMPILER

Class:	System Variable
Function:	Pushes to the stack the address of the compiler variable which points to the last entry in the COMPILER vocabulary.
Input/Output:	None/One stack entry.
Usage:	Used to access the link to the last COMPILER vocabulary entry.
Code:	Not applicable.
Bytes:	9
Notes:	In the SYS users block. The code body is an offset number and there is no return address. See *SYS.

CONSTANT

Class:	Defining Word
Function:	Creates a word-length constant keyword dictionary entry whose name is the token following CONSTANT and whose value equals the top stack entry.
Input/Output:	One stack entry/None.
Usage:	Defining word-length named constants.
Z80 Code:	CREATE ;CREATE PRIMITIVE HEADER
	, ;STORE NUMBER IN CODE BODY
	SCODE ;REPLACE CODE ADDRESS

```
EX     DE,HL      ;WORD ADDRESS TO HL
LD     E,{HL}     ;GET LOW BYTE IN CODE BODY
INC    HL         ;BUMP POINTER
LD     D,{HL}     ;GET HIGH BYTE
PUSH   DE         ;NUMBER TO STACK
JP     {IY}       ;JUMP TO NEXT
```

Bytes: 21

Formal Definition:
  : ■CONSTANT■CREATE■, ■;CODE■....

Notes: The "...." is the assembly or machine code.

CONTEXT

Class: System Variable

Function: Pushes to the stack the address of the system context variable.

Input/Output: None/One stack entry.

Usage: Used to access the system variable which contains the address of the vocabulary that will be searched to locate keywords.

Code: Not applicable.

Notes: In the SYS user block. The code body contains an offset number and there is no return address.

CORE

Class: Vocabulary

Function: Sets the CONTEXT system variable to the address of the code body of CORE which contains the address of the latest entry in the vocabulary.

Input/Output: None/None.

Usage: Evokes the CORE vocabulary.

Code: Not applicable.

Bytes: 12

Notes: Predefined but exactly as if defined using the VOCABULARY defining keyword.

CR>

Class:	Interstack
Function:	Pops the byte at the top of the return stack and pushes it to the stack in sign-extended format.
Input/Output:	One return stack byte entry/One stack entry.
Usage:	Retrieval of temporary data stored on the return stack to the stack in a format compatible with signed 16-bit arithmetic.

Z80 Code:

```
        LD    L,{IX+0}    ;GET TOP RETURN BYTE
        INC   IX          ;ADJUST RSP
        LD    H,0         ;ASSUME BYTE POSITIVE
        BIT   7,L         ;TEST BYTE SIGN
        JR    Z,SKIP      ;IF ZERO, POSITIVE
        DEC   H           ;MAKE NEGATIVE
SKIP:   PUSH  HL          ;PUSH 16 BIT WORD
```

Bytes: 23

CREATE

Class:	Defining Word
Function:	Creates a dictionary header for a primitive keyword whose name is the token following CREATE and links it to the CURRENT vocabulary.
Input/Output:	None/None.
Usage:	Used to create all dictionary headers.

Code:

```
        ENTRY       ;POINTER TO LATEST HEADER
        ASPACE      ;SET THE SEPARATOR
        TOKEN       ;TOKEN TO DICTIONARY SPACE
        HERE        ;POINTS TO THE TOKEN
        CURRENT     ;ADDRESS OF CURRENT VOCABULARY
        @           ;VOCABULARY LINK
        !           ;UPDATE LINK TO NEW TOKEN
        *C# 4       ;FOUR IDENTIFIER CHARACTERS
        DP          ;DICTIONARY POINTER
        +!          ;ENCLOSE FOUR CHARACTERS
        ,           ;ADD LINK ADDRESS TO NEW
                     HEADER
        HERE        ;WORD ADDRESS OF NEW HEADER
        2+          ;POINTS TO CODE BODY
        ,           ;STORE AT WORD ADDRESS
```

Bytes: 39

Formal Definition:

: ■CREATE■ENTRY■ASPACE■TOKEN■HERE■CURRENT■@■!■
4■DP■+!■,■HERE■2+■,■;

CRET

Class:	I/O
Function:	Issues a carriage-return line-feed sequence to the display.
Input/Output:	None/None.
Usage:	Display formatting.
Z80 Code:	CALL $CRLF ;CALL CR-LF
Bytes:	13

CSPLIT

Class:	Stack
Function:	Pops the top stack entry and creates two 16-bit numbers. The high-order byte is moved to the low-order byte of the second entry in sign-extended format. The low-order byte is returned as the top stack entry as a positive 16-bit number.
Input/Output:	One stack entry/Two stack entries.
Usage:	Stack manipulation of multi-byte integers.

Z80 Code:

```
        POP   HL          ;GET 16 BIT NUMBER
        LD    E,H         ;MOVE HIGH BYTE
        LD    H,0         ;MAKE LOW + 16 BIT
        LD    D,H         ;ASSUME POSITIVE
        BIT   7,E         ;TEST SIGN
        JR    Z,OUT1      ;IF +, IT'S OK
        DEC   D           ;ELSE MAKE NEGATIVE
OUT1:   PUSH  DE          ;PUSH SIGNED BYTE
        PUSH  HL          ;PUSH REMAINDER
```

Bytes:	22

CURRENT

Class:	System Variable
Function:	Pushes to the stack the address of the current vocabulary variable.
Input/Output:	None/One stack entry.
Usage:	Used to access the current vocabulary variable which contains the address of the vocabulary where new keywords will be added.
Code:	Not applicable.
Bytes:	9
Notes:	In the SYS user block. The code body is an offset number and there is no return address. See *SYS.

CVARIABLE

Class:	Defining Word
Function:	Creates a byte variable keyword dictionary entry whose name is the token following CVARIABLE and whose initial value is the low-order byte of the entry popped from the stack.
Input/Output:	One stack entry/None.
Usage:	Defining byte-length named variables and initializing them.

Z80 Code:

```
CCONSTANT         ;CREATE HEADER AND INITIALIZE
SCODE             :REPLACE CODE ADDRESS AND EXIT
      PUSH  DE          ;PUSH WORD ADDRESS
      JP    {IY}        ;JUMP TO NEXT
```

Bytes: 15

Formal Definition:

: ■CVARIABLE■CCONSTANT■;CODE■....

Notes: The "...." is assembly or machine code.

D*

Class:	Arithmetic
Function:	Does a signed multiply of the second stack word by the low-order byte of the top stack entry and replaces both entries by the 24-bit product with the 8 most significant bits sign extended as the second stack entry and the 16 least significant bits as the top stack entry.
Input/Output:	Two stack entries/Two stack entries.
Usage:	Signed integer arithmetic.

Z80 Code:

```
      EXX                    ;SAVE IR
      POP   BC               ;GET 8 BIT NUMBER
      POP   DE               ;GET 16 BIT NUMBER
      CALL  $ISIGN           ;FIELD INPUT SIGNS
      CALL  $UD*             ;MULTIPLY 16X8
      EX    AF,AF'           ;RETRIEVE SIGN FLAG
      JP    P,OUT*           ;IF +, IT'S OK
      LD    A,C              ;MOVE 8 MOST SIGNIFI-
                             CANT
      CPL                    ;COMPLEMENT
      LD    C,A              ;RESTORE
      EX    DE,HL            ;MOVE 16 LEAST
      LD    HL,0             ;GET ZERO
      SBC   HL,DE            ;NEGATE 16 LEAST
      JR    NZ,OUT           ;IF NOT ZERO, IT'S OK
      INC   C                ;ELSE 2'S COMP MOST
```

OUT*	PUSH	HL	;16 LEAST TO STACK
	PUSH	BC	;8 MOST TO STACK
	EXX		;RESTORE IR

Bytes: 39

Notes: Does not test the top stack entry to insure it is a valid 8-bit number. The 16 least significant bits are an unsigned number on the stack.

D/MOD

Class: Arithmetic

Function: Does a signed divide of the 24-bit number in the third (16 least significant bits) and second (8 most significant bits) stack entries by the low-order byte of the top stack entry. Replaces these entries with the 16-bit quotient as the second stack entry and the positive 8-bit remainder expanded to 16 bits as the top entry.

Input/Output: Three stack entries/Two stack entries.

Usage: Signed integer arithmetic.

Z80 Code:

	EXX		;SAVE IR
	POP	HL	;GET 8 BIT DIVISOR
	POP	DE	;8 MOST SIGNIFICANT
	POP	BC	;GET 16 LEAST
	LD	A,H	;DIVISOR SIGN
	XOR	D	;RESULT SIGN
	EX	AF,AF'	;SAVE SIGN FLAG
	LD	A,L	;GET DIVIDEND SIGN
	AND	A	;TEST SIGN
	JP	P,MOV1	;IF +, IT'S OK
	NEG		;MAKE POSITIVE
MOV1:	LD	D,A	;STORE DIVISOR
	LD	H,B	;GET 16 LEAST
	LD	L,C	;TO HL
	LD	A,E	;GET 8 MOST
	LD	E,D	;MOVE DIVISOR TO E
	AND	A	;TEST SIGN
	JP	P,MOV2	;IF +, IT'S OK
	CPL		;COMPLEMENT HIGH 8
	LD	HL,0	;ELSE GET ZERO
	SBC	HL,BC	;NEGATE LOW 16
	JPC	NZ,MOV2	;IF NON-ZERO, IT'S OK
	INC	A	;ELSE BUMP HIGH
MOV2:	LD	D,A	;MOVE HIGH 8
	CALL	$UD/	;DIVIDE 24X8
	CALL	$OSIGN	;JUSTIFY RESULT

```
                    PUSH   HL          ;QUOTIENT TO STACK
                    PUSH   BC          ;REMAINDER TO STACK
                    EXX                ;RESTORE IR
```

Bytes: 48
Notes: Does not test the top stack entry to insure it is a valid 8-bit
                    number. No test is made to insure a valid 16-bit quotient.

DECIMAL

Class: System
Function: Sets the system variable BASE to 10 decimal to evoke
                    decimal I/O.
Input/Output: None/None.
Usage: Evokes radix 10 I/O.
Z80 Code:
```
                    LD     A,0A        ;GET 10 DECIMAL
                    LD     {BASE},A    ;STORE IT AT BASE
```
Bytes: 15

DEFINITIONS

Class: System Directive
Function: Sets the system variable CURRENT to the value in the
                    system variable CONTEXT.
Input/Output: None/None.
Usage: Sets the vocabulary into which new definitions will be
                    linked.
Z80 Code:
```
                    LD     HL,{CONTEXT}    ;CONTEXT VOCABULA
                    LD     {CURRENT},HL    ;TO CURRENT
```
Bytes: 16

DISPLAY

Class: I/O
Function: Outputs to the display the low-order byte of successive top
                    stack entries until a non-ASCII code is output (a character
                    with the high-order bit 1 set).
Input/Output: One to N stack entries/None.
Usage: Output to display the stack string data.
Z80 Code:
```
          $DISPLAY:     EXX                ;SAVE IR
          DLOOP;        POP    HL          ;GET TOP STACK WORD
                        LD     A,L         ;LOW BYTE
```

```
            CALL   $ECHO      ;DISPLAY IT
            AND    A          ;TEST CODE FOR BIT 7
            JP     P,DLOOP    ;IF POSITIVE, LOOP
            EXX               ;RESTORE IR
```

Bytes: 21

Notes: Entered from #> (to display number strings) at the $DISPLAY entrance.

DO

Class:	Compiler Directive (Immediate)
Function:	Encloses the word address of the program control directive *DO in the dictionary and then pushes to the stack the address of the next free dictionary location.
Input/Output:	None/One stack entry.
Usage:	Used to initiate a DO . . . LOOP or DO . . . +LOOP construct in the compile mode.

Code:

```
      *# XX        ;WORD ADDRESS OF *DO {LITERAL}
      DO,          ;STORE ADDRESS AND GET POINTER
```

Bytes: 16

Formal Definition:

   : ■DO■XX■DO,■;■IMMEDIATE

DO,

Class:	System
Function:	Stores the program control directive at the top of the stack to the dictionary and returns the address of the next free dictionary location on the stack.
Input/Output:	One stack entry/One stack entry.
Usage:	Used to define compiler directive immediate keywords.

Code:

```
      ,            ;STORE DIRECTIVE
      HERE         ;PUSH FREE ADDRESS
```

Bytes: 14

Formal Definition:

   : ■DO,■,■HERE■;

DOES>

Class:	Program Control Directive
Function:	Replaces the first word in the code body of the latest entry

in the CURRENT vocabulary with the top return stack word and then replaces its code address with the second return stack entry.

Input/Output: Two return stack word entries/None.

Usage: Used to terminate the compile time code of a high-level defining word definition. Always followed by keywords that constitute the execution time generic code definition.

Z80 Code:

```
R>              ;GET TOP RETURN ADDRESS
ENTRY           ;LATEST HEADER ADDRESS
*C# 8           ;PLUS 8
+               ;POINTS TO CODE BODY
!               ;STORE RETURN TO CODE BODY
SCODE           ;REPLACE CODE ADDRESS AND RETURN
      DEC   IX              ;ADJUST RSP
      LD    {IX+0},B        ;IR LOW BYTE TO RETURN
      DEC   IX              ;ADJUST RSP
      LD    {IX+0},C        ;IR HIGH BYTE TO RETURN
      EX    DE,HL           ;WA REGISTER TO HL
      LD    C,{HL}          ;@WA LOW INTO IR
      INC   HL              ;BUMP WA
      LD    B,{HL}          ;@WA HIGH INTO IR
      INC   HL              ;BUMP WA
      PUSH  HL              ;PUSH POINTER
```

Bytes: 39

Formal Definition:

: ■DOES> ■R> ■ENTRY■8■ + ■!■;CODE■....

Notes: The "...." is assembly or machine code.

DP

Class: System Variable

Function: Pushes to the stack the address of the dictionary pointer variable.

Input/Output: None/One stack entry.

Usage: Used to access the system variable which contains the address of the next free dictionary location.

Code: Not applicable.

Bytes: 9

Notes: In the SYS user block. The code body contains an offset number and there is no return address. See *SYS.

DROP

Class: Stack

Function:	Pops the top stack entry and discards it.
Input/Output:	One stack entry/None.
Usage:	Stack clean up.
Z80 Code:	POP HL ;DROP TOP
Bytes:	11

DUMP

Class:	I/O
Function:	Does a memory dump using the second stack entry as the starting address and the top stack entry as the ending address. Displays a line consisting of the address, eight numbers, a space, and eight more numbers. Removes both entries.
Input/Output:	Two stack entries/None.
Usage:	Examining memory.
Code:	OVER ;GET LOOP STARTING ADDRESS
	*DO ;INITIALIZE DO LOOP
	CRET ;ISSUE CR-LF
	DUP ;DUPLICATE LINE ADDRESS
	*C# 4 ;FOUR CHARACTER LINE ADDRESS MINIMUM
	.R ;PRINT LINE ADDRESS
	PART ;ISSUE FIRST 8
	PART ;ISSUE SECOND 8
	WAIT ;TIME TO STOP AND WAIT?
	*C# 10 ;16 NUMBERS PER LINE
	*+LOOP EC ;LOOP UNTIL DONE
	DROP ;DROP ADDRESS
Bytes:	37

Formal Definition:

: ■DUMP■OVER■DO■CRET■DUP■4■.R■PART■PART■WAIT■
10■+LOOP■DROP■;

DUP

Class:	Stack
Function:	Duplicates the top stack entry and pushes it to the stack.
Input/Output:	One stack entry/Two stack entries.
Usage:	Stack management.
Z80 Code:	POP HL ;GET TOP WORD
	PUSH HL ;RESTORE TOP
	PUSH HL ;AND PUSH IT AGAIN
Bytes:	13

ECHO

Class:	I/O
Function:	Pops the top stack entry and outputs the low-order byte to the display.
Input/Output:	One stack entry/None.
Usage:	Direct control of the display for formatting.

Z80 Code:

```
POP   HL          ;GET TOP
LD    A,L         ;GET LOW-ORDER BYTE
CALL  $ECHO       ;DISPLAY IT
```

Bytes: 15

ELSE

Class:	Compiler Directive (Immediate)
Function:	Encloses the word address of the program control directive *ELSE in the dictionary, saves the address of the next free dictionary location on the stack, reserves 1 byte in the dictionary, swaps the top two stack entries, computes the difference between the top stack entry and the current free dictionary location and encloses the low-order byte in the dictionary as a relative jump byte.
Input/Output:	One stack entry/One stack entry.
Usage:	Used to terminate the True code portion in an IF...ELSE ...THEN construct in the compile mode.

Code:

```
*# XX         ;WORD ADDRESS OF *ELSE {LITERAL}
DO,           ;STORE ADDRESS AND GET POINTER
0             ;GET ZERO
C,            ;RESERVE BYTE
SWAP          ;SWAP TOP TWO ADDRESSES
THEN          ;EXECUTE THEN CODE
```

Bytes: 24

Notes: See definition of THEN.

Formal Definition:

: ■ELSE■XX■DO,■0■C,■SWAP■THEN■;■IMMEDIATE

END

Class:	Compiler Directive (Immediate)
Function:	Encloses the word address of the program control directive *END in the dictionary, pops the top stack address, computes the difference between this address and address of the current free dictionary location and encloses the low-order byte in dictionary as a relative jump byte.
Input/Output:	One stack entry/None.

Usage: Used to terminate a BEGIN . . . END loop structure in the compile mode.

Code: *# XX   ;WORD ADDRESS OF *END {LITERAL}
          END,   ;STORE AND COMPUTE JUMP

Bytes: 16

Formal Definition:
 : ■END ■XX ■END, ■; ■IMMEDIATE

END,

Class: System

Function: Encloses the address of the program control directive at the top of the stack in the dictionary, computes the relative jump byte using the top stack entry and the current free dictionary location and encloses the low-order byte in the dictionary.

Input/Output: Two stack entries/None.

Usage: Used in defining compiler directive immediate keywords.

Code: ,   ;STORE DIRECTIVE WORD ADDRESS
        HERE   ;CURRENT FREE ADDRESS
        −   ;COMPUTE RELATIVE OFFSET
        C,   ;ENCLOSE IT IN DICTIONARY

Bytes: 18

ENTRY

Class: System

Function: Pushes to the stack the address of the first header byte of the latest entry in the CURRENT vocabulary.

Input/Output: None/One stack entry.

Usage: Used to locate the address of the latest vocabulary definition which will become the link address of the next keyword.

Code: CURRENT ;CURRENT ADDRESS
        @   ;VOCABULARY ADDRESS
        @   ;HEADER ADDRESS

Bytes: 16

ERASE

Class: Utility

Function:	Fills a region of memory with ASCII spaces. The starting memory address is the second stack entry and the ending memory address is the top entry. Removes both entries.
Input/Output:	Two stack entries/None.
Usage:	Clearing string data.
Code:	1+ ;BUMP LAST ADDRESS FOR LOOPING
	SWAP ;GET LOOP ORDER CORRECT
	*DO ;INITIALIZE LOOP
	ASPACE ;GET SPACE CODE
	I> ;INDEX EQUALS MEMORY ADDRESS
	C! ;SPACE TO MEMORY
	*LOOP F8 ;LOOP UNTIL DONE
Bytes:	25

EXECUTE

Class:	System
Function:	Pops the top stack entry to the word address register and jumps to the inner interpreter RUN routine to cause the execution of a keyword.
Input/Output:	One stack entry/None.
Usage:	Used by the system for keyword execution and by operator for defining conditional execution keywords.
Z80 Code:	POP HL ;GET KEYWORD WORD ADDRESS
	JP RUN ;EXECUTE IT
Bytes:	12
Notes:	EXECUTE does not have a return address.

FILL

Class:	Utility
Function:	Fill a region of memory with a specified byte. The byte is the third stack entry low-order byte. The starting memory address is the second stack entry and the ending memory address is the top entry. Removes all three entries.
Input/Output:	Three stack entries/None.
Usage:	Loading memory to some initial value.
Code:	1+ ;BUMP LAST ADDRESS FOR LOOPING
	SWAP ;GET RIGHT LOOP ORDER
	*DO ;INITIALIZE LOOP
	DUP ;DUPLICATE BYTE
	I> ;GET MEMORY ADDRESS
	C! ;STORE BYTE
	*LOOP F8 ;LOOP UNTIL DONE

DROP   ;REMOVE BYTE FROM STACK

Bytes: 27

Formal Definition:

: ■FILL■1+ ■SWAP■DO■DUP■I> ■C!■LOOP■DROP■;

FORGET

Class:	Vocabulary
Function:	Searches the current vocabulary for the token following FORGET. If located, the current link address is set to the address of the link in the keyword located and the dictionary pointer is reset to the start of the header of the located keyword. If not located, the token is echo displayed and followed by a "?".
Input/Output:	None/None.
Usage:	Used to delete keyword definitions in a spatial sense.

Code:

CURRENT	;GET CURRENT ADDRESS
@	;POINTS TO LATEST ENTRY IN CURRENT
CONTEXT	;GET CONTEXT ADDRESS
!	;SET TO SEARCH CURRENT
'	;SEARCH FOR TOKEN {KEYWORD}
DUP	;NEED WORD ADDRESS TWICE
*C# 2	;WORD ADDRESS LESS 2 POINTS
−	;TO THE LINK ADDRESS
@	;THE LINK ADDRESS
CURRENT	;GET CURRENT ADDRESS
@	;POINTS TO THE LINK
!	;RESET LINK TO TOKEN LINK
*C# 6	;WORD ADDRESS LESS 6 POINTS TO THE
−	;FIRST HEADER BYTE OF THE TOKEN
DP	;GET FREE DICTIONARY ADDRESS
!	;RESET DICTIONARY FREE LOCATION

Bytes: 44

Notes: Caution is advised. It is possible to forget part or all of the context vocabulary. The end result is an unusable language since nothing can be located.

Formal Definition:

: ■FORGET■CURRENT■@ ■CONTEXT■!■'■DUP■2■ − ■@ ■
CURRENT■@ ■!■6■ − ■DP■!■;

HERE

Class:	System

Function:	Pushes the address of the next free dictionary location to the stack (the address stored at the system variable DP).
Input/Output:	None/One stack entry.
Usage:	Used by the system in building dictionary entries and by the operator to determine dictionary space usage.

Z80 Code:	LD	HL,{DP}	;GET @DP
	PUSH	HL	;FREE LOCATION TO STACK

Bytes:	14

HEX

Class:	System
Function:	Sets the system variable BASE to 16 decimal to evoke hexadecimal I/O.
Input/Output:	None/None.
Usage:	Evokes radix 16 I/O.

Z80 Code:	LD	A,10	;GET 16 DECIMAL
	LD	{BASE},A	;STORE IT AT BASE

Bytes:	15
Notes:	Base 16 I/O is the base on start-up.

I>

Class:	Interstack
Function:	Pushes to the stack the loop index for the innermost word-length loop which is the top return stack word.
Input/Output:	One return stack word/One return stack word and one stack word.
Usage:	Retrieval of the current word loop index.

Z80 Code:	LD	L,{IX+0}	;GET LOW INDEX
	LD	H,{IX+1}	;GET HIGH BYTE
	PUSH	HL	;INDEX TO STACK

Bytes:	17
Notes:	Presumes nothing else on the return stack except loop index.

IF

Class:	Compiler Directive (Immediate)
Function:	Encloses the word address of the program control directive *IF in the dictionary, pushes the address of the next free dictionary location to the stack and reserves 1 byte in the

dictionary for a relative jump byte.

Input/Output:	None/One stack entry.
Usage:	Used to initiate a conditional branch construct in the compile mode.

Code:	*# XX	;WORD ADDRESS OF *IF {LITERAL}
	DO,	;STORE ADDRESS AND SAVE POINTER
	0	;GET A ZERO
	C,	;RESERVE A BYTE

Bytes: 20

Formal Definition:
   : ■IF■XX■DO, ■0■C, ■; ■IMMEDIATE

IMMEDIATE

Class:	Vocabulary
Function:	Delinks the latest entry from the current vocabulary and links it to the compiler vocabulary. The previous second entry in the current vocabulary becomes the latest entry.
Input/Output:	None/None.
Usage:	Adding keywords to the compiler vocabulary.

Code:	ENTRY	;POINTS TO LATEST CURRENT KEYWORD
	DUP	;SAVE IT FOR COMPILER LINK
	*C# 4	;CURRENT HEADER + 4 POINTS TO THE
	+	;LATEST KEYWORDS LINK
	DUP	;SAVE AS NEW LINK ADDRESS
	@	;GET THE LINK
	CURRENT	;POINTS TO CURRENT
	@	;POINTS TO VOCABULARY
	!	;UPDATE CURRENT TO 2ND KEYWORD
	COMPILER	;COMPILERS ADDRESS
	@	;POINTS TO LAST COMPILER ENTRY
	SWAP	;ADDRESS THEN LINK
	!	;STORE LINK IN PREVIOUS CURRENT
	COMPILER	;COMPILER ADDRESS
	!	;PREVIOUS CURRENT TOP OF COMPILER

Bytes: 39

Formal Definition:
   : ■IMMEDIATE■ENTRY■DUP■4■ + ■DUP■@■CURRENT■@■!■
COMPILER■@■SWAP■!■COMPILER■!■;

IOR

Class:	Logical

Function:	Replaces the top two stack entries by the logical inclusive or of the entries on a bit-by-bit basis.
Input/Output:	Two stack entries/One stack entry.
Usage:	Logical operations.

Z80 Code:

```
POP   HL        ;GET TOP WORD
POP   DE        ;GET NEXT WORD
LD    A,L       ;MOVE TOP LOW BYTE
OR    E         ;OR IN 2ND LOW BYTE
LD    L,A       ;SAVE LOW OR
LD    A,H       MOVE TOP HIGH BYTE
OR    D         ;OR IN 2ND HIGH BYTE
LD    H,A       ;SAVE HIGH OR
PUSH  HL        ;PUSH RESULT
```

Bytes: 19

J>

Class:	Interstack
Function:	Pushes to the stack the loop index for the second innermost word-length loop.
Input/Output:	Three return stack word entries/Three return stack word entries and one stack entry.
Usage:	Retrieval of the second level word-length loop index.

Z80 Code:

```
LD    L,{IX+4}    ;GET LOW INDEX
LD    H,{IX+5}    ;GET HIGH INDEX
PUSH  HL          ;INDEX TO STACK
```

Bytes: 17

Notes: Presumes only word-length loop parameters on the return stack.

K>

Class:	Interstack
Function:	Pushes to the stack the loop index for the third innermost word-length loop.
Input/Output:	Five return stack word entries/Five return stack word entries and one stack entry.
Usage:	Retrieval of the third level word-length loop index.

Z80 Code:

```
LD    L,{IX+8}    ;GET LOW INDEX BYTE
LD    H,{IX+9}    ;GET HIGH INDEX BYTE
PUSH  HL          ;INDEX TO STACK
```

Bytes: 17

Notes: Presumes only word-length loop parameters on the stack.

KEY

Class:	I/O
Function:	Pushes to the stack in the low-order byte position the next ASCII code entered via the keyboard.
Input/Output:	None/One stack entry.
Usage:	Interfaces the keyboard to the system.
Z80 Code:	CALL $KEY
	LD L,A
	PUSH HL
Bytes:	15
Notes:	Presumes transfer via the A register.

LBP

Class:	System Variable
Function:	Pushes to the stack the address of the line buffer pointer variable.
Input/Output:	None/One stack entry.
Usage:	Used to access the line buffer pointer variable which contains the address of the start of the next token in the input line buffer.
Code:	Not applicable.
Bytes:	9
Notes:	In the SYS users block. The code body is an offset number and there is no return address. See *SYS.

LEAVE

Class:	Compiler Directive (Immediate)
Function:	Encloses the word address of the program control directive *LEAVE in the dictionary.
Input/Output:	None/None.
Usage:	Compiles a command to cause an immediate exit from a word-length loop construct at execution time. Used within a conditional branch construct.
Code:	*# XX ;WORD ADDRESS OF *LEAVE {LITERAL}
	;ENCLOSE IT
	,
Bytes:	16
Formal Definition:	

    : ■LEAVE■XX■,■; ■IMMEDIATE

LOOP

Class:	Compiler Directive (Immediate)
Function:	Encloses the word address of the program control directive *LOOP in the dictionary, then pops the stacks and computes the difference between this address and the next free dictionary address and encloses the low-order byte in the dictionary as the relative jump byte.
Input/Output:	One stack entry/None.
Usage:	Used to terminate a DO . . . LOOP construct in the compile mode.

Code:

```
*# XX      ;WORD ADDRESS OF *LOOP
           {LITERAL}
END,       ;STORE ADDRESS AND JUMP
```

Bytes:	16

Formal Definition:

  : ■LOOP■XX■END, ■; ■IMMEDIATE

LROT

Class:	Stack
Function:	Rotates the top three stack entries left in an infix cyclic sense (input A B C into B C A with A the final top stack entry).
Input/Output:	Three stack entries/Three stack entries.
Usage:	Control of stack order.

Z80 Code:

```
POP    DE              ;GET TOP
POP    HL              ;GET 2ND
EX     {SP},HL         ;EXCHANGE 3RD AND 2ND
PUSH   DE              ;PUSH OLD TOP
PUSH   HL              ;PUSH OLD 3RD
```

Bytes:	15

MAX

Class:	Arithmetic
Function:	Replaces the top two stack entries by the entry with the higher value (signed).
Input/Output:	Two stack entries/One stack entry.
Usage:	Signed integer arithmetic tests.

Z80 Code:

```
POP    DE              ;GET TOP
POP    HL              ;GET 2ND
PUSH   HL              ;ASSUME 2ND GREATER
```

```
              AND    A          ;RESET CARRY
              SBC    HL,DE      ;2ND-TOP
              JP     P,OUT      ;2ND GREATER, EXIT
              POP    HL         ;DROP 2ND
              PUSH   DE         ;PUSH TOP
       OUT:   JP     {IY}       ;JUMP TO NEXT
```
Bytes: 21

MIN

Class:	Arithmetic
Function:	Replaces the top two stack entries with the entry with the smaller value (signed).
Input/Output:	Two stack entries/One stack entry.
Usage:	Signed integer arithmetic tests.
Z80 Code:	

```
              POP    DE         ;GET TOP
              POP    HL         ;GET 2ND
              PUSH   HL         ;ASSUME 2ND SMALLER
              AND    A          ;RESET CARRY
              SBC    HL,DE      ;2ND-TOP
              JP     N,OUT      ;2ND SMALLER, EXIT
              POP    HL         ;DROP 2ND
              PUSH   DE         ;PUSH TOP
       OUT:   JP     {IY}       ;JUMP TO NEXT
```
Bytes: 21

MINUS

Class:	Arithmetic
Function:	Replaces the top stack entry with its two's complement.
Input/Output:	One stack entry/One stack entry.
Usage:	Signed integer arithmetic.
Z80 Code:	

```
              LD     HL,0       ;GET ZERO
              POP    DE         ;GET NUMBER
              AND    A          ;RESET CARRY
              SBC    HL,DE      ;0-NUMBER
              PUSH   HL         ;PUSH 2'S COMPLEMENT
```
Bytes: 18

MOD

Class:	Arithmetic

Function:	Does a signed divide of the second stack word by the low-order byte of the top stack entry. Replaces both entries with the 8-bit remainder expanded to 16 bits.
Input/Output:	Two stack entries/One stack entry.
Usage:	Signed integer arithmetic.
Z80 Code:	

```
EXX                ;SAVE IR
POP    DE          ;GET 8 BIT DIVISOR
POP    BC          ;GET 16 BIT DIVIDEND
CALL   $ISIGN      ;FIELD INPUT SIGNS
CALL   $US/        ;DIVIDE 16X8
PUSH   BC          ;PUSH REMAINDER
EXX                ;RESTORE IR
```

Bytes:	21
Notes:	No test is made to insure a valid 8-bit divisor.

MODE

Class:	System Variable
Function:	Pushes to the stack the address of the system mode variable.
Input/Output:	None/One stack entry.
Usage:	Used to access the system variable which contains the system execution state.
Code:	Not applicable.
Bytes:	9
Notes:	In the SYS user block. The code body contains an offset number and there is no return address. See *SYS. If MODE contains 0, the execute mode is in effect and if 1, the compile mode is in effect. MODE is a CVARIABLE and must be referenced using keywords for byte-length addressing.

MODU/

Class:	Arithmetic
Function:	Does a signed divide of the second stack entry by the low-order byte of the top stack entry. Replaces both entries with the positive 8-bit remainder expanded to 16 bits as the second stack entry and the 8-bit quotient expanded to 16 bits as the top stack entry.
Input/Output:	Two stack entries/Two stack entries.
Usage:	Signed integer arithmetic.
Z80 Code:	

```
EXX                ;SAVE IR
POP    DE          ;GET 8 BIT DIVISOR
```

```
                        POP    BC           ;GET 16 BIT DIVIDEND
                        CALL   $ISIGN       ;FIELD INPUT SIGNS
                        CALL   $US/         ;DIVIDE 16X8
                        CALL   $OSIGN       ;FIELD OUTPUT SIGN
                        PUSH   BC           ;REMAINDER TO STACK
                        PUSH   HL           ;QUOTIENT TO STACK
                        EXX                 ;RESTORE IR
```

Bytes: 25
Notes: Does not test the divisor to insure it is a valid 8-bit
                  number. No test is made to insure a valid 8-bit quotient.

MOVE

Class: Utility
Function: Move the region of memory specified by the starting ad-
                   dress of the third stack entry and the ending address of the
                   second stack entry to the memory region specified by the
                   starting address of the top stack entry. Removes all three
                   entries.
Input/Output: Three stack entries/None.
Usage: Used to move memory data.
Z80 Code:

```
                 EXX                   ;SAVE IR
                 POP    DE             ;NEW STARTING ADDRESS
                 POP    HL             ;OLD ENDING ADDRESS
                 POP    BC             ;OLD STARTING ADDRESS
                 AND    A              ;RESET CARRY
                 SBC    HL,BC          ;COUNT−1
                 PUSH   BC             ;OLD STARTING
                 EX     {SP},HL        ;SAVE COUNT−1
                 POP    BC             ;BC=COUNT−1
                 EX     DE,HL          ;HL=NEW STARTING
                 PUSH   HL             ;SAVE IT
                 AND    A              ;RESET CARRY
                 SBC    HL,DE          ;MOVE FROM TOP?
                 POP    HL             ;GET IT BACK
                 JR     NC,BOTTOM      ;NO, BOTTOM
                 EX     DE,HL          ;HL=OLD START
                 INC    BC             ;BC=COUNT
                 LDIR                  ;MOVE THE BLOCK
OUTM:            EXX                   ;RESTORE IR
                 JP     {IY}           ;RETURN TO NEXT
BOTTOM:          ADD    HL,BC          ;NEW ENDING ADDRESS
                 EX     DE,HL          ;OLD STARTING ADDRESS
                 ADD    HL,BC          ;OLD ENDING ADDRESS
                 INC    BC             ;BC+COUNT
```

	LDDR		;MOVE THE BLOCK
	JR	OUTM	;JUMP TO RETURN

Bytes: 40

Notes: The memory blocks may be overlapping, but this routine will correctly move them.

NEXT

Class: Program Control Directive

Function: Encloses a jump to the inner interpreter NEXT routine in the dictionary

Input/Output: None/None.

Usage: Used to terminate keywords defined using machine code.

Z80 Code: *# E9FD   ;FDE9 INSTRUCTION {LITERAL}
            ,   ;ENCLOSE THE JP {IY}

Bytes: 16

Formal Definition:
    HEX ■ : ■NEXT ■E9FD ■ , ■ ;

NOT

Class: Logical

Function: Inverts the logic state of the flag at the top of the stack.

Input/Output: One stack entry/One stack entry.

Usage: Inverting the results of relational test or other flags.

Z80 Code:

	POP	HL	;GET THE FLAG
	LD	A,L	;MOVE LOW BYTE
	OR	H	;OR IN HIGH BYTE
	LD	DE,0	;ASSUME FALSE RESULT
	JR	NZ,OUT	;IF NONZERO, FALSE
	INC	E	;MAKE TRUE
OUT:	PUSH	DE	;FLAG TO STACK

Bytes: 20

OCTAL

Class: System

Function: Sets the system variable BASE to 8 decimal to evoke octal I/O.

Input/Output: None/None.

Usage: Evokes radix 8 I/O.

Z80 Code:		LD	A,8	;GET 8 DECIMAL
		LD	{BASE},A	;STORE IT AT BASE
Bytes:	15			

OVER

Class:	Stack
Function:	Duplicates the second stack entry and pushes it to the top of the stack.
Input/Output:	Two stack entries/Three stack entries.
Usage:	Control of stack order.
Z80 Code:	POP HL ;GET TOP
	POP DE ;GET 2ND
	PUSH DE ;RESTORE 2ND AS 3RD
	PUSH HL ;RESTORE TOP AS 2ND
	PUSH DE ;RESTORE 2ND AS TOP
Bytes:	15

PART

Class:	I/O
Function:	Pops an address from the stack and displays eight numbers to the operator from the 8 bytes following the initial address. The address pointer is left on the stack.
Input/Output:	One stack entry/One stack entry.
Usage:	Used by DUMP to display memory.
Code:	SPACE ;ISSUE SPACE TO DISPLAY
	*C# 8 ;LOOP ENDING INDEX
	0 ;LOOP STARTING INDEX
	*CDO ;INITIALIZE LOOP
	DUP ;DUPLICATE POINTER
	C@ ;GET MEMORY BYTE
	*C# 3 ;SET TO DISPLAY 3 CHARACTERS
	.R ;DISPLAY AT LEAST 3
	1+ ;INCREMENT MEMORY POINTER
	*CLOOP F3 ;LOOP UNTIL DONE
Bytes:	33

Formal Definition:
: ■PART■SPACE■8■0■CDO ■DUP■C@■3■.R■1+■CLOOP■;

R>

Class:	Interstack

Function:	Pops the word at the top of the return stack and pushes it to the stack.
Input/Output:	One return stack word entry/One stack entry.
Usage:	Retrieval of temporary data stored on the return stack or direct control of return stack addresses.

Z80 Code:

```
LD    L,{IX+0}    ;GET RETURN LOW BYTE
INC   IX          ;ADJUST RSP
LD    H,{IX+0}    ;GET RETURN HIGH BYTE
INC   IX          ;ADJUST RSP
PUSH  HL          ;PUSH TO STACK
```

Bytes:	21

RROT

Class:	Stack
Function:	Rotates the top three stack entries right in an infix cyclic sense (input A B C into C A B with B the top stack entry).
Input/Output:	Three stack entries/Three stack entries.
Usage:	Control of stack order.

Z80 Code:

```
POP   HL          ;GET TOP
POP   DE          ;GET 2ND
EX    {SP},HL     ;TOP TO 3RD
PUSH  HL          ;3RD TO 2ND
PUSH  DE          ;2ND TO TOP
```

Bytes:	15

S*

Class:	Arithmetic
Function:	Does a signed multiply of the low-order byte of the second stack entry by the low-order byte of the top stack entry and replaces both entries by the 16-bit product.
Input/Output:	Two stack entries/One stack entry.
Usage:	Signed integer arithmetic.

Z80 Code:

```
EXX                 ;SAVE IR
POP   BC            ;GET FIRST 8 BITS
POP   DE            ;GET 2ND 8 BITS
CALL  $ISIGN        ;FIELD INPUT SIGNS
CALL  $US*          ;MULTIPLY 8X8
CALL  $OSIGN        ;JUSTIFY RESULT
PUSH  HL            ;QUOTIENT TO STACK
EXX                 ;RESTORE IR
```

Bytes:	24

Notes: No test is made to insure that either stack entry is a valid 8-bit number.

SCODE

Class: Program Control Directive (Headerless)

Function: Resets the code address of the latest keyword in the CURRENT vocabulary to the address at the top of the return stack.

Input/Output: One return stack word entry/None.

Usage: Used by the system to load the generic code address for defining words at execution time and then return to the outer interpreter.

Code:
```
R>      ;GET RETURN ADDRESS
CA!     ;STORE IT AS CODE ADDRESS
```

Bytes: 8

Formal Definition:
: ■SCODE■R> ■CA!■;

SIGN

Class: I/O

Function: Pushes the ASCII code for a minus sign to the stack (in the low-order byte position) if the top byte on the return stack is two's complement negative.

Input/Output: One return stack byte entry/One return stack byte entry and zero or one stack entries.

Usage: Adds a leading negative sign to the stack string number if the original binary number was negative. Used in designing formatted displays.

Z80 Code:
```
         BIT   7,{IX+0}   ;GET RETURN SIGN BIT
         JR    Z,OUT      ;IF ZERO +, EXIT
         LD    L,2D       ;- ASCII CODE
         PUSH  HL         ;MINUS SIGN TO STACK
OUT:     JP    {IY}       ;JUMP TO NEXT
```

Bytes: 19

SINGLE

Class: System

Function: If the top stack entry is a valid 8-bit number (the high-order byte is all zeros or all ones), a False flag is pushed to the stack. Otherwise a True flag is pushed to the stack.

Input/Output: One stack entry/Two stack entries.

Usage: Used to determine storage or display requirements for stack numbers.

Z80 Code:

```
        POP   HL        ;GET WORD
        PUSH  HL        ;RESTORE WORD
        LD    L,H       ;IF SINGLE, 0 OR FFFF
        LD    A,H       ;GET HIGH BYTE
        AND   A         ;TEST IT
        JR    Z,OUT     ;IF ZERO, PUSH FALSE
        INC   HL        ;SEE NOTE BELOW
OUT:    PUSH  HL        ;PUSH FLAG
```

Bytes: 19

Notes: If the top byte is single, the INC HL instruction will yield a False flag since FFFF+1=0 if and only if the original value of H was FF.

SPACE

Class:	I/O
Function:	Echo displays a space to the display.
Input/Output:	None/None.
Usage:	Display formatting.
Z80 Code:	

```
        LD    A,20      ;GET ASCII SPACE CODE
        CALL  $ECHO     ;ECHO DISPLAY IT
```

Bytes: 15

STATE

Class:	System Variable
Function:	Pushes to the stack the address of the system state variable.
Input/Output:	None/One stack entry.
Usage:	Used to access the system variable which contains the compiler immediate state.
Code:	Not applicable.
Bytes:	9

Notes: In the SYS user block. The code body contains an offset number and there is no return address. See *SYS. STATE is 1 set if a compiler immediate keyword is located in the compile mode and is 0 set when the keyword is executed. STATE is a CVARIABLE and must be referenced using keywords for byte-length addressing.

SWAP

Class:	Stack
Function:	Interchanges the order of the top two stack entries.
Input/Output:	Two stack entries/Two stack entries.
Usage:	Stack data management.
Z80 Code:	

```
POP   HL          ;GET TOP
EX    {SP},HL     ;TOP TO 2ND
PUSH  HL          ;2ND TO TOP
```

Bytes: 13

THEN

Class:	Compiler Directive (Immediate)
Function:	Pops the address from the stack, computes the difference between this address and the current free dictionary location as the relative jump byte, and stores the byte at the address popped from the stack initially.
Input/Output:	Used to terminate a branch construct in the compile mode.
Code:	

```
HERE      ;GET FREE ADDRESS
OVER      ;COPY JUMP ADDRESS OVER HERE
−         ;COMPUTE JUMP BYTE
SWAP      ;REVERSE ORDER
C!        ;STORE JUMP BYTE
```

Bytes: 20

Notes: Loads a previously reserved byte in the dictionary. Define THEN as a normal keyword, then define ELSE and WHILE as IMMEDIATES, and finally make THEN an IMMEDIATE.

Formal Definition:
: ■THEN■HERE■OVER■ − ■SWAP■C!■;

TYPE

Class:	I/O
Function:	Pops the top stack entry which points to a string consisting of a length argument followed by that many ASCII characters. Outputs the string characters to the display.
Input/Output:	One stack entry/None.
Usage:	Display of system messages to the operator.
Z80 Code:	

```
        POP   HL          ;GET STRING ADDRESS
$TYPE:  LD    E,{HL}      ;GET LENGTH
LOOP:   INC   HL          ;BUMP POINTER
```

```
LD      A,{HL}       ;GET CHARACTER
CALL    $ECHO        ;ECHO DISPLAY IT
DEC     E            ;DECREMENT LENGTH
JR      NZ,LOOP      ;IF LENGTH≠0, LOOP
```

Bytes: 20

VARIABLE

Class:	Defining Word
Function:	Creates a word-length variable dictionary keyword entry whose name is the token following VARIABLE and whose initial value is the value popped from the stack.
Input/Output:	One stack entry/None.
Usage:	Defining and initializing word-length named variables.
Z80 Code:	CONSTANT :CREATE HEADER AND INITIALIZE

```
SCODE       :REPLACE CODE ADDRESS AND EXIT
            PUSH   DE            ;PUSH WORD ADDRESS
            JP     {IY}          ;JUMP TO NEXT
```

Bytes: 15

Formal Definition:
: ■VARIABLE■CONSTANT■;CODE■....

Notes: The "...." is the assembly or machine code.

VOCABULARY

Class:	Defining Word
Function:	Creates a vocabulary keyword dictionary entry whose name is the token following VOCABULARY, with an initial link to the latest entry in the CURRENT vocabulary. and which, when the vocabulary name is executed, sets the system variable CONTEXT to the link address.
Input/Output:	None/None.
Usage:	Defining vocabularies.
Code:	

```
<BUILDS   ;CREATE THE HEADER AND BODY
ENTRY     ;GET CONTEXT LINK
,         ;STORE IN BODY
DOES>     ;RESET CODE ADDRESS, BODY AND EXIT
CONTEXT   ;GET CONTEXT ADDRESS
!         ;STORE LINK TO CONTEXT
```

Bytes: 22

Formal Definition:
: ■VOCABULARY■ < BUILDS■ENTRY■,■DOES> ■CONTEXT■!■;

WAIT

Class:	Utility
Function:	If a keyboard entry (any) has been received, a loop is entered waiting for the next keyboard entry.
Input/Output:	None/None.
Usage:	Used to hold the display screen fixed to allow inspection.
Code:	See notes.
Bytes:	See notes.
Notes:	A system specific keyword which first reads the keyboard port without an initial rest. If an entry has been received, the keyboard is sampled until the next entry is received. No keyboard return is expected. The routine should not manipulate the cursor but should simply await the next entry. Very system specific.

WHILE

Class:	Compiler Directive (Immediate)
Function:	Encloses the word address of the program control directive *WHILE in the dictionary. The top two stack entries are swapped, the top stack entry is popped. The offset from this address to the current free dictionary location is enclosed in the dictionary as a relative jump byte. The function also pops the top stack entry, computes the difference between this address and the current free dictionary location and stores the low-order byte to the address popped from the stack as a relative jump byte.
Input/Output:	Two stack entries/None.
Usage:	Used to terminate a loop construct containing a *WHILE.
Code:	SWAP ;CHANGE STACK ORDER
	*# XX ;WORD ADDRESS OF *WHILE
	END, ;STORE ADDRESS AND OFFSET FOR BEGIN
	THEN ;STORE OFFSET FOR IF OR ELSE
Bytes:	20

Formal Definition:
: ■WHILE■SWAP■XX■END,■THEN■;■IMMEDIATE

Notes:	See definition for THEN.

XOR

Class:	Logical
Function:	Replaces the top two stack entries by the logical exclusive

or of the entries on a bit-by-bit basis.

Input/Output: Two stack entries/One stack entry.

Usage: Logical operations.

Z80 Code:

```
POP    HL        ;GET TOP WORD
POP    DE        ;GET 2ND WORD
LD     A,L       ;MOVE TOP LOW BYTE
XOR    E         ;XOR IN 2ND LOW BYTE
LD     L,A       ;MOVE TO RESULT
LD     A,H       ;GET TOP HIGH BYTE
XOR    D         ;XOR IN 2ND HIGH BYTE
LD     H,A       ;MOVE TO RESULT
PUSH   HL        ;RESULT TO STACK
```

Bytes: 19

[

Class: Compiler Directive (Immediate)

Function: Encloses the literal handler *[in the dictionary, changes the token separator to] and scans the next token from the input buffer and then encloses the token in extended header format in the dictionary.

Input/Output: None/None.

Usage: Compiling literal strings into secondary keywords or display formatting.

Code:

```
*# *[        ;WORD ADDRESS OF *[ {LITERAL}
,            ;ENCLOSE IT IN THE DICTIONARY
*C# 5D       ;GET THE SEPARATOR ]
TOKEN        ;MOVE TOKEN TO THE DICTIONARY
HERE         ;GET START OF TOKEN
C@           ;TOKEN LENGTH
1+           ;ADDRESS OF LENGTH OF TOKEN
DP           :DICTIONARY ADDRESS
+!           ;ENCLOSE TOKEN IN DICTIONARY
```

Bytes: 31

Formal Definition:

: ■[■XX ■, ■5D ■TOKEN ■HERE ■C@ ■1+ ■DP ■+! ■; ■IMMEDIATE

6.2 A Classy Cross-Reference ───────────────

What would you expect to find in a classy cross-reference? A cross-reference by class, of course. Following are all the keywords arranged alphabetically by class.

Arithmetic Keywords

*	2−
*/	2/
*/MOD	ABS
+	D*
−	D/MOD
/	MAX
/MOD	MIN
1+	MINUS
1−	MOD
2*	MODU/
2+	S*

Compiler Directives

+LOOP	END
BEGIN	IF
C+LOOP	LEAVE
CDO	LOOP
CLEAVE	THEN
CLOOP	WHILE
DO	[
ELSE	

Compile Mode Terminators

;
;CODE

Defining Words

:	CREATE
<BUILDS	CVARIABLE
CCONSTANT	VARIABLE
CONSTANT	VOCABULARY

I/O

#	CLEAR
#>	CRET
#S	DISPLAY
.	DUMP
.R	ECHO
<#	KEY
?	PART
ADUMP	SIGN
APART	SPACE
ASCII	TYPE
C?	

Interstack

<R	CR>
C<R	I>
CI>	J>
CJ>	K>
CK>	R>

Literal Handlers

*#
*C#
*[

Logical

AND	NOT
IOR	XOR

Memory Reference

!	C!
+!	C+!
0SET	C0SET
1SET	C1SET
@	C@

Program Control Directives

*+LOOP	*IF
*C+LOOP	*LEAVE
*CDO	*LOOP
*CLEAVE	*WHILE
*CLOOP	DOES>
*DO	NEXT
*ELSE	SCODE
*END	

Relational

0<
0=
<
=
>

Stack

2DUP	DUP
2OVER	LROT
2SWAP	OVER
CJOIN	RROT
CSPLIT	SWAP
DROP	

Subroutine

$CRLF	$UD*
$ECHO	$US*
$ISIGN	$UD/
$KEY	$US/
$OSIGN	

System

'(tick)	CA!
*SYS	DECIMAL
+SP	DO,
,(comma)	END,
−SP	ENTRY
?RS	EXECUTE
?SP	HERE
ABORT	HEX
ASPACE	OCTAL
BINARY	SINGLE
C,	

System Directives

DEFINITIONS

System Variables

BASE	DP
COMPILER	LBP
CONTEXT	MODE
CURRENT	STATE

Utility

ERASE
FILL
MOVE
WAIT

Vocabulary

CORE
FORGET
IMMEDIATE

6.3 Sum Total

There are roughly 150 user-available keywords in the design presented. The memory requirement to implement the keywords in the Section 6.1 description is about 3200 bytes. The total design, including the inner interpreter, the outer interpreter, and the routine of Section 5.3, can be easily coded in less than 4 K bytes. Well, maybe not easily, but it will fit.

7 | Extension Please

There are any number of extensions that may be added to the TIL language. All depend only on defining the problem, defining the keywords and extending the language. The utility of the extension is the sole criteria. For example, an important keyword in my system is an ASCII file called SANDI. It contains our anniversary, her birthday, my mother-in-law's phone number, and other critical data-base parameters. One can never be too safe.

Some of the more useful extensions to the basic (not BASIC) TIL will be considered in this section. Incorporation of all of these extensions will extend the TIL from a language to a programming system. The extensions are not totally unrelated among themselves, although it is possible to incorporate some features and not others. The level of presentation of the material in this section is higher than in previous sections. The reader is assumed to have a working knowledge of more advanced software concepts and a broader knowledge of hardware interfacing.

7.1 Introductions

The majority of the extensions to the TIL are predicated on a system configuration of 16 K bytes of programmable memory and a floppy disk/controller combination. It is presumed that a more sophisticated operating system is available to support the system input/output to the disk system. The system designer (you) is faced with many more decisions on how to configure the overall software system. Depending on the idiosyncrasies of the disk system designer, a total rewrite of the disk controller software may be in order. This generally arises because the equipment manufacturer presumes that the disk operating system should reside at some strange location in memory, and the bootstrap read-only memory he supplies does not contain all of the fundamental disk input, output and control functions.

The three main extensions to be considered are an assembler, a virtual memory system, and an editor. These three functions are complimentary but caution is advised; the functions are only similar in nature to what their names imply. This will become clearer when the functions are discussed.

A TIL assembler is different from the normal concept of an assembler. It still translates from "assembly language" to "machine language" but it has restrictions on how programs can be structured. Rather than using a symbol table to resolve forward and backward references, it passes addresses on the stack. It contains structured constructs to accomplish this semi-automatically. This is generally adequate for resolving references in the short programs encountered in TIL keyword definitions but not for general assembly language programming. The target memory for the assembled code is the TIL dictionary since the assembler is specifically designed for defining new keywords. The assembler extension does not depend on the disk system and is very useful even in small systems. The assembler is always evoked with the system in the execution mode rather than the compile mode. This is true even when the assembly source code is disk resident and is loaded to the system to extend the language.

The TIL virtual memory extension is a method for integrating a floppy disk into the basic system. The disk is used to store both TIL source text and program data. Disk accesses are accomplished in a manner that is totally transparent to the operator. Source text on the disk may include both primitive and secondary keywords that are assembled/compiled to the free dictionary space when the source text is evoked. The primitive keywords in the source text must contain totally relocatable code if defined using a "," or C, keyword, or they must be defined in assembly language (which allows relocation by its very nature). A virtual memory system without an associated TIL assembler is restrictive. Program data accesses are provided by the virtual memory system, but the data formatting is strictly application-dependent.

The TIL editor is designed to allow generation and modification of TIL source text files. Source text files allow individual keywords, classes of keywords, or entire vocabularies to be stored in source form on the disk rather than demanding resident TIL memory space. When the keywords are needed, they can be loaded to the system and are compiled/assembled to the resident dictionary. The editor is specifically designed to simplify source text manipulation. Although it has limited general text editor features, it is not designed to be the last word in an editor. If it is desired or required, it is certainly possible to add general text editing features.

In discussing the extensions, I will usually give an overview of how to proceed with the design, rather than a detailed discussion of a precise design. This is mostly a fallout of the hardware- specific nature of the designs. A Z80 assembler description is of limited use if you have some other microcomputer, but the design approach is still similar. Note that, in order to proceed, the designer of the assembler must be familiar with both the microcomputer and the assembly language process. This is typical of all of the extensions; a degree of sophistication is required to proceed with a design.

7.2 Assemblers

An extension of great utility is the TIL assembler. The assembler consists of a group of keywords which are usually spatially intermixed with the core language but contained in a separate vocabulary. A TIL assembler materially eases the generation of the full core language by allowing more easily remembered keyword mnemonics to be used (instead of direct machine code) in defining primitives. A TIL assembler is evoked in the execute mode and the system never enters the compile mode while the assembler is in effect.

A TIL assembler is very different from the usual concept of an assembler. The TIL assembler is specifically designed to allow the addition of keywords to the TIL rather than to produce stand-alone programs or subroutines. The target memory for the assembler is the free dictionary space since this is where keyword extensions are always added. The TIL assembler does not use a symbol table but rather uses the stack to store addresses needed to resolve both forward and backward references. This is generally adequate given the brevity of most keyword definitions.

7.2.1 Assembler Overview

The problem with describing the assembler is the machine-specific nature of the beast. Although the general design procedure for producing an assembler is universal, the product is not. The design techniques will be illustrated relative to the Z80.

The assembler for the threaded interpretive language is a translator. It translates more easily remembered instruction mnemonics into machine code. Like all TIL code entry, the assembler is a reverse Polish notation entry design. A non-TIL assembler entry usually consists of a line number, an optional label, an instruction mnemonic and one or more operands. The operands are usually register designators, numbers, or labels. The TIL assembler does not support line numbers and demands that the operands precede the instruction mnemonic. Only limited label operands are supported.

The mnemonics for the TIL assembler will not necessarily be those suggested by the manufacturer of the microprocessor. The manufacturer's mnemonics generally presume a symbol table which can be used to resolve ambiguities within a single mnemonic instruction regarding the addressing mode. It is far easier in a TIL to assign individual mnemonic names to the various addressing modes. As an example, the Zilog mnemonic ADD will generate 1-, 2-, or 3-byte instructions for implied register addressing, immediate addressing, register pair addressing and indexed addressing. In the TIL, separate mnemonics are used to evoke the different addressing modes.

Strictly from personal preference, the mnemonics (keywords) that I use for the Z80 are all three letters followed by a comma. The instruction names are a cross-breed of Z80 and 8080 mnemonics and a personal quirk that names should be related to the action and the addressing modes. For example, the mnemonics STA (store accumulator) and LDA (load accumulator) a la the 8080 are very descriptive and are retained. The mnemonic EX DE,HL (Z80) or XCHG (8080) that interchange the DE and HL register pair is simplified to XDH,. The Z80 mnemonic suggests that other register pairs could be interchanged by using different operands (not true) while the 8080 mnemonic does not indicate which items are to be exchanged (and there are several with the Z80). I will leave the design of your mnemonics to you but will perforce use my own in the design presentation.

7.2.2 Architecture and the Assembler

Any assembler must make use of the central processing unit architecture to define a reasonable set of mnemonics. The machine-code instructions of a given processor generally have a regularity that results from the logic design of the unit. Individual bits within the machine instruction determine the operation type, the register(s) involved, the conditional options depending on the internal status, and the addressing mode. Some central processing units are very regular in their architecture (the 6809) and some are very irregular (the Z80). The goal is to find the regular instructions that will allow the definition of instruction classes. A careful inspection of the manufacturer's documentation will most often reveal this regularity. Almost all of the regular instructions in a given processor can be built from bit mask patterns. The bit patterns represent registers, conditions, operation types, or other parameters used by the central processing unit to direct its internal operations.

To illustrate this pattern regularity, the Z80 internal architecture will be briefly described first. Figure 7.1 shows the main register of the Z80. The

Figure 7.1: *Z80 processor registers.*

H	L	H′	L′
D	E	D′	E′
B	C	B′	C′
A	F	A′	F′
IX			
IY			
PC			
SP			
I	R		

registers A, B, C, D, E, H, and L may be individually addressed as 8-bit registers with the A register as the accumulator. The register pairs AF, BC, DE, HL, IX, IY, SP, and PC are 16-bit registers with the HL, IX, and IY registers serving as accumulators with limited scope. The F register is a program status word that contains flag bits which are set by the central processing unit. The state of the bits depends on the results from executing given instructions.

Ignore for the moment the addressing modes of the Z80; the mask patterns that address registers, register pairs, and condition codes in the Z80 are depicted below in table 7.1:

Pattern	Register	Register Pair	Condition	
0 0 0	B	BC	NZ	(non-zero)
0 0 1	C	DE	Z	(zero)
0 1 0	D	HL,IX,IY	NC	(non-carry)
0 1 1	E	AF,SP	CY	(carry)
1 0 0	H		PO	(parity odd)
1 0 1	L		PE	(parity even)
1 1 0	M,@X,@Y or default		P	(positive)
1 1 1	A		N	(negative)

Table 7.1: *Mask patterns that address registers, register pairs, and condition codes.*

Note that the register pairs are 2-bit masks rather than 3-bit masks. So what are M, @X, and @Y you ask, and why are there several register pairs evoked by the same mask pattern? The addressing modes just landed.

The designation M (8080 derived), or in Z80 parlance {HL}, refers to the fact that the HL register pair can be used as a pointer to a memory location which can be accessed like a register (implied register pair indirect addressing). The Z80 allows the IX and IY registers to be used to determine an effective address using the value in the register plus a signed displacement embedded in the instruction. This is a form of indexed indirect addressing that is evoked by @X or @Y, as opposed to the Z80 {IX+d} or {IY+d}. The form of these instructions consists of 1 byte (DD for an @X or FD for an @Y), the first byte of the equivalent M instruction, the signed displacement byte (-126 to $+129$), and the second byte of the equivalent M instruction, if applicable. When used in this fashion the M, @X and @Y, along with displacement in the later two cases, specify a memory location which is accessed as if it were an 8-bit "register".

When the HL, IX or IY keywords are used as register pair designators, the instruction formats for all three are the same except that the IX instruction is preceded by a DD byte and the IY by an FD byte. The mask patterns for all three register designators are the same, however.

One further factor is important relative to the mask patterns. The register pair mask patterns always fall in bit position b5b4 in the instruction (with b0 the least significant bit). The condition code patterns always fall in positions b5b4b3 and the register patterns may be in positions b5b4b3 or b2b1b0. These facts are important when the assembler is designed.

The regularity of the mask patterns for register designations and condition flags is typical for most processors. This regularity often extends into instruction groups as well. For example the entire Z80 ALG (arithmetic and logic group) of instructions are of the form:

	b7	b6	b5	b4	b3	b2	b1	b0
Register	1	0	←	f	→	←	r	→
Immediate	1	1	←	f	→	1	1	0	← n →

Here r is one of the 3-bit register masks, f is a 3-bit function code and n is an 8-bit byte following the instruction. The arithmetic and logic register instructions perform some operation between the register designated by r and the A register (accumulator) and leave the result in the A register and/or the condition flags of F set appropriately. The immediate arithmetic and logic instructions perform similar operations using the immediate byte instead of a register. The f-bit mask pattern evokes the following functions:

f	Function
0 0 0	Add
0 0 1	Add with carry
0 1 0	Subtract
0 1 1	Subtract with carry
1 0 0	AND
1 0 1	Exclusive OR
1 1 0	Inclusive OR
1 1 1	Compare

Other microcomputers have similar instruction designator bits.

The object of the assembly keyword designs is to produce coding sequence from input of the form:

> keyword
> operand.1 keyword
> operand.1 operand.2 keyword
> operand.1 operand.2 operand.3 keyword

The operands are either register designations, condition codes, or numbers, all of which leave numbers (or masks) on the stack. The keywords are the instruction mnemonic and they expect any required input data on the stack. The keywords combine the operand masks with the basic instruction masks as appropriate and enclose the resulting machine code instruction in the dictionary. The mnemonics produce 1-, 2-, 3-, or 4-byte machine-code instructions in the Z80 case.

Since the assembler always operates in the execute mode, numbers entered as operands are always pushed to the stack. By defining the register and condition codes as CCONSTANTs, the mask patterns can also be pushed to the stack. The mnemonic keywords then evoke instruction skeletons, add in mask patterns as appropriate, and enclose the results in the dictionary. If the instructions are regular, it is usually possible to define the keywords using a high-level defining word. In this case the specific mask is stored with the mnemonic keyword and the generic instruction build code follows the defining word (see 1BYTE of Section 4.5.5 as an example).

7.2.3 The Z80 Assembler

The code for producing a subset of the Z80 assembler will be given in the following pages. It is not a "complete" assembler since some possible Z80 instructions are not produced. Generally this is because more than one form of the instruction exists.

One of the more difficult aspects of the design of the Z80 TIL assembler is designing a method for handling the indexed addressing mode. The inclusion of these instructions considerably complicates the design of keywords. This will become obvious when the design is presented. It is possible to produce a less complex assembler by totally ignoring the indexed instructions. They are still available via the "," and C, keywords if needed.

There are several ways to present the design: by addressing mode, by functional group, or by the number of bytes in the instruction. Because of the irregularity of the Z80 instruction set, a mixture of the different design approaches will be used. The result will be total coverage but in a nonstandard way.

7.2.3.1 The Operands

The object of the game at this point is to define the operand keywords. The design is not complex. Consider the following:

```
: ■8* ■2* ■2* ■2* ■ ;

0 ■CCONSTANT ■B
1 ■CCONSTANT ■C
2 ■CCONSTANT ■D
3 ■CCONSTANT ■E
4 ■CCONSTANT ■H
5 ■CCONSTANT ■L
```

```
6 ■CCONSTANT■M
7 ■CCONSTANT■A

00■CCONSTANT■BC
10■CCONSTANT■DE
20■CCONSTANT■HL
30■CCONSTANT■AF
30■CCONSTANT■SP

00■CCONSTANT■NZ
08■CCONSTANT■Z
10■CCONSTANT■NC
18■CCONSTANT■CY
20■CCONSTANT■PO
28■CCONSTANT■PE
30■CCONSTANT■P
38■CCONSTANT■N
```

Several points should be noted. The carry and minus keywords are defined as CY and N to prevent contention with register designators. The 8* keyword will be used to shift the register masks to position b5b4b3 from the b2b1b0 position of the definitions. The use of A, B, C, D, and E as keyword names in the ASSEMBLER vocabulary will force the use of leading zeros during equivalent hexadecimal number entry. There are alternate naming conventions that could be used to prevent these problems. The choice is yours, but I personally prefer C as the register designator rather than C. or C{ or some other convention.

The register pair keywords @X and @Y will load the initial byte which indicates the index mode and will leave a negative-valued mask on the stack. The mask is designed such that the low-order byte position contains a positive 07 (the mask pattern for M) but the high-order bit is set to 1. The negative value is easy to test to determine if the index mode special store of the displacement value is required. Thus:

```
: ■@X■DD■C,■8007■;
: ■@Y■FD■C,■8007■;
```

The register pair keywords are simply:

```
: ■IX■DD■C,■HL■;
: ■IY■FD■C,■HL■;
```

Having the operand enclosing the indexed byte simplifies the design somewhat. Trouble arises in only one case with this design.

7.2.3.2 The Constants ──────────────────────

There are several Z80 instructions that have no required operands or are irregular enough to preclude the use of operands. These instructions are either 1 or 2 bytes long but the first byte of the 2 byte instructions is always hexadecimal ED. The 1-byte instructions are defined using the 1BYTE defining word of Section 4.5.5. The definition is:

: ■1BYTE■ < BUILDS■C, ■DOES > ■C@■C, ■;

The mnemonic keywords are then defined as:

3F■1BYTE■CCF,	Complement carry flag
AF■1BYTE■CLA,	Clear accumulator {XOR A}
2F■1BYTE■CPL,	Complement accumulator (1's complement)
27■1BYTE■DAA,	Decimal adjust accumulator
F3 ■1BYTE■DSI,	Disable interrupts
FB■1BYTE■ENI,	Enable interrupts
76■1BYTE■HLT,	Halt
00■1BYTE■NOP,	No operation
A7■1BYTE■RCF,	Reset carry flag {AND A}
37■1BYTE■SCF,	Set carry flag
C9■1BYTE■RET,	Return from subroutine
08■1BYTE■XAA,	Exchange AF and AF'
D9■1BYTE■XAL,	Exchange all three register pairs
EB■1BYTE■XDH,	Exchange DE and HL

Two-byte instructions are defined using the high-level defining keyword:

: ■2BYTES■ < BUILDS■C, ■DOES > ■ED■C, ■C@■C, ■;

With this defining keyword, the mnemonic keywords are:

46■2BYTE■IM0,	Set interrupt mode 0
56■2BYTE■IM1,	Set interrupt mode 1
5E■2BYTE■IM2,	Set interrupt mode 2
44■2BYTE■NEG,	Complement A (2's)
4D■2BYTE■RTI,	Return from interrupt
45■2BYTE■RTN,	Return from non-maskable interrupt
6F■2BYTE■RLD,	Rotate left digit
67■2BYTE■RRD,	Rotate right digit
57■2BYTE■LAI,	A = I
5F■2BYTE■LAR,	A = R
4F■2BYTE■LRA,	R = A
47■2BYTE■LIA,	I = A

Several of these instructions are so useless (R = A) that they are included for drill rather than utility.

7.2.3.3 8-Bit Move Group

The 8-bit move group simply moves data around the machine in byte-sized hunks. There are several addressing modes allowed.

The register to register move basic instruction is of the form:

b7	b6	b5	b4	b3	b2	b1	b0
0	1	←	r	→	←	r′	→

Here r and r′ are register masks, and the r′ register is moved to the r register. One of the "registers" may be M, @X, or @Y. There are ninety-one forms of this type — forty-nine involving only the 8-bit registers, fourteen involving the indirect HL register (M) and twenty-eight involving the indirect indexed registers (@X and @Y). The indirect indexed forms are 3-byte instructions and all others are 1-byte instructions.

The sequence to assemble an instruction to move the M register to the C register is:

$$C\blacksquare M\blacksquare MOV,\blacksquare$$

The C register is input first to retain the infix notation form C = M, which would equate C to the value of M. The sequence to assemble an instruction to move the A register to the memory location whose address is four more than the value in the IX register is:

$$4\blacksquare @X\blacksquare A\blacksquare MOV,\blacksquare$$

The keyword MOV, is defined as:

: ■MOV, ■OVER■8* ■OVER■ + ■40■ + ■C, ■ + ■0< ■IF■C, ■THEN■;

The OVER■8* extracts the r register mask and shifts it over to b5b4b3. The OVER■ + then adds the r and r′ masks. The 40■ + adds in the register-to-register move mask and the C, encloses the result in the dictionary. At this point the stack still contains at least the r and r′ masks. Remember if @X or @Y precede the MOV, the first DD or FD byte will have already been enclosed prior to the execution of MOV,. The + ■0< adds the r and r′ mask and leaves a true value on the stack if the result is negative. Only the @X or @Y register masks are negative so that the IF■C, ■THEN will drop the flag and store the displacement only for the indexed indirect cases. One note should be mentioned. There is no test to prevent using two M, @X, or @Y operands. Using two M operands will assemble a 76 (HALT) instruction. Any other combination leads to nonsense and should be avoided.

The instruction group to move a given 8-bit number to some register is of the form:

b7	b6	b5	b4	b3	b2	b1	b0
0	0	←	r	→	1	1	0	←	n	→

Here n is the 8-bit number. The register may be the M @X, or @Y "register." The calling sequence is of the form:

$$d■r■n■MVI,■$$

Here d is the indexed displacement used only for the @X or @Y register options, r is the register, and n is the byte number. The keyword MVI, is defined as:

: ■MVI, ■OVER■8*■06■ + ■C, ■SWAP■0< ■IF■SWAP■C, ■
THEN■C, ■ ;

There are eight possible instructions of this type with the indexed forms being 4 bytes long and all others being 2 bytes long.

The Z80 has six instructions that move the A register to the memory location whose address is the contents of the BC, DE, or HL register pair, or move the memory location to the A register. Those involving the HL register pair are evoked using the MOV, mnemonic keyword with M as an operand. The other four instructions are all 1-byte instructions. These four instructions and two other extended addressing instructions, which also load or store to the A register using the memory location whose address is embedded in the instruction, complete the 8-bit move group. One would like to evoke these six instructions via LDA, and STA, keywords. This can be done but at the expense of some restrictions in the extended addressing mode. Specifically, a test is made to see if the top stack value is 0000 (a BC operand result) or 0010 (a DE operand result), rather than some other number that would indicate an extended address. This eliminates two out of sixty-four K memory locations which could be addressed in the extended mode.

To use this approach, first define a keyword that will leave a True flag on the stack only if the top stack entry is a BC or DE register pair mask. This keyword can be defined as:

: ■BCORDE■2DUP ■BC■ = ■SWAP■DE■ = ■OR■ ;

The four mask patterns involved are:

	b7	b6	b5	b4	b3	b2	b1	b0						
Load	$\{$ 0	0	$\leftarrow r_p \rightarrow$		1	0	1	0						
	0	0	1	1	1	0	1	0	$\leftarrow$	n_L	$\rightarrow$	$\leftarrow$	n_H	$\rightarrow$
Store	$\{$ 0	0	$\leftarrow r_p \rightarrow$		0	0	1	0						
	0	0	1	1	0	0	1	0	$\leftarrow$	n_L	$\rightarrow$	$\leftarrow$	n_H	$\rightarrow$

The keywords for the mnemonics are:

: ■LDA, ■BCORDE■IF■0A■ + ■C, ■ELSE■3A■C, ■, ■THEN■;
: ■STA, ■BCORDE■IF■02■ + ■C, ■ELSE■32■C, ■, ■THEN■;

Although this may appear unduly complex, it is the price one pays for an irregular set of machine instructions.

7.2.3.4. 16-Bit Move Group

The 16-bit move group moves data around the machine in word-sized hunks. As in the 8-bit move group, there are several addressing modes.

The extended addressing, 16-bit move instructions load register pairs with a word embedded in the instruction. The BC, DE, HL, and SP instructions are 3 bytes long while the IX and IY forms are 4 bytes long. The basic instruction has the following form:

b7	b6	b5	b4	b3	b2	b1	b0						
0	0	$\leftarrow$ rp $\rightarrow$		0	0	0	1	$\leftarrow$	n_L	$\rightarrow$	$\leftarrow$	n_H	$\rightarrow$

Here rp is a register pair mask, n_L is the low-order byte and n_H is the high-order byte. This instruction may be preceded by a DD or FD byte in the case of the IX or IY register designation. The calling sequence is:

rp■n■DMI,

The DMI, (double move immediate) is fairly descriptive of the action. The keyword DMI, is defined as:

: ■DMI, ■SWAP■01■ + ■C, ■, ■;

The register pair to memory and memory to register pair move instructions are fairly regular except that two forms exist for those involving the HL pair. The odd forms of these two instructions are unfortunately both faster and shorter than the regular forms and are the preferred forms. The register pair to memory move instructions are of the form:

		b7	b6	b5	b4	b3	b2	b1	b0				
Regular	ED	0	1	← rp →		0	0	1	1	← n_L →		← n_H →	
Irregular		0	0	1	0	0	0	1	0	← n_L →		← n_H →	

The irregular HL form is different from the regular form and there is no leading ED byte. The irregular form may be preceded by a DD or FD byte if the IX and IY register pair is involved. The calling sequence for these instructions is:

$$n\ ■\ rp\ ■\ DSM,$$

The DSM, (double store to memory) keyword is defined as:

: ■DSM, ■DUP ■HL ■ = ■IF ■22 ■C, ■DROP ■ELSE ■ED ■C, ■43 ■ + ■C, ■THEN ■, ■;

Note that this sequence will not allow the regular form of the HL move instruction to be assembled.

The memory to register pair instructions have the form:

		b7	b6	b5	b4	b3	b2	b1	b0				
Regular	ED	0	1	← r_p →		1	0	1	1	← n_L →		← n_H →	
Irregular		0	0	1	0	1	0	1	0	← n_L →		← n_H →	

The DLM, (double load from memory) keyword is called using the following protocol:

$$rp\ ■\ n\ ■\ DLM,$$

The DLM, mnemonic keyword is defined as follows:

: ■DLM, ■SWAP ■DUP ■HL ■ = ■IF ■2A ■C, ■DROP ■ELSE ■ED ■ C, ■4B ■ + ■C, ■THEN ■, ■;

Again the regular form of the instruction referencing the HL register cannot be generated.

The Z80 has sixteen instructions to push 16-bit words from register pairs to the stack and six instructions to pop 16-bit words from the stack to register pairs. The instructions are of the form:

	b7	b6	b5	b4	b3	b2	b1	b0
Push	1	1	← r_p →		0	1	0	1
Pop	1	1	← r_p →		0	0	0	1

These instructions may be preceded by the indexed byte indicator DD or FD. The keywords necessary are part of a group of keywords that use the high-level defining keyword defined as follows:

: ■1MASK■ < BUILDS ■C, ■DOES > ■C@ ■SWAP ■8* ■ + ■C, ■;

The keywords are defined as:

C5 ■1MASK ■PSH,
C1 ■1MASK ■POP,

7.2.3.5 Arithmetic and Logic Group —————————————

The arithmetic and logic group includes both 8- and 16-bit operations. The accumulator for the 8-bit instructions is the A register, and for the 16-bit instructions is either the HL, IX, or IY register. Condition flags are contained in F.

There are eighty 8-bit instructions that operate on registers where registers include the indirect M and indexed registers @X and @Y. The machine-code forms for these instructions was given in Section 7.2.2. The mnemonic keywords are defined using a high-level definition. The defining sequence is:

: ■8ALG■ < BUILDS ■C, ■DOES > ■C@ ■OVER ■
+ ■C, ■0< ■IF ■C, ■THEN ■;

80 ■8ALG ■ADD,
88 ■8ALG ■ADC,
90 ■8ALG ■SUB,
98 ■8ALG ■SBC,
A0 ■8ALG ■AND,
A8 ■8ALG ■XOR,
B0 ■8ALG ■IOR,
B8 ■8ALG ■CMP,

The generic code in the defining word encloses the displacement byte if the @X or @Y forms are used.

The immediate forms of the 8-bit arithmetic and logic instructions are again defined using a high-level keyword. Eight possible instructions can be generated. The defining sequence is:

: ■8IM■ < BUILDS ■C, ■DOES > ■C@ ■C, ■C, ■;

C6 ■8IM ■ADI,
CE ■8IM ■ACI,
D6 ■8IM ■SUI,
DE ■8IM ■SCI,

```
E6■8IM■ANI,
EE■8IM■XOI,
F6■8IM■ORI,
FE■8IM■CPI,
```

There is nothing magic about the sequence, and the mnemonics are strictly personal preference.

The 8-bit register increment and decrement instructions again allow the extended definition of a register. The bit patterns for these instructions are:

	b7	b6	b5	b4	b3	b2	b1	b0
Increment	0	0	←	r	→	1	0	0
Decrement	0	0	←	r	→	1	0	1

The keywords are simply:

```
:■INC,■DUP■8*■04■+■C,■IF■C,■THEN■;
:■DEC,■DUP■8*■05■+■C,■IF■C,■THEN■;
```

The 16-bit arithmetic instructions in the Z80 are:

	BC	DE	HL	SP	IX	IY
Add to HL	09	19	29	39	—	—
Add to IX	DD09	DD19	—	DD39	DD29	—
Add to IY	FD09	FD19	—	FD39	—	FD29
Add with carry to HL	ED4A	ED5A	ED6A	ED7A	—	—
Subtract with carry to HL	ED42	ED52	ED62	ED72	—	—

The problem with this instruction set arises in part from our definition of the IX and IY keywords. The other part results from some type of indicator being required for the indexed accumulator case. By defining the keywords such that only the indexed keywords require two operands, a reasonable design results. The following sequence of definitions will do the job:

```
:■DAD,■09■+■C,■;
:■DAI,■SWAP■OVER■=■IF■−1■DP■+!■THEN■DAD,■;
:■DAC,■ED■C,■4A■+■C,■;
:■DSC,■ED■C,■42■+■C,■;
```

The double-add indexed instruction moves the dictionary pointer back if an IX■IX or an IY■IY operand sequence is input, since in this case two index bytes are incorrectly enclosed in the dictionary.

Since the Z80 does not directly support a double subtract without carry instructions, an instruction of this type is generated by defining the sequence:

```
:■DSB,■EDA7■,■42■+■C,■;
```

The sequence EDA7■, encloses first the A7 byte and then the ED. The A7 instruction is a A■AND, instruction which resets the carry flag but leaves A unchanged. (This instruction also exists as RCF,.)

The technique of defining macroinstructions, such as DSB, is very useful. It is quite common in microcomputers to encounter sequences of instructions which occur regularly. In the 8080, for example, it is possible to define a double length subtract instruction as a macroinstruction in the assembler since the basic instruction set does not contain such an instruction. Macroinstructions are easy to define and implement in a TIL assembler. It is even possible to define instructions such as multiply and divide if you want to generate these sequences as in-line code.

The double precision register pair increment and decrement instructions are:

	b7	b6	b5	b4	b3	b2	b1	b0
Increment	0	0	←	r_p	→	0	0	1	1
Decrement	0	0	←	r_p	→	1	0	1	1

These instructions may be preceded by the indexed byte indicator DD or FD. The keyword mnemonic is defined using the 1MASK defining word as follows:

$$03■1MASK■DIN,$$
$$0B■1MASK■DDC,$$

7.2.3.6 Rotate and Shift Group

The rotate and shift group is fairly regular except that there are four 1-byte instructions that are duplicates of the regular 2-byte instructions. The 1-byte versions do not have the leading CB byte (which is standard for the 2-byte regular instructions), but are otherwise identical except for status flag results. The form of the second byte is:

b7	b6	b5	b4	b3	b2	b1	b0
0	0	←	f	→	←	r	→

Here r is one of the extended register definitions. The f code is as follows:

Mask	Function
000	Rotate left circular
001	Rotate right circular

010	Rotate left through carry
011	Rotate right through carry
100	Shift left register
101	Shift right register
110	Not defined
111	Shift right logical

The choice to patch the four odd rotate instructions is optional but will be considered here.

The keyword mnemonics are defined using a high-level defining word as follows:

```
:■RSG■<BUILDS■C,■DOES>■CB■C,■C@■DUP■20■−■0<■
IF■OVER■07■=■IF■−1■DP■+!■THEN■THEN■OVER■0<■
IF■LROT■C,■THEN■+■C,■;
```

The mnemonic keywords are:

```
00■RSG■RLC,
08■RSG■RRC,
10■RSG■RLT,
18■RSG■RRT,
20■RSG■SLR,
28■RSG■SRR,
38■RSG■SRL,
```

The majority of the code in the defining word is devoted to dropping the leading CB byte in the four odd cases. The third IF clause tests for indexing and inserts the displacement in the third byte location, if so.

7.2.3.7 Bit Addressing

The Z80 bit addressing mode allows testing, setting, or resetting of any bit in any register where the extended "register" definition is used. The forms of these instructions are:

		b7	b6	b5	b4	b3	b2	b1	b0
Bit test	CB	0	1	←	b	→	←	r	→
Set	CB	1	1	←	b	→	←	r	→
Reset	CB	1	0	←	b	→	←	r	→

Here b is the bit number ranging from 0 to 7. If the register is @X or @Y, the

CB is the second byte in the instructions, the dispacement is the third byte and the fourth byte is the specific instruction byte. The calling sequences are:

$$b■r■mnemonic$$
$$d■b■r■mnemonic$$

The keyword mnemonics are defined as follows:

:■BITAD■ <BUILDS■C, ■DOES> ■CB■C, ■C@ ■LROT■8*■
+ ■OVER■ + ■SWAP ■0< ■IF■SWAP■C, ■THEN■C, ■;

        40■BITAD■BIT,
        80■BITAD■RES,
        C0■BITAD■SET,

7.2.3.8 Block-Directed Instructions ────────────────

Although it is not obvious from the ZILOG Z80 manual, the block move, compare, input, and output instructions can be classified into one group. The general forms of these instructions are:

b7	b6	b5	b4	b3	b2	b1	b0
ED	1	0	1	← C →		0	← f′ →

Here the condition mask and function masks have the following significance:

C Mask	Condition
00	Increment
01	Decrement
10	Increment and repeat
11	Decrement and repeat

f′ Mask	Function
00	Load
01	Compare
10	Input
11	Output

The sixteen instructions can be defined as follows:

```
00■CCONSTANT■IC
01■CCONSTANT■DC
10■CCONSTANT■IR
11■CCONSTANT■DR
```

```
:■BDIR■<BUILDS■C,■DOES>■ED■C,■C@■+■C,■;
```

```
A0■BDIR■CLD,
A1■BDIR■CCP,
A2■BDIR■CIN,
A3■BDIR■COT,
```

Here the constants are the conditional operands for the four basic mnemonic types.

7.2.3.9 Miscellaneous Instructions

Several instructions, however, fall into no clearly defined category when building the assembler. Consider the following: the Z80 restart instruction has this form:

b7	b6	b5	b4	b3	b2	b1	b0
1	1	←	n'	→	1	1	1

Here n' refers to the restart number (0 to 7). These are modified page zero addressing mode instructions. They are equivalent to a subroutine call to a page zero address whose address is eight times the restart number. The eight instructions are assembled by the keyword:

```
:■RST,■8*■C7■+■C,■;
```

Operands not in the set 0 thru 7 will obviously lead to problems.

The input and output mnemonic keywords expect an I/O port number on the stack. These port numbers are in the set 0 to FF (0 to 255 decimal). The basic instructions have no variables and are defined:

```
DB■8IM■INA,
D3■8IM■OTA,
```

There are three groups of instructions that assemble very different instructions but in a similar manner. One group assembles instructions that exchange the top stack parameter with a register pair. Another group loads the stack pointer register with the register pair. The last group loads the central processing unit program counter with the register pair contents. The register pairs are the HL, IX, or IY only. In all cases the basic instructions are the same with indexed bytes preceding the group instruction. The keywords are defined as:

$$: \blacksquare XST, \blacksquare E3 \blacksquare C, \blacksquare DROP \blacksquare;$$
$$: \blacksquare JPM, \blacksquare E9 \blacksquare C, \blacksquare DROP \blacksquare;$$
$$: \blacksquare LSP, \blacksquare F9 \blacksquare C, \blacksquare DROP \blacksquare;$$

In all cases, the keyword expects a register pair operand. The only purpose for this is to load the index bytes where applicable.

7.2.3.10 Call and Return Group

The call and return group of instructions assembles calls to subroutines or returns from subroutines. The problem with using these instructions is knowing what the call address is. One cannot stop in the middle of assembling a definition and define a label keyword to save the current stack pointer. This would lead to disastrous results.

There are several methods of keeping track of critical system addresses. One method is to simply use a HERE■. sequence at the critical point in the assembly code followed by a quick resort to a pencil to note the address on a laundry ticket or some other handy surface. The problem with this method is the transient nature of such notations and the fact that the system does not know the data. Another method is to define the entrance points as CONSTANTs before the definition is started. The CONSTANTs may be filled with the required address data using a LABEL keyword defined as follows:

$$: \blacksquare LABEL \blacksquare ' \blacksquare 2 + \blacksquare HERE \blacksquare SWAP \blacksquare ! \blacksquare;$$

At the point in the code where the dictionary pointer is to be saved, the sequence LABEL followed by the name of the label is inserted in the assembly stream. The keyword LABEL uses the sequence '■2+ to locate the code body of the constant and then fills it with the current dictionary free space address.

The unconditional subroutine call instruction expects an address on the stack left there by a number or label (CONSTANT) operand. The call instruction will simply assemble a CD byte followed by the 2-byte address. The keyword mnemonic is defined as:

$$: \blacksquare CAL, \blacksquare CD \blacksquare C, \blacksquare, \blacksquare;$$

The unconditional return from a subroutine is a 1-byte instruction already defined in Section 7.2.3.2.

The conditional call and return instructions have the formats:

	b7	b6	b5	b4	b3	b2	b1	b0		
Call	1	1	←	cc	→	1	0	0	n_L	n_H
Return	1	1	←	cc	→	0	0	0	n_L	n_H

Here cc is one of the condition code masks. The calling sequence is of the form:

$$n\;■\;cc\;■\;mnemonic$$

The keyword mnemonics are defined using the following sequence:

: ■CCODE■ < BUILDS■C, ■DOES > ■C@■ + ■C, ■, ■;

C4■CCODE■CLC,
C0■CCODE■RTC,

7.2.3.11 Jump Instructions

The jump instruction includes both conditional and unconditional jumps to either an absolute address or to an address relative to the instructions address. The problem of using these instructions is obviously knowing the target address of the jump. The mnemonic keywords do not care how the address data got on the stack; it simply must be there. I shall consider methods of accomplishing this semi-automatically in a later section.

The conditional and unconditional absolute jump instructions are of the form:

	b7	b6	b5	b4	b3	b2	b1	b0		
Unconditional	1	1	0	0	0	0	1	1	n_L	n_H
Conditional	1	1	←	cc	→	0	1	0	n_L	n_H

Like the call *conditional instruction*, the operand order is *address* then *condition code*. The instruction mnemonic keywords are defined as follows:

: ■JMP, ■C3■C, ■, ■;
C2■CCODE■JPC,

The relative jump instructions have the following forms:

	b7	b6	b5	b4	b3	b2	b1	b0		
Unconditional	0	0	0	1	1	0	0	0	← n →	
Conditional	0	0	1	← cc′ →		0	0	0	← n →	

Here the cc' conditions are the low-order 2 bits of the CY, NC, Z, and NZ condition (only), and n is the relative-jump offset from the address following the address of n. The value n is treated as a signed 8-bit value allowing relative jumps of −128 to +127 bytes relative to the next instruction following the jump. The required keywords are defined as follows:

18■8IM■JPR,
: ■JRC,■10■+■C,■C,■;

The Z80 has a relative jump instruction that first decrements the B register and performs the relative jump only if the B register is not zero. If the B register is zero after the decrement, the next instruction is executed. This instruction keyword is defined as:

10■8IM■DJN,

7.2.3.12 Summary

The Z80 assembler presented here is a fairly complete, fundamental assembler. The design requires about 1800 bytes in this form. The major disadvantage of the design is its weak error detection and protection. The only real error detection is stack underflow. Adding the protective code is certainly feasible but requires more memory. The design does contain extra code to optimize the assembled code where two instruction forms exist. Additionally, all of the possible Z80 instructions are covered. Many instructions are scarcely used, so including them is of limited utility. It is certainly possible to define a limited subset of the design in about 1 K bytes of memory that will provide well over 95% percent of the instructions usually used. The remaining instructions can be assembled using C, and "," keywords when encountered.

7.2.4 Structured Assembly Code

Up to this point, the forward and backward reference problem has not been addressed. First, a brief explanation of the problem is in order. The problem arises because it is sometimes necessary to execute code only if some event occurs or to repeat code execution until some event occurs. If the code is to be skipped over, the address where execution is to be continued must be known to allow the forward jump. At assembly time, however, the address of the continuation point is not known until the intervening code is assembled in place. If the code is to be repeated, a jump backwards to some point in the code is required. This implies that someone or something must remember an address to allow this backward reference.

A non-TIL assembler usually handles the forward and backward reference problem in one of two ways. One solution is to employ a two-pass arrangement. The code is written using labels instead of addresses. The first pass through the code counts instruction bytes and builds a symbol table with the address of each label noted. The second pass can then assemble the code since all addresses are known. Another common method is to use a forward reference table. This allows a one-pass assembler to be built. Each time a label is encountered, a symbol table entry is opened with the address of the label noted. If an operand label is encountered, the symbol table is checked to see if the label is in the table. If it is, the address is known and the backward reference can be resolved. If the label is not in the symbol table, the reference must be a forward reference. In this event, the assembler stores the address where a patch to the code is required in a forward reference table along with the label itself. After each symbol table entry is made, the forward reference table is tested to see if there are occurrences of the label just entered. If there are, the code at the patch addresses is corrected and the patch address and labels are removed from the forward reference table. At the end of the assembly the forward reference table is checked to insure that it is empty or that all forward references have been resolved.

Actually, implementation of these techniques depends on the available jump instructions of the microcomputer in question. If only absolute jump instructions are available, the process is fairly simple since the number of bytes to be counted or to be patched is fixed. Some microcomputers, such as the Z80, have relative jump instructions that are shorter than the absolute jump instructions. In this case, the assembler designer is faced with the additional problem of deciding which type of jump to employ. Most relative jumps are limited in how far they can jump (-126 to $+129$ bytes in the Z80 case). In the backwards reference case, it is easy to test and assemble the right type of jump. In the forward jump case, the length of the jump is unknown when the byte count for the instruction must be set. One method of resolving this dilemma is to always assume the longer absolute jump. Another is to allow the programmer to specify the jump byte and to trust his judgment on the length of the jump required.

The LABEL keyword introduced in Section 7.2.3.10 is one method that could be used for resolving backward jumps. The problem with the technique is that the associated CONSTANT keyword must be defined before the assembly, and it will remain a part of the dictionary. In the case of a subroutine, this is usually a desirable condition. For a simple backward jump during program assembly, it is not a good technique.

The forward and backward reference problem in a TIL assembler is resolved via the stack using constructs similar to those used in the language itself. This technique is somewhat different from the usual assembler techniques. The fundamental difference is that a symbol table is never generated and cannot be recovered after the assembly process. In a TIL assembler, the backward reference address is pushed to the stack using a special keyword. Other keywords are defined to retrieve the address from the stack and assemble the backward jump. In forward references, the patch address is pushed to the stack, and space is allocated for the jump instruction using a special keyword. At the target location of the forward jump, other keywords retrieve the patch address (but only one time) and assemble the address to this location. The construct keywords are designed to assemble the constructs semi-automatically. By semi-automatically I mean that in some cases the programmer must decide whether to use an absolute or relative jump.

7.2.4.1 BEGIN---END Loops

The simplest construct is the BEGIN---END loop. The loop differs somewhat in form and usage from the equivalent TIL form. Instead of expecting a flag on the stack, the END form keyword expects a condition code. Further, there are several different END forms possible. Since the jump is a backward jump, the keyword could decide between a relative and absolute jump depending on the length of the jump, or two keywords could be defined which would require the operator to select the address mode.

In all cases, the BEGIN keyword simply pushes the next free dictionary address to the stack. The keyword is defined in the assembler vocabulary as:

:■BEGIN■HERE■;

This keyword simply saves the address of the next instruction to be assembled by pushing it to the stack.

The END form to be considered for the Z80 will consider the automatic generation of the jump instruction depending on the jump length and the condition code. The condition codes considered in the basic assembler did not include an unconditional condition but only eight specific conditions (Z, NZ, CY, NC, PE, PO, P, N). The first step is to define the unconditional "condition" as:

−1■CCONSTANT■U

This allows the assembly sequence to be:

...■BEGIN■...■condition■END■...

The END keyword will assemble a relative jump instruction back to the first assembler instruction following BEGIN if the backward jump is less than 126 bytes and the condition code is U, Z, NZ, CY, or NC. Otherwise, the END keyword will assemble an absolute address.

To generate the required END keyword, the first step is to define two keywords that will decide whether to assemble a conditional or unconditional jump address, given that the addressing mode has already been decided. The keywords are:

: ■JRC ■DUP ■0< ■IF ■DROP ■JPR, ■ELSE ■JRC, ■THEN ■;
: ■JAC ■DUP ■0< ■IF ■DROP ■JMP, ■ELSE ■JPC, ■THEN ■;

Both keywords expect the condition code on the top of the stack and the address or relative address as the second stack entry. The END keyword can then be defined as:

: ■END ■DUP ■20 ■ − ■0< ■IF ■OVER ■HERE ■2 + ■ − ■DUP ■80 ■
− ■0< ■IF ■2SWAP ■DROP ■JRC ■ELSE ■DROP ■JAC ■THEN ■
ELSE ■JAC ■THEN ■;

The outer conditional branch selects the absolute addressing mode if the condition code calls for PE, PO, P, or N condition since there are no relative jumps for these conditions. The inner conditional branch tests the jump length and assembles a relative jump if the jump is −128 bytes, or assembles an absolute jump otherwise.

The keywords defined in this fashion are somewhat slow but very convenient. The programmer never needs to consider which addressing modes are applicable or how far the jump may be. The alternative is to define a sequence of keywords that requires the programmer to specify the type of backward jump required or to default all backward jumps to absolute jumps.

One final note. The unconditional END construct can lead to an endless loop since it is the analog of the TIL 0 ■END form.

7.2.4.2 IF . . . ELSE . . . THEN ───────────────────────────

The IF . . . ELSE . . . THEN assembler construct is similar in concept to the TIL constructs. The problem is that both the IF and ELSE forms assemble forward jumps. The IF forms always assemble conditional forward jumps, and the ELSE forms always assemble unconditional forward jumps. The only reasonable way out of the dilemma is to trust to the programmer's judgment on the length of the jump.

The decision to trust the programmer's judgment implies separate keywords for both absolute and relative IF forms. The ELSE form must then be informed as to which type of IF form it must fill in an address, and whether its forward jump is an absolute or relative jump. The THEN form must similarly know the addressing type of the IF or ELSE form. The forms are then:

RIF — A relative if
AIF — An absolute if
RRELSE — Assumes a RIF and a relative else
RAELSE — Assumes a RIF and an absolute else
ARELSE — Assumes an AIF and a relative else
AAELSE — Assumes an AIF and an absolute else
RTHEN — Assumes a RIF or RRELSE or ARELSE
ATHEN — Assumes an AIF or RAELSE or AAELSE

The ELSE forms are optional as in the TIL constructs.
Given the IF forms, the idea is to assemble a forward jump instruction, given a condition code operand preceding the mnemonic, and to leave a pointer to the jump instruction variable field on the stack. The variable jump field will be filled with a 0 until filled in by an ELSE or THEN form. The definitions are:

: ■RIF■0■SWAP■JRC,■HERE■ ;
: ■AIF■0■SWAP■JPC,■HERE■2+ ■ ;

The ELSE forms must assemble an unconditional forward jump, fill in the variable field of the IF form and leave a pointer to the unconditional forward jump variable field on the stack. This variable field is again filled with a 0 until filled in by the THEN form. The ELSE form does not have any operands. The keywords are defined as:

: ■ATHEN■HERE■SWAP■!■ ;
: ■RTHEN■OVER■ − ■SWAP■1− ■C!■ ;
: ■RRELSE■HERE■2+ ■RTHEN■18■ ,■HERE■ ;
: ■RAELSE■HERE■3■ + ■RTHEN■0■JMP,■HERE■2− ■
: ■ARELSE■ATHEN■18■ ,■HERE■ ;
: ■AAELSE ■ATHEN■0■JMP,■HERE■2− ■ ;

Observant of you to notice that the THEN forms were whiffled in and used to define the ELSE forms. After all, both the ELSE and THEN are used to patch forward jump variable fields and should look similar. It should also be realized that the THEN forms do not actually assemble any code at the point that they are evoked but merely fill in the previously reserved locations.
There is actually one important fact about the conditional branch constructs which you may have noted. The True code and False code bodies are reversed from the usual TIL constructs. This results from the fact that the Z80, like most microcomputers, jumps if the condition is met. The syntax diagrams are:

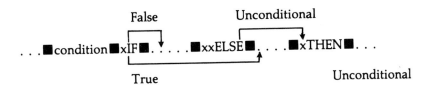

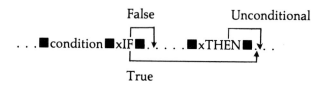

Actually this does not represent a problem with the Z80 since both senses of condition codes are available, which can effectively reverse the sense of the code bodies.

7.2.4.3 WHILE

The assembler WHILE construct is the exact analog of the TIL WHILE construct. It does need to know, however, the addressing mode of the ELSE or IF form it is to patch. This leads to the following forms:

> : ■RWHILE■SWAP■U■END■HERE■RTHEN■;
> : ■AWHILE■SWAP■U■END■HERE■ATHEN■;

These keywords expect the address stored by BEGIN to be the second stack entry and the pointer stored by the IF or ELSE form to be the top stack entry. The SWAP■U■END sequence will assemble an absolute or relative conditional jump back to the address stored by BEGIN. The remaining code then patches the IF or ELSE form as appropriate.

The construct syntax of Section 4.4.3 applies with minor variation. The differences involve the condition code, the use of the relative or absolute forms and the reverse code body sense in the IF form.

7.2.4.4 DO ... LOOP

The assembler DO . . . LOOP construct is substantially different from the TIL construct. It is specifically designed in the Z80 assembler to utilize the DJNZ (decrement and jump non-zero) instruction (the DJN, in our notation). This instruction decrements the B register and does a relative jump if the register is non-zero. Otherwise, it executes the next instruction. The evoking sequence for the assembler DO . . . LOOP construct is:

...n■DO■....■LOOP■...

Here the LOOP code will be repeated n times. An initial value of 0 will cause a 256-count loop, so that the loop may be executed from 1 to 256 times. The keywords required for the construct are:

:■DO■HERE■B■LROT■MVI,■;
:■LOOP■HERE■2+■−■DJN,■;

It is possible to use the LOOP keyword in a construct of the form:

....BEGIN....LOOP....

This construct presumes that the B register was suitably loaded by some other means (say by the result of some computation followed by a B■A■MOV,) prior to the occurrence of BEGIN.

It must be noted that loop constructs of this form are not specific to the Z80 with its DJNZ instruction. The operation can just as easily be emulated on other central processing units by defining a suitable macroinstruction. For example, an 8080 assembler DJN, keyword could be defined as:

:■DJN,■B■DEC,■NZ■JPC,■;

This, of course, presumes that the mnemonics for the 8080 are selected to conform to the design presented.

Other loop constructs could be defined for the Z80 using macroinstructions. This will not be done in the basic assembler since there are no fundamental machine instructions which they support. Other loop structures are applications specific.

7.2.4.5 Construct Summary

Implementing the structured constructs for the assembler requires an additional 375 bytes or so. The assembly language programmer job is eased somewhat by the presence of these simple constructs, since they can keep track of the addresses on the stack without effort on the programmer's part. The constructs can be nested as long as entire constructs are defined in one code section. A validity test on nesting is simply that removal of any construct in its entirety cannot remove *part* of another construct. This must be true for *all* constructs.

If the constructs available do not match the programmer's needs, the BEGIN keyword plus the stack keywords of the CORE vocabulary can be used to suitably manipulate addresses for the assembler jump keywords. As with all TIL keywords, the assembler keywords do not care how their expected stack entries arrived; they just assume they are there.

7.2.5 Assembler Design Notes

The TIL assembler keywords are normally defined in the ASSEMBLER vocabulary. The vocabulary is linked to the CORE vocabulary and is usually intermixed spatially with the CORE vocabulary. Keywords to be defined in assembly code are primitives. The defining word that creates the keyword is called CODE. This keyword not only creates a primitive header but also sets the CONTEXT vocabulary to ASSEMBLER. In my personal system, CODE also sets the hexadecimal number base since I prefer to code using hexadecimal numbers. The keyword CODE is thus defined as:

: ■CODE■CREATE■HEX■ASSEMBLER■;

All of these keywords exist in the CORE vocabulary. The keyword that terminates the definition is NEXT. This keyword encloses in the dictionary the instructions necessary to return to the inner interpreter (IY ■ JPM, for the Z80) and then sets the CONTEXT vocabulary to the CURRENT vocabulary. In effect, this restores the vocabulary before the keyword was defined. A formal definition of NEXT is:

: ■NEXT■IY■JPM, ■DEFINITIONS■;

NEXT exists in the ASSEMBLER vocabulary and differs from the NEXT defined in the CORE vocabulary.

Inevitably the question arises about the viability of building a "real" assembler using the TIL assembler. It is possible, but not easily accomplished, and not without several modifications and extensions to the TIL assembler. The modifications necessary are to solve problems that also arise in a non-TIL assembler. Fundamentally, the non-TIL assembler is designed to input an assembly code source file, generate machine code that is to reside and execute at some given address but is stored at assembly time at some different location, and, finally, to store the resulting machine-code file in some mass storage device. A TIL-based real assembler must perform similar tasks.

The capability to store a file on some mass media and to load a file to the system has been assumed just to build the TIL. The ability to generate an assembly language source text file has not been considered. This requires some type of editor program to generate and update the source test. This requirement is not really necessary for the short definitions encountered in a TIL assembler. There is a vast difference between a 3-line keyword definition and a long assembly language program. With the interactive TIL assembler, the assembly "source" disappears when the line it is entered on is scrolled off the display. An editor to generate an assembler source file and a virtual memory system to access the files will be considered later.

The usual problem is relocating the assembly code. TIL source assembly code is always assembled to the free dictionary space. All of the assembler keywords are constructed using the "," and C, keywords which accomplish this action. A more general scenario is to allow the starting location of the desired program to be specified, but to actually save the program at some different location. This implies that a program could begin at any memory address, including an address which is occupied by the assembler at assembly time.

There are two basic changes needed to allow a TIL assembler to be of more general-purpose value. The keywords "," and C, must be redefined prior to defining any of the assembler keywords. The keywords that assemble absolute addresses must also be modified. These include both the assembler mnemonic keywords and the assembler construct keywords. The reason for these modifications is almost self-evident.

The keywords "," and C, must be modified to pop words or bytes from the stack and enclose them at the next consecutive assembler file location rather than the next free dictionary location. The assembler file location can be set equal to the dictionary pointer to assemble TIL keywords or to any available free memory space to support either direct assembly to the true target location or to a file location which will later be stored on the mass media. The address where the stack data is enclosed is referred to as the program counter (PC). The CODE keyword could be designed to set PC to DP to assemble TIL keywords.

The keywords that assemble absolute addresses to the program must also be modified to support the assembly of a program to a different area of memory than it will occupy at execution time. For example, the TIL may start with a PC value of 4000, but the program may execute with the assembled program at 1000. Thus, the absolute address stored by the assembler must be 3000 less than the PC value reference for the loading address at assembly time. The offset between the program origin and the initial value of the PC is always a constant. To assemble TIL keywords or to assemble a program that will execute at its assembly address, set this offset to 0. The CODE keyword could also be designed to zero this offset value for assembling TIL keywords.

A "real" assembler does have some restrictions and disadvantages. The real problem is that the programs must be fairly short due to the lack of a symbol table. For those cases where the built-in constructs are inadequate, stack management can become a very real problem. The interactive building of an assembly program will not allow program documentation. If the editor and virtual memory system are not supported, program debug and modification really implies program re-entry via the keyboard and not correction of some source text.

One final note about threaded interpretive language assemblers. Some instructions are used so rarely that the memory required to implement them exceeds their utility. The right answer is to ignore these instructions. The "," and C, keywords can always be used in the event the unimplemented instructions are required. The TIL assembler should be designed for utility rather than formal completeness.

7.3 Virtual Memory ────────────────────────────

Virtual memory is a technique for transparently extending the addressing space of a computer by using a combination of actual system memory and a direct access storage device. A user could have an effective addressable memory space of several hundred thousand bytes in a system that only has 12 K to 16 K bytes of actual memory. The direct access storage device could be any of a number of devices. I will constrain this discussion to a floppy disk system rather than opening Pandora's box. This is the most popular type of microcomputer system direct access storage device.

There are roughly forty skillion ways to implement a virtual memory system. I won't even scratch the surface but will direct the presentation to a particular philosophy. Because of the extreme hardware dependence of the device interface, the level of the presentation will be somewhat sketchy. The design of the virtual memory system is not extremely difficult if one is intimately familiar with both the disk system hardware and its associated software. If not, it is almost impossible unless the disk system documentation is absolutely superb.

7.3.1 The Device ────────────────────────────

A disk system usually consists of a disk controller board and an actual disk drive mechanization. The object of the disk system is to allow storage of data on the diskette media. The important point about the disk system is that the data are stored in *blocks* of bytes which are accessed from consecutive memory locations. The actual number of bytes in a block is usually 128, but systems with 256 bytes per block are common and 4 K-byte blocks are not unheard of.

The format the system uses to record the blocks on the diskette media is device-dependent. The blocks are stored on tracks or circular areas on the diskette. The mini-floppy diskette usually has thirty-five tracks and the floppy seventy-six tracks for storage of data. The concentric tracks are usually numbered from 0 upward, with 0 the outermost track. Within a track there are a number of sectors defined. Depending on the device, a sector consists of data used to synchronize and/or identify the sector, the actual data block, and some type of block validation data. The most common sector formats consist of twenty-six sectors of 128 data bytes or ten sectors of 256 data bytes, but many other formats exist.

The total number of data blocks the disk system can contain is the number of tracks times the number of sectors per track. The disk controller always addresses the blocks by track number and sector number. This addressing is applicable between the system and the disk controller.

Disk controllers are extremely variable in design. Some are very simple devices that depend on the central processing unit for initialization and simply signal the arrival of each data block byte at the interface and expect the processor to store to the proper memory location. Other controllers have their own processor on the controller board and quite sophisticated file management software in read-only memory. Most controllers are somewhere between these extremes.

A common problem with disk controllers is that presumptions about the location of a supporting disk operating system (DOS) are embedded in the controller design. This may force the system designer to either patch the controller software (generally read-only memory resident) or build the threaded interpretive language around the disk operating system. Exactly how this will be accomplished is so system-dependent that no more can be said.

7.3.2 Disk Access

The object of the virtual memory system is to access disk blocks by some addressing scheme such that the access is transparent to the operator. Correct access will occur regardless of whether the block is currently system resident or disk resident. If a block is not resident in the system when it is accessed, it is automatically loaded to the system memory. If a block has been modified while system resident, it will be updated by the system under operator direction such that the operator never needs to know which blocks are to be updated.

Disk data blocks that are system resident are stored in buffers. There are usually sufficient buffers defined to hold one or two *screens* of data. A screen is 1 K bytes of data (which will just fill a display screen of 16 lines of 64 characters per line). For a block length of 128 bytes there are thus eight to sixteen block buffers of 128 bytes each required. Data screens are a convenient form for storing TIL source text. The block buffers are usually defined at some convenient memory address out of the way of the main TIL language area.

The block buffers are used for temporary storage of data read from the disk or to be written to the disk. Blocks of data are read from the disk and stored to some block buffer using the keyword GETIT. Data in a block buffer are written to the disks using the keyword PUTIT. These two keywords are the primitives needed to implement all disk accesses. The target disk blocks for the accesses are addressed by a block number. There is a mapping between the disk block number and the disk track and sector number. The relationship is:

$$\text{Block\#} = (\text{Track\#}) \times (\text{Sectors/Track}) + (\text{Sector\#}) + 1$$

The block numbers are thus in the set $[1-N]$ where N is system-dependent.

The primitives GETIT and PUTIT will interface with the system disk I/O routines to actually perform the disk read/write. These routines usually require a buffer address, a block number (or sector and track number) and a drive number as input parameters. The drive number is usually stored in the system variable DRIVE if multiple drives are available. The buffer address and block number are passed to the keywords on the stack. The availability of these keywords will be presumed.

Typically both GETIT and PUTIT are designed to reserve disk space at the low end of the disk which is used to store the core language. This disk is usually placed in disk drive number 0 in a multidrive system. By defining a system variable named OFFSET, the amount of reserved area can be stored as a system parameter. The keywords DR0, DR1, . . . can be defined to both set the DRIVE system variable and the OFFSET system variable as appropriate for the given system configuration. This can be somewhat risky in a single drive system.

Two other factors are important about GETIT. The keyword leaves a buffer address at the top of the stack when it completes. This allows for convenient recovery of the address where the data is located. GETIT also tests the block number to insure that a valid block is requested. If it detects an error, the error routine is called by GETIT, with the address of a disk addressing error message as a parameter. A similar scheme is employed in PUTIT. Depending on the available disk software, read or write errors may be handled by the system disk software or may need to be fielded by routines within the TIL code.

To implement GETIT and PUTIT in a somewhat uniform manner, it is usual to segment the software tasks between the TIL and the system I/O code. Typically the TIL code is designed to pass the data needed by the system I/O code in the system user area. For example, a typical scheme is for the TIL code to set the following parameters:

TARGET — The starting address of the block buffer.
DRIVE — The drive number.
TRACK — The track number.
SECTOR — The sector number.
OPER — The operation (0 = Write, 1 = Read).

The definition of GETIT and PUTIT are then something like:

```
: ■GETIT ■SETUP ■OPER ■C1SET ■DISKI/O ■ ;
: ■PUTIT ■SETUP ■OPER ■C0SET ■DISKI/O ■ ;
```

Here SETUP pops the block number and the buffer address from the stack; computes TRACK and SECTOR from the block number, OFFSET, and the number of sectors per track; calls an error routine if the track number computed is outside the boundaries of the disk; and exits with TARGET, TRACK and SECTOR set. The DISKI/O routine then calls a system I/O routine which actually performs the reading and writing of the I/O operation. Alternately, GETIT and PUTIT can be written as primitives which perform the same operation using a subroutine $SETUP.

7.3.3 Buffer Control

By knowing the definition of the keywords GETIT and PUTIT, the actual design of the virtual memory scheme can be considered. This involves laying out the buffer area and designing keywords to load a specific disk block to a specific block buffer or vice versa. This implies a control structure but the control should be invisible to the operator.

Buffers can have several states. They can be empty or otherwise available to the system. They can contain some specific disk block exactly as contained on the disk. They can contain either new data or modified versions of blocks that are contained on the disk. The system needs to know the status of the buffers to properly manage the system resources. One relatively simple way to store the information is in a keyword called SBUF which contains the current status of the block buffers.

The keyword SBUF is an array that contains two words for each block buffer in the system. The first word is a status word and the second word is the address of the starting location of the block buffer. The status word contains 0 if the buffer is empty, or if it is in use, contains the block number of the block currently located in the buffer. The high-order bit of the status word is 1 set if the block is modified or updated. The array is a convenient way to store the data the system needs to hide the disk accesses from the operation.

The keyword the operator uses to access any block is BLOCK. This keyword expects the desired block number on the stack when it is evoked and replaces the block number with the address of the first byte of the block. This address is always the starting address of one of the block buffers. The definition of BLOCK is:

: ■BLOCK■RESIDENT■IF■BUFFER■GETIT■THEN■;

The keyword RESIDENT searches the array SBUF looking for a status word that matches the block number at the top of the stack (ignoring the most significant bit). If a match is found, the block number is replaced by the address of the starting location of the block buffer associated with the status word and a False flag is then pushed to the stack. If a match is not found, a True flag is pushed to the stack leaving the block number as the second stack entry. The keyword BUFFER searches the array SBUF looking for a 0 status word. If an empty buffer is located, the address of the starting location of the block buffer associated with the 0 status word is pushed to the stack and the buffer is loaded by GETIT. If there are no available buffers, the error routine is called by BUFFER with the address of a buffer full message as a parameter.

With the advent of BLOCK, a virtual memory scheme is at hand. Reading of disk blocks to the disk is totally transparent to the operator. The operator simply treats all blocks as if they were system-resident. There is no file directory and no "named" files except as defined by the operator. Named files can be created by the operator as follows:

: ■FILENAME■i■BLOCK■j■BLOCK■....■n■BLOCK■;

Here i . . . n are block numbers. As many blocks can be defined in FILENAME as there are block buffers. However, named files are strictly applications-dependent.

The storage of updated block buffers back to the disk is not done automatically. The operator must evoke this action manually using the keyword SAVE. SAVE searches the array SBUF looking for status words with their high-order bit set. If the update bit is set, the associated buffer is written to the disk block using PUTIT and the status word is set to 0. If the update bit is not set, the status word is simply 0 set. A keyword named ZBUF is also defined; it merely sets all the status words in SBUF to 0. This implementation does not change any block buffer contents when either SAVE or ZBUF is evoked. This is sometimes helpful when the operator makes an error. The important point is that the operator does not need to concern himself about which blocks need to be updated. The system will perform the task semi-automatically. The system needs to be directed to perform the task to prevent overwriting of disk blocks when this action is undesirable.

Setting of the update bit in the SBUF array status words is done by the system using special keywords. The design of these special keywords hides the activity from the operator. For example, if the operator is updating a data file, the keyword D! is usually based instead of the "!" keyword. D! is defined as:

$$: \blacksquare D! \blacksquare UPDATE \blacksquare ! \blacksquare ;$$

Just like "!", D! expects an address at the top of the stack and a number as the second stack entry. The keyword UPDATE searches the SBUF array starting address locations. If the address at the top of the stack is within the block buffer range of one of the buffer areas, the update bit of the associated status word is 1 set. Other methods of setting the update bit will be considered later.

7.3.4 Screens ————————————————————————————

Source text for special vocabularies can be stored on the disk in screens. A screen may be loaded to the system and assembled/compiled to the dictionary space that exists when the load occurs. Typical applications for this technique are language extensions that are required for some applications but are usually not needed. A floating point package or an editor are examples. The source text may be either primitives (defined using assembly language or numbers followed by "," or C,) or secondaries. Primitives may not contain absolute address references unless the address is known to be invariant (a system variable for example) since the assembly origin is not known *a priori*. Listing 7.1 gives examples of typical screens.

```
( SCREEN 0 - EDITOR, SCREEN 1 OF 2 ) : EDITOR ; HEX
( 1 ) 40 CCONSTANT LENGTH
( 2 ) 12 CCONSTANT LBUF 160 CA!
( 3 ) : LLBUF LBUF @ LENGTH + 1- ;
( 4 ) : LCLEAR LBUF @ DUP 7F + ERASE ;
( 5 ) : 15TH SCREEN @ @ 3C0 + ;
( 6 ) : L15TH 15TH LENGTH + 1- ;
( 7 ) : BSTART DUP 0< OVER F > OR IF QUESTION ELSE LENGTH *
        SCREEN @ DUP -1 = IF QUESTION ELSE @ + THEN THEN ;
( 9 ) CREATE INLINE 2EB CA!
( 10 ) : REPLACE BSTART INLINE LBUF @ LLBUF LROT MOVE LCLEAR ;
( 11 ) : CLEAR BSTART DUP LENGTH + 1- ERASE ;
( 12 ) : DELETE BSTART DUP LENGTH + L15TH LROT MOVE F CLEAR
        LCLEAR ;
( 14 ) : INSERT DUP BSTART 15TH = IF REPLACE ELSE DUP BSTART
        15TH 1- OVER LENGTH + MOVE REPLACE THEN ; 1 LOAD




( SCREEN 1 - EDITOR, SCREEN 2 OF 2 )
( 1 ) : TYPE CRET BSTART DUP LENGTH + SWAP DO I> C@ ECHO LOOP ;
( 2 ) : SHOW CRET L15TH SCREEN @ @ DO I> C@ ECHO LOOP HIDE ;
( 3 ) : LIST 1+ SWAP CRET CDO CI> 4 * 1+ @LBUF GETIT DUP 40 +
        SWAP DO I> C@ ECHO LOOP CLOOP LCLEAR ;




( 14 ) : EMSG CRET [ EDITOR LOADED, DECIMAL BASE ] ; DECIMAL
( 15 ) EMSG
```

Listing 7.1: *EDITOR screens.*

The method of addressing screens is by screen number. Screen numbers are in the set (0...N) where N is a system configuration-dependent number. Screens are always stored on the disk in consecutive disk blocks. There is a mapping between screen numbers and the block number of the first of the contiguous blocks that form the screen. The mapping is:

$$\text{Block \#} = (\text{Screen \#}) \times 8 + (\text{Offset \#}) + 1$$

The offset number is a system variable used to control the location of the first defined screen. Typically this is desirable to allocate low-order blocks as data blocks and high-order blocks as a screen block area. Usually the offset is contained in the system variable SCRNOFF but is sometimes arbitrarily set to a constant. In any event remember that OFFSET is also applied by GETIT and PUTIT.

The purpose of having text screens is to use them as system inputs precisely as if they had been typed in by the operator. The outer interpreter of Section 2 (figure 2.2) had provisions for loading the input buffer from a mass storage device and for echo displaying the OK message when the input buffer is empty, only if the keyboard is the input device. Consider this outer interpreter and the design of the MASS keyword: in our present design, MASS will perform the input from the disk screen to the input buffer . . . not a block buffer.

To begin our design, first consider the initiation of the screen loading event. A keyword name LOAD is defined to initiate the loading of the screen number that is the top stack entry. The LOAD keyword simply sets two system variables. The system variable SCRN is set equal to the screen number at the top of the stack. The system variable LINE is set to 0. When the line in which the keyword LOAD appears is complete, the outer interpreter returns to get the next input. It first tests LINE to see if it is positive. If it is, MASS is called. Otherwise, the keyboard input routine INLINE is called.

The keyword MASS can be defined many ways, one of which follows:

> : ■MASS■?LINE■IF■LBUF■@■GETIT■DROP■ELSE■
> BTOL■THEN■LBUF■@■LBP■!■;

A fairly careful look at the undefined keywords should reveal the game plan.

The keyword ?LINE first computes a block number based on LINE, SCRN and SCRNOFF. It next increments LINE by one and resets LINE to −1 if it equals 8. ?LINE then searches SBUF to see if the block is already system-resident. If it is, the address of the block buffer and a False flag are pushed to the stack. This will cause a branch to BTOL which will move the block buffer to the input buffer. If the block is not system-resident, the block number and a True flag are pushed to the stack. This will cause a branch to LBUF■@■GETIT■DROP which will load the line buffer with the disk block. The DROP removes the input buffer address, which was returned by GETIT, from the stack. Finally, the line buffer pointer is reset to point to the start of the input buffer.

When the outer interpreter regains control from MASS, it cannot tell how the input line buffer was loaded. Whatever is in the line will be executed precisely in accordance with the TIL syntax. If an executable token is scanned, it will be executed just as if it had been typed by the operator. When the input line is entirely scanned, the LINE variable is tested to insure it is negative before the OK message is displayed. This prevents a sequence of OK messages from appearing as the lines are executed. One final note: the error routine must set SCRN negative if an error is detected. This forces operator response if an error occurs during screen loading.

The above scheme allows eight successive blocks (or sixteen display lines) to be executed. After the eighth block is executed, LINE will be negative and the OK message will be displayed. If only a partial screen of source text is available, a method to cause early return to the INLINE input can be designed. Consider a ;S keyword that sets LINE to −1. By embedding ;S in a screen block, forced exit to INLINE occurs on the completion of block execution. If a

LOAD command is embedded in a screen, it will terminate loading of the current screen and initiate loading of the new screen. This allows screens to be chained together so that vocabularies or user programs are not constrained to be a single screen in length.

One feature that is important in a virtual memory system of this type is some means of identifying screen contents. This can be done by defining a comment medium, placing descriptive comments on the first line of each screen and defining a keyword that will display the first line of successive screens.

Since there is no way to retain source text, a comment keyword makes little sense in a system without the virtual memory mechanization. Assume that the comment keyword is defined as "(" (left parenthesis). The keyword "(" sets the token separator to ")" and scans the next token from the input line. It does nothing with the token it scans. This allows text to be entered in a screen following the ■ after the initial "(" until terminated by a ")" or the end of the line. This text will be ignored by the system when the comment is encountered in the input buffer. I usually include the screen number in the comment as well as a brief description of the screen contents and note if more than one screen is chained by the screen. See listing 7.1 for typical screen comment usage.

The keyword that displays the first line of successive screens is LIST. This keyword expects a starting and ending screen in the input range. To allow the operator to stop the display, a call to the WAIT keyword is coded after each line is output. LIST needs at least one empty buffer to hold the first block of each screen as it is read from the disk. The first sixty-four characters of each block are then displayed. Since there is no reason to make the first lines of the screens permanently system resident, the buffer is marked empty after each access.

A keyword that is very similar to LIST is SHOW. This keyword shows the entire screen contents on the display rather than just the first line. At the end of each screen display, a keyword named HIDE is called rather than WAIT. HIDE not only waits for the next keyboard entry but also suppresses the cursor. This allows the entire screen to be displayed without a hole at the cursor point.

The protocol for screen residency is somewhat analogous to block residency. The keyword that loads a screen to the system is OPEN. OPEN expects a screen number on the stack and will attempt to load the screen to one of two sets of eight contiguous blocks. There are four important system variables associated with the operation as follows:

SCRN — The target screen.
SCRN0 — SCRN1 — The screen number of the screen resident in the nth set of eight blocks (if resident) or -1 (if not).
SCREEN — A pointer to the start of the SBUF low-order or high-order set of block buffers of the current screen.

OPEN will first test SCRN0 and SCRN1 to determine if the screen is resident. If it is, SCREEN is set to point to the start of the appropriate set of buffers. If the screen is not resident, and one of the two available screens is open, the screen is loaded to the system and both SCREEN and SCRNn are updated with the screen number. If both screens are in use, an error message is called indicating that the screens are full. The operator is thus forced to free a screen area to load the new screen.

The screens, when loaded to the system, result in the block number of each screen block being stored in SBUF. This effectively prevents BLOCK calls from overwriting screens. Both one screen and one or more blocks can be system-resident if at least two screen buffers are available. Screens differ somewhat from blocks in that screen keywords do not set update bits in SBUF. Screen can be written to the disk only by explicitly calling the WRITE command.

The keyword WRITE will always write eight consecutive blocks to the disk. The target screen number is assumed to be on the stack and whichever screen was opened last will be written to the disk. In short, SCREEN is used as the pointer to the appropriate screen to write. This particular scheme will allow easy duplication of screens (ie:]■OPEN■4■WRITE will duplicate screen 0 as screen 4). When screens are written to the disk, no changes to the residency status of the screens takes place. Screens are deleted from the system only by using the CLOSE keyword. CLOSE expects a screen number on the stack and will set SCRN0 and SCRN1 to -1 if the screen is system-resident. If the screen is not resident, an error message results.

There are a number of additional keywords that can be defined to manipulate screens. For example, SCREENS could be defined to display which screens are currently resident. There are any number of additional keywords that can be defined. Remember too that screens need not be accessed simply by number but may be given aliases. For example, the editor vocabulary is accessed simply by the EDITOR keyword which is defined as:

: ■EDITOR■n■LOAD■;

The keyword that accesses the ASCII file SANDI is defined as:

: ■SANDI■n■OPEN■SHOW■;

This definition both loads the file (screen) to the system and displays the entire file.

7.3.5 Data Manipulation

The virtual memory system contains the core keywords for transparent disk accessing. These keywords will allow easy data manipulation just as they allow easy screen manipulation. Data storage is very applications-dependent. Several techniques for using data blocks will be considered, albeit lightly.

Data files can be defined to hold either ASCII data or numerical data. The format is fully controlled by the application. Actually, the main reason that block numbers start at 1 rather than 0 is that the system uses block 0 as an ASCII data file. Block 0 is used to store operator messages that are seldom used but need to be available somewhere. The messages that are displayed to the operator on system start-up or when a system error occurs are examples. The error message block is loaded to the input line buffer and an offset number is expected on the stack when the message is evoked. The message keyword is:

: ■DISKMESSAGE■0■LBUF■@■■GETIT■+■TYPE■;

This is a typical application of a block as a special file. Actually this block contains records where each record is a message which is evoked by the address offset loaded to the stack by the error-handling routine which calls DISKMESSAGE.

Although the basic unit of storage is a block of 128 bytes, it is easy to define data files of different sizes. A record is a subunit of a file where a file consists of some multiple number of blocks. An integer number of records may not completely fill a file. The easiest case to consider is the case where an integer number of records of n bytes each equals 128 bytes or one block. The more difficult case is where a record crosses a block boundry.

To consider the easier case, assume that records consist of 32 bytes. The records will be stored in consecutive blocks on the disk starting at the block number stored in the constant DATA. A record can be transparently accessed by the operator given the following definition sequence:

n■CONSTANT■DATA
DECIMAL■:■RECORD■32■128■*/MOD■
SWAP■DATA■+■BLOCK■+■;

The sequence n■RECORD will leave the address of the first byte of the record on the stack. The operator need not worry about the residence status of the block, since the system will load the correct block if it is not system-resident using the RECORD keyword via the BLOCK call.

Accessing records that cross a block boundary is a much more difficult feat. There are several ways to attack the problem. They fall into two categories. One method is to design the record allocation scheme so that records always begin on block boundaries and must contain an integer number of records. The other procedure is to always load two disk blocks to two consecutive block buffers if the boundary could be crossed. The design of the keywords is not extremely difficult. The intent is to always load a complete record to the system.

In turn, a record can contain subfields where specific items in the record are stored. These subfields can also be accessed transparently with a suitable set of keyword definitions. The fundamental reason for always loading a complete record is to insure that all record subfields are available. The overall intent is to allow record and subfield definitions that always return the address of the data regardless of its location in the system when it is requested. Thus blocks, records, and subfields are precisely like arrays defined in the core, always available simply by their keyword names.

When a data block, record, or subfield is updated it is important that D! be used rather than "!" if the update is to be marked for later storage to the disk. As previously described, a SAVE command is required to actually update the disk.

7.3.6 Loose Ends

At this point we have considered most of what is required to implement the virtual memory system. There are, however, still a few loose ends to tidy up.

The virtual memory system is usually made a part of the CORE vocabulary. There is little point in establishing a separate vocabulary for the basic disk accessing routines. When the editor is discussed, several other disk (as opposed to purely editing) functions will also be covered. This is simply a convenient place to hide the routines, since the editor vocabulary is usually disk-resident.

A system is usually designed from its inception to include the virtual memory extension. This isn't surprising since most people remember spending the several hundreds of dollars that disk hardware costs. Even if the expensive part isn't acquired until later, the existing language is not lost. The INLINE keyword address of the outer interpreter of Section 5 could be replaced by the word address of the keyword INPUT as an example. INPUT is a secondary which is designed to choose between INLINE and MASS. A change to QUESTION also needs to be implemented to suppress the OK message appropriately.

7.4 Editor

The threaded interpretive language editor is the tool for generating and modifying screens of source text. Unlike the assembler and virtual memory keywords, the EDITOR vocabulary keywords are not system-resident but must be loaded to the system when needed. The keyword EDITOR accomplishes this by pushing the screen number of the initial editor screen to the stack and then calling LOAD. The first definition in the editor screen is a redefinition of the keyword EDITOR so that the EDITOR vocabulary can be discarded using FORGET when all editing tasks are completed.

7.4.1 Line by Line

The basic (not BASIC) editor is line-oriented. That is, it manipulates entire lines of text rather than the characters within a line. The editor always operates on a screen of data which is loaded to the block buffers using the OPEN command. To modify an existing screen or to generate a new screen, the screen must be loaded to the buffers before editing begins. To locate screens or display screens, the keywords LIST and SHOW are available.

The editor commands are fairly simple. The commands all assume that a line number between 0 and 15 is on the stack when the command is evoked. Any textual data to be input to the block buffers is done by calling the normal INLINE input routine. If INLINE was implemented in the core language as a headerless primitive, it can be given a header in the EDITOR vocabulary as follows:

CREATE■INLINE■nn■CA!■;

Here nn is the address of the first instruction of the INLINE primitive, not its word address. (See line 9 of screen 1 in listing 7.1). One other point does bear on this use of INLINE; only the first 64 characters may be used rather than the usual 128 input characters. For example, the command to replace line 0 of the current screen is:

0■REPLACE■

Note that a carriage return follows REPLACE and the cursor point will immediately drop to the start of the next line. Any text following REPLACE will be ignored by the system since the input buffer is first cleared by INLINE. At the occurrence of the next carriage return, the contents of the first sixty-four characters in the input buffer are moved to the appropriate block buffer half.

As a result of the manner in which INLINE was designed, the backspace, line delete, and carriage return functions work as always. In fact, an editor command to clear a line is not required since a replaced line with a single carriage return will clear the line. The line editing commands include:

REPLACE — Pops a line number from the stack, fills the line with spaces, and then replaces the line with the textual string following the REPLACE. Also used to clear a line.

INSERT — Pops a line number from the stack, moves all lines from this line through line 14 down one line, and replaces the line originally popped from the stack with textual string following as if the REPLACE command were used. The fifteenth (last) line is lost.

DELETE — Pops a line number from the stack, moves all lines from this line number plus one up one line, and clears line 15.

TYPE — Pops a line number from the stack and displays the line.

To write the completed screen back to disk, the WRITE command must be used. The keyword CLOSE is used to free the screen area.

Although the LIST and SHOW were presented as screen keywords, I usually embed them in the EDITOR vocabulary. Since screens are seldom played with except in the edit mode, this is not a very restrictive feature.

Actually the editor vocabulary is used to generate itself. The editor keywords are first designed and then the following sequence is typed in the execute mode:

: ■EDITOR■n■LOAD■;■ : ■EDITOR■;■ ■n■OPEN

This opens screen n (ie: makes it system-resident). Next, the keywords that constitute the editor vocabulary are entered in the system. These keywords are then used to generate the screen which contains the same definitions. The first line of the screen is defined as:

(■SCREEN■n■ − ■EDITOR■)■ : ■EDITOR■;

Note that EDITOR in both this definition and the second occurrence in the previous definition are simply placeholders used to forget the definitions after the EDITOR screen(s) are generated. This editor is the minimum configuration that should be considered. It can be assembled/compiled to the current dictionary space in less than one second (typically) and occupies about 350 bytes.

Listing 7.1 lists the two editor screens associated with ZIPD. The editor is loaded by typing EDITOR and responds:

EDITOR LOADED, DECIMAL BASE

when loading completes. Note that ZIPD disk blocks are 256-bytes long.

7.4.2 In a Line

A more advanced line editor can be easily added to the line-oriented editor. The line editor will allow the characters within a line to be modified without retyping the whole line. The editor does not directly modify the block buffer. Rather it is used to generate a new line. When the new line is correct, it is moved to the block buffer to incorporate the line in the screen.

The line editor function requires a sixty-four character array and two pointers. The line pointer points to the block buffer where the line being edited is stored. The array pointer points to the array where the modified line is being built. The line editor is called from the EDITOR using the command keyword EDIT. The keyword will first display the line whose address is on the stack, clear the array to ASCII spaces, set the line pointer to the first address of the buffer half where the line to be modified is stored, set the array pointer to the first address of the array, and enter a special input mode. In this special input mode, all commands to the editor are ASCII control codes. The control codes and the action they evoke follow:

CNTL-@(At). Echoes a CRLF, the screen line, a CRLF, and the array line up to the array entry point. Neither pointer is changed.

CNTL-A (Advance). Moves the character pointed to by the line pointer to the location pointed to by the array pointer; echo displays the character and advances both pointers.

CNTL-B (Back). Enters a space at the current array point, decrements both pointers, and echo displays the backspace command. This command will not allow either pointer to be decremented past its starting address.

CNTL-C (Copy). Moves the remaining characters in the line from the block buffer to the array buffer. Terminates when the end of either buffer is reached.

CNTL-D (Delete). Advances only the line pointer and echo displays a delete symbol to the screen. (I use an ⊠ symbol, but this is arbitrary.)

CNTL-E (Enter). Echoes a < symbol to the display and enters an entry mode. All characters entered via the keyboard except CNTL-E are moved to the array buffer at the array pointer location and the array pointer is advanced. A CNTL-E input results in the display of a > symbol and the entry mode is terminated.

CNTL-F (Find). The command expects a second keyboard input. When the input is received the line buffer characters are copied to the array buffer until the line buffer character equals the second keyboard input character. Always terminates if the end of either buffer is reached.

CNTL-G (Go). Moves the array buffer to the line buffer (sixty-four characters) and exits the line edit mode.

CNTL-H (Home). Exits the line edit mode.

The line editor design sketched above is but one of many approaches. It has one very important feature: the original line is not modified until all editing functions are complete. An escape command (CNTL-H) allows the current line to remain untouched and returns control to the editor to allow for a re-edit in case one becomes totally confused. For me, such touches are a requirement.

In case you didn't notice, the commands are in the set 0 thru 8 (the ASCII codes for CNTL-@ thru CNTL-H). This allows a case construct to be built to control the calls to the various keywords that implement the actions. It is not important that the editor be either super-fast or super-small. It can be defined using existing CORE keywords rather than using a group of primitives. After all, its main use is to generate and modify source text which is to be saved on the disk. It is seldom called when any task program is actually system-resident. More time is lost due to the operator's snail-like pace than to keyword execution.

7.5 Cross-Compilation

Cross-compilation of a threaded interpretive language program refers to the process of generating a stand-alone program capable of executing some given task. The program is always generated and stored on the disk rather than in memory. The target address for the program being cross-compiled may be any memory location in the system in which it will be resident, including the memory space of the TIL being used to generate the program. The object of the cross-compilation is to generate a threaded program which can be loaded to the target system and which will autonomously perform some specific task. The programs may be developed and tested using the TIL before being cross-compiled. The intent is to delete all of the unnecessary features of the CORE language and produce the smallest possible object program. For example, the entire outer interpreter is the executive for the TIL and is not required by most programs. It need not be resident in the autonomous program.

7.5.1 The End Result

The easiest way to understand the cross-compilation process is to consider what the final object program will be like. Obviously the object program will contain an inner interpreter, primitive and secondary keywords, and some type of executive program to control execution. It will not contain the TIL outer interpreter (the TIL executive) nor will it contain any keyword headers. Keyword headers are designed to allow the TIL to thread keywords together. This is not required of the object program since the scope of the program is fixed.

The program being generated will be stored on the disk rather than in memory. Actually it will be built in the block buffers and transferred to the disk. The target address of the program maps directly to a disk block address. That is, if the target address of the object program is hexadecimal 0000 to 01FF, and the program is to be stored in block 6, there is a constant offset of hexadecimal 0600 between the block "address" and target memory address (ie: the program will be stored in blocks 6, 7, 8, and 9).

Since the object program does not have headers in its keyword definitions, the "dictionary" for the object program is not available in the usual sense. The vocabulary for the object program is actually stored in the generating system. When it is searched, it will return the word address of some keyword in the object program. The object program vocabulary is essentially a symbol table of the word addresses for the object program.

Because object program headers will be created in the resident vocabulary but the code addresses will be stored in the object virtual space, all defining words are redefined in the cross-assembler. The keyword CREATE in the cross-assembler generates a header in the OBJECT vocabulary and saves the address of the next available location in the free object program space at word address location of the keyword. It then stores a pointer to the word that follows the next free object location at the build address and increments the free object space location pointer. This creates a primitive code address in the object program code whose word address is stored in the word address of the header in the OBJECT vocabulary. This is diagrammed in figure 7.2. Note that the virtual address where the object code is stored (the build address) is not the same as the target memory address where the object code will be located but is offset. This offset is the offset from object to virtual memory (0300 in our example).

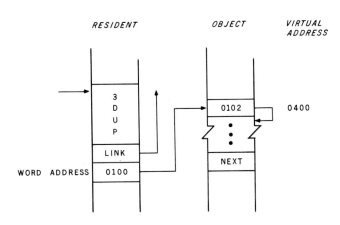

Figure 7.2: *A cross-compiled DUP primitive example.*

The point of all of this is not nearly as strange as it first appears. To build a secondary implies locating a word address to be enclosed in the object dictionary space. This word address is the word address of the keyword in the object program when it is the resident program. The dictionary headers are, however, being added to the TIL free dictionary space, not the object space. Further, the virtual address of the place where the code is to be stored is different from the object address where it will finally be located. This concept is central to understanding the cross-assembler.

The keywords that enclose data in the object dictionary ("," and C,) also must be redefined in the cross-compiler. This impacts the entire assembly process. A cross-assembler must be available to build entries to the object program and store them to the virtual memory build space. Defining words such as VARIABLE and CONSTANT must also be redefined. Even the number-handling routines of the outer interpreter are different in the cross-compilation mode, since the literal handlers are differently located. The cross-compiler is very different from the normal compiler/assembler.

7.5.2 The Process

The cross-compilation of TIL programs requires a substantial redefinition of the resident TIL program. The cross-compiler is usually disk-resident. When it is evoked, the cross-compiler and cross-assembler are loaded to the system. Effectively an entirely new outer interpreter is contained in the cross-compiler. The object program to be cross-compiled is also resident on the disk in source text form.

The usual technique is to define a special load screen for cross-compiler object program generation. This screen includes the source text for an inner interpreter and several of the most useful keywords. These include the keywords to support the branch and loop constructs, the defining words, literals, some basic arithmetic, memory reference, relational, stack and interstack keywords. (If some of the keywords are known to be unnecessary, this general-purpose screen can be copied and edited first.) The screen is loaded by the cross-compiler and becomes the core of the object program.

A second general-purpose screen is then loaded to establish the variable storage policy for the object program. If the object code will be placed in read-only memory, special provision for correctly allocating variables to the programmable memory must be included. Otherwise the variable storage can be in-line. One of two screens is loaded to the system to establish the variable storage protocol.

Unless you are very lucky, the keywords embedded in the object program to this point do not match the requirements of the object program load screen. If the object program was generated by redefining all those keywords needed to support the object code except those known to exist in the core object screen, the object program screen can be loaded to produce the final object program. In either event, remember that all keywords must be defined before they are used in another definition.

It should be noted that the object program cannot be tested in the normal system environment in its final form. The load screen used to generate the final object program can be checked out interactively but the final object program cannot. By including definition of all the keywords except those known to exist in the core object screen, a fairly high degree of assurance that the object program is correct can be achieved before cross-generation.

7.6 Widget Sorters

Because the etiology of widgets is an obscure science, I won't even discuss widgets here. Instead, I will discuss something even more vague.

The system software necessary to control the hardware is generally referred to as the system monitor or the operating system. This software may be written in threaded code just as easily as any other program. The I/O routines should still be coded as subroutines to allow access by other programs, but this is a minor point. A review of the keywords and extensions will reveal that most of the features of a general-purpose system monitor program are available in the TIL.

There are several functions that are usually available in a system monitor that have not been considered in the TIL. These include several debugging features and utility functions. The core monitor features include the ability to generate, display, and test programs, the ability to load programs to memory and save programs on mass media, the ability to test the system hardware, and the ability to perform housekeeping chores of various types (such as I/O).

There are several ways to generate a threaded system monitor. The most simplistic approach is to design an outer interpreter that has the ability to execute keywords but does not have a compile mode. This approach results in a substantially smaller outer interpreter with far fewer keywords needed to support the outer interpreter. This fixes the scope of the monitor at build time. A 2 K-byte monitor of this type will support an amazing number of features. Only the keyword directly available to the operator needs headers, which helps shoehorn the system into 2 K-bytes of memory.

Using this approach, the full-blown compiling outer interpreter must be a separate program. The inner interpreter for the system monitor can be used by the more comprehensive language exactly as if it were a utility program. All of the keywords with headers can also be used if this is done. The primitive keywords without headers in the system monitor can be given headers in the main language with suitably defined coding addresses.

It should be noted that even though the system monitor is a threaded interpreter, this does not imply that only threaded code can be supported by the system. The monitor must be capable of loading a program to memory. It does not care what the contents of the memory load are. By defining an unconditional jump keyword to the address at the top of the stack, any program can be executed. I do run BASIC in a system with a threaded system monitor.

A saner but larger monitor can be constructed using a full compiling version of the outer interpreter. The virtual memory features can be included in this type of a monitor. Not all of the language features of the general purpose language need be contained in the monitor. By concentrating the resources on I/O and other essential features, a subset of the language will suffice. The full language can be called into play via a load screen. This is somewhat of an advantage in that only the monitor software need be in a fixed location. By setting the dictionary pointer before calling the load screen, the language may be relocated at will to any area of programmable memory.

There are several tacks that can be taken to achieve the desired goal. Most involve bootstrapping. For example, the initial bootstrapping operation for my Z80 system started with a 1 K-byte read-only memory monitor on the central processing unit board. The monitor was debugged on an 8080 system; the read-only memory was programmed and then installed in the Z80 system. Using this monitor, the disk system (with its own read-only memory bootstrap loader and disk operating system) was then installed. The disk operating software was then specialized to the Z80 I/O using the 1 K-byte read-only memory monitor. Using the combined disk operating system/1 K-byte monitor, a new system disk was generated that bootstrapped not the disk operating system, but a more extensive system monitor. This monitor was then used to develop the threaded system monitor. Finally, a more extensive disk bootstrap loader was generated and burned into a 1 K-byte read-only memory, and the disk read-only memory and original system monitor read-only memory were removed. In the end, a power-on or master reset boot loads the threaded monitor from the disk. Other programs, such as BASIC, have their own individual bootstrap loaders. They can be loaded autonomously or by the threaded system monitor.

By suitable trickery, a fairly universal operating system can be developed. The compiling version of the system can even allow the development of relocatable system utility software. As an example, a disassembler can be written in threaded source code as a load screen. The advantage of this is fairly simple to see. A program to be disassembled can generally be located at its intended load point (unless it is located in the system monitor area). The disassembler can be loaded to any free memory area by setting the dictionary pointer prior to loading the appropriate screen. This leaves the source to be disassembled where it should be, resulting in an easier disassembler design.

The ability to extend the language to system software has a subtle advantage. There exists only one protocol and one set of input commands for both the system and the language itself. There is no question about separators being commas for one command language and spaces for another. The keywords evoke the same response in both languages unless purposefully changed. Uniformity has its advantages.

7.7 Floating Point

All of the arithmetic keywords considered so far have been restricted to signed integers. There is no fundamental reason for not building a floating-point arithmetic package for the TIL if it is required. If scientific computations are needed, the TIL will certainly support your requirements. The only reason that my current TIL does not support floating-point is my lack of time to teach the beast the basics. A quick sketch of the fundamentals should point the more ambitious in the right direction.

7.7.1 Formats

There are as many floating-point formats kicking around as there are opinions about what constitutes beauty. All of the formats eventually reduce to the form:

$$N = \pm A \times B^{\pm C}$$

In this form A is called the mantissa, B is called the exponent base and C is called the exponent. After this simple fact is stated, all sanity disappears and emotion ensues.

The mantissa is usually constrained to be in the range:

$$B^i < |A| < B^{i+1}$$

where i is an integer. Simply because computers are usually (but not always) implemented as binary machines, the exponent base B is usually selected to be some power of 2. Because B is selected *a priori*, it is not explicitly carried within the floating-point number format but is implicit in the computational routines. What needs to be carried in the floating-point representation is: the sign of the mantissa, the mantissa magnitude, the sign of the exponent, the exponent magnitude, and, finally (because of the mantissa constraint), some indicator of a zero mantissa condition.

Since computers are computers and generally recognize only integers (and usually binary integers at that), there are some fundamentally rational ways to define floating-point number formats. The way the format is designed affects the attributes of the numbers to be represented. Two common choices for the exponent base are 2 and 16. The numbers can be represented for the case $i = -1$ as:

$$\pm A_1 \times 2^{\pm C} \qquad\qquad \pm A_2 \times 16^{\pm C}$$

$$0.5 < |A_1| < 1.0 \qquad\qquad 0.0625 < |A_2| < 1.0$$

Given a maximum integer value for C, the dynamic range of the A_1 format is much less than that of the A_2 format. This is easy to see since $2^{128} \cong 10^{38}$ but $16^{128} \cong 10^{154}$. The larger the value of B, the fewer bits needed for C in order to achieve the same dynamic range. The dynamic range advantage for a larger value of B does not come for free. As a scaled binary number, the A_1 format always has a 1 to the right of the binary radix point. The A_2 format may have up to three leading zeros to the right of the binary radix point before the appearance of a 1. Given the same number of bits to define A, the A_1 format always has the same number of significant digits but the A_2 format does not. To illustrate this, consider a floating point number which is first divided by 2 and then multiplied by 2. In the A_1 format, the value of A_1 would not change since the divide and multiply affect the value C only. In the A_2 format, the divide could result in a right shift of A_2 and no change to C. The least significant bit of A_2, if it were 1 set, would be lost by the divide and not recovered by the multiply. In fact, there are variations of up to 3 bits in the significance of the A_2 format due to the choice of C.

Two common formats for floating-point numbers are given in figure 7.3.

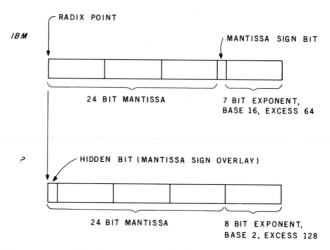

Figure 7.3: *Two common floating-point number formats. One is used by IBM, the other is in general use.*

In both formats, the exponent is carried as an excess number and the special case of C = 0 indicates that A = 0. For example:

	Exponent Value in Hex	Exponent	Mantissa
	FF	2^{+127}	
	.	.	
	.	.	
	.	.	
?Format	80	2^0	$0.5 \le A < 1.0$
	.	.	
	.	.	
	.	.	
	01	2^{-127}	
	00	—	A = 0

In the IBM format, the mantissa is allocated 24 bits but may have only 21 significant bits. In the "?" format, the MSB (most significant bit) is known to be a 1 so that it is hidden by the sign bit which overlays the MSB. In both formats a mantissa sign bit of 0 indicates a positive mantissa and a mantissa sign bit of 1 indicates a negative mantissa.

If your computer supports hardware floating point, all of this is moot since it fixes the format to be used. If not, the ideal format depends on your requirements for precision, dynamic range and the ease with which your format can be mechanized on your machine. Since some microcomputers support BCD (binary coded decimal) arithmetic, even these forms of floating-point arithmetic are feasible (ie: an exponent base C of 10).

Within the constraints of most microcomputer instruction sets, the fastest floating-point arithmetic routines are usually exponent base 2 formats. If speed is not the important criteria, select the format with the right attributes for your application. Whatever the criteria, the use of formats with multiples of 16-bits are generally preferred for TILs since the stack is 16 bits wide.

There are actually four different formats associated with TIL floating-point numbers: the conceptual format, the format used to store floating-point numbers in code bodies or when in threaded code lists as literals, the format when the number is on the data stack, and the I/O (input/output) format. There are no fixed rules for designing these formats. The "right" answer depends on the microcomputer and the ease of the implementation.

7.7.2 Floating Keywords

The keywords required for floating-point manipulation are remarkably similar to those required for integer manipulation. The biggest potential change to the TIL in adding floating-point involves the I/O. None of the outer interpreters considered to this point allowed for the possibility that an input number could be a floating-point number rather than an integer number. There are several ways to correct the I/O to allow this eventuality.

The floating-point philosophy is exactly the same as the integer philosophy: data type resolution is incumbent on the programmer. All floating-point keywords are predicated on the stack being preloaded before the keyword is evoked. The necessary keywords for general programming are relatively easy to predict.

The stack-oriented keywords consist of FDROP, FDUP, FOVER and FSWAP as a minimum. The only essential difference between these keywords and the equivalent integer versions is that a single floating-point number occupies two (or more) consecutive stack entries. The interstack floating-point operators F<R and FR> are simply multiple transfers of floating numbers.

The memory reference operators F@, F! and F+! involve conversions between floating-point stack and memory formats. The F+! operator does not have the utility of the +! operator and may not be needed.

The floating arithmetic operators include FABS, FMINUS, F+, F−, F*, F/, F/MOD, FMOD, FMAX, FMIN, and F10*. Obviously this is where the nitty-gritty of the floating-point resides. Oddly enough, FABS and FMINUS are easier to implement than ABS and MINUS. If only the remainder were! The floating-point relational operator includes F=, F>, F<, F0=, and F0<. The first three of these routines are mildly complex.

Clearly, floating-point defining words FCONSTANT and FVARIABLE and a floating-point number literal handler *F# are required. Routines to convert signed integers to floating-point (ITOF) and floating-point to integer (FTOI) are also desirable. A floating-point output routine such as F. would be nice too. Except for ITOF and FTOI, these routines are concerned with I/O and I/O formats.

There are several ways to implement the I/O routines. One method is to change the outer interpreter to allow floating-point input numbers to be generated if a token is one of the following forms:

$$N = \begin{cases} X \\ XEY \end{cases}$$

where:

$$X = \begin{cases} i. \\ i.J \\ .J \\ -i. \\ -i.J \\ - .J \end{cases} \quad \text{for i and j integer base 10}$$

$$Y = \begin{cases} i \\ -i \end{cases} \quad \text{for i integer base 10}$$

This change to the outer interpreter is clearly the preferred implementation since the system can decide whether to push the result to the stack (execute mode) or add the floating-point literal handler plus the floating-point number to the threaded list (compile mode).

An alternate approach is to define two separate keywords. A keyword named FLOAT could be defined to scan the next token from the input buffer, convert the token to the internal floating-point stack format and leave the result on the stack. An immediate keyword could perform a similar conversion in the compile mode except it would enclose the floating-point literal handler plus the converted number to the threaded list of code being compiled. This method works but does have the potential for error.

7.7.3 Summary

Clearly, there are many additional operands that could be defined to extend the system capabilities beyond the level supported by these relatively simplistic operands. Once a floating-point capability is available, trigonometric and other mathematical functions are reasonable candidates. All of this is in the works for my TIL, with a floating-point design half complete and my eye on cordic-based mathematical algorithms.

7.8 Extension Summary

The extensions to the language are a somewhat mixed blessing. As more and more features are added, the language becomes bigger and bigger. On the other hand the language utility increases. However, the good part is that an initial threaded interpretive language of size 4 K can grow and grow as the system grows. A 12 K-byte TIL should support an absolutely incredible set of capabilities. I simply cannot imagine a TIL of that size.

8 | Life With a TIL

When it comes down to brass tacks, living with most pro-
gramming languages is like living with your mother-in-law:
tranquility interspersed with moments of incredible rage.
The most insidious aspect is getting the "thing" to do what
you want. For "thing" read mother-in-law, BASIC, FOR-
TRAN, . . . , but not TIL.

8.1 Starting Out

The aspect of the TIL which is most enjoyable and also the most hazardous is its interactive nature. TILs love to "talk" to people and are extremely adept at learning (given proper guidance). TILs are very happy to reveal their inner-most secrets and show you their home. There is no part of the system which can't be displayed, changed, manipulated, and occasionally messed up in your conversations with the TIL. The problem is the very ease with which new keywords can be added to the language. It leads to the "design-at-the-keyboard" (DATK) syndrome.

The only known cure for the "design-at-the-keyboard" syndrome is a deliberate effort on the part of the programmer to design a program before the keyboard is touched. Designing a TIL program is not much different than designing in other languages. A TIL does demand a modest amount of struc-ture in a program: that is, a keyword cannot be used before it is defined, and it does demand that the structured construct syntax be complete (ie: a LOOP or +LOOP must terminate a DO). The actual structure of a program must be en-forced by the programmer.

In designing a TIL program, I generally attack the problem in a very rigid fashion; design the keywords from the top-down and then enter the program in a fixed format. The fixed format for program entry is a self-enforced, disciplined technique, rather than something demanded by the language itself. The other steps are simply common sense. (Programming does demand a cer-tain amount of common sense, although I will admit that some programs reflect more than others.) It should be pointed out that the techniques I will espouse are designed to preserve my sanity, since they work and work very well.

8.2 Program Structure

There are several reasons for insisting on a fixed structure for a program. Fundamentally it allows one to reconstruct the crime at some later point in time from the scattered remnants of keywords covering the battleground. There is nothing worse than trying to figure out some program *post-facto.* Ideally the program should be a source code version stored on the mass media rather than an embedded program in some vocabulary. In any event some type of listing of the program should be created during the build process to allow later program modification or simply to allow precise determination of what the code actually does.

The structural aspects of the program are designed both to satisfy the undefined keyword problem and to put items that are declared in a logical order. All programs are arranged as follows:

- Vocabulary definitions.
- Data type definitions.
- Global data definitions.
- Procedure definitions.
- Main program.

While this is the general format of a program, a certain amount of precedence must exist within each category. This will become obvious later (hopefully), since it is part of the design process.

8.2.1 Vocabulary Definition

Defining the vocabulary is fundamental to determining the resources available for program design. Almost all programs (except for cross-compiled, stand-alone programs) are linked back to the core vocabulary. How the program is linked to the core language can seriously affect the attributes of the program. For example, consider that a complete floating-point arithmetic package exists as a separate vocabulary that is linked to the core vocabulary. The floating-point vocabulary could contain a complete set of keywords for the generation, manipulation, and display of floating-point data types. By linking the new program vocabulary to the floating-point vocabulary rather than directly to the core vocabulary, the new program could contain both integer and floating-point data types.

The rationale for linking indirectly to the core vocabulary through a vocabulary such as the floating-point vocabulary only makes sense if the linking vocabulary is always system-resident or if the linking vocabulary redefines keywords that also exist in the core vocabulary. In the case of the floating-point vocabulary, both the floating-point data declaration types and other definitions are contained in the vocabulary. The data declaration types need to be available before global data definitions are attempted.

In cases where it is desired to include an entire library of standard functions in a new program, an alternate technique to vocabulary linking can also be used. How this is done is dependent upon whether the new program is being built on disk or is being interactively defined. If the program is being built on the disk, the library screens are first duplicated, the first screen of the library routine is reidentified as the first screen of new program and the screen load linkages are redefined to incorporate all of the library screens. The reidentification should include the name of the new program as a keyword definition to allow FORGET < new program > to delete the entire program. It is simply required to type in the names of the library functions desired after the vocabulary is established. Simply including the names of the desired library functions on a screen will not work. The screen calls are not nested so that the appearance of the library-loading keyword in another screen will load the library but will not return to the calling screen. If you want, a routine called LIBRARY could be defined to initiate a screen-load nesting operation. The final screens in each library vocabulary would have to contain the denesting code to complete this scenario.

The important point about the vocabulary definition step is that it defines the basic capabilities available to the new program. Keywords that are unique to the new program are not placed in libraries or added to the resident vocabularies to allow linking via the unique vocabulary. The vocabulary definition simply establishes the basic keywords available as resources to define the unique keywords of the new program.

8.2.2 Data Type Definitions

The basic TIL language contains only limited predefined data types. Depending on how you have defined the language, arrays, strings, user blocks, and other data types may not be available to a particular applications program. If required, they must be added. Data files unique to the program and the record structure of the data files must be defined along with any unique data type definitions. The keywords for the data and file definitions must precede the definition of the global data. In this case the appearance of the data type definitions before data declaration is required. Simply demanding that they all appear in one place is not required; it is common sense.

8.2.3 Global Data Definitions

Although it has not been stressed to this point, a TIL distinguishes between local and global data. Any named data such as a variable is globally available via its keyword name and occupies dictionary memory space. Data passed to a procedure or program on the stack or stack data internal to the procedure is local to the procedure and occupies stack memory space. Local data may be nothing more than a copy of global data, but once the quantity is on the stack, it is local data.

One other interesting feature of a TIL is that it allows data passage by value, by address, by pointer to an address, or by any other conceivable means. Examples of the first three methods are constants, variables, and user variables. In all cases the correct resolution of the data rests with the programmer and not the system.

In defining global data, I generally define the keywords in the order of increasing complexity. Constants are defined first, followed by variables, arrays, pointers, strings (messages), data files and records, etc. An important point about defining data keyword names is to make them descriptive. Proper keyword names and suitable usage of the keywords in subsidiary definitions lead to much more lucid programs. The use of a constant keyword with a descriptive name is much preferred, for example, over the isolated appearance of some number in the middle of a keyword definition. Although this is at odds with the desire to conserve memory, a self-documenting keyword is a boon to understanding the intent of the program.

8.2.4 Procedure Definitions

The procedural definition phase is where all of the keywords required to support the main program are defined. Procedures may be operands, functions, subroutines, program control directives, or other actions required by the main program. Because a keyword cannot be referenced before it is defined, it is not unusual to observe a natural precedence in the entry order for procedures. The "natural" precedence order is from the most primitive level to the most sophisticated level. Usually this is precisely the order demanded by the define-before-use criteria.

During the procedure definition phase, it is not unusual to incorporate library routines by stealing the source code from the disk and merging it with the program source code. A library of such source code routines is very helpful in generating programs. As an example, trigonometric floating point routines could be stored on the disk in a library file. Those routines required by a given application program could be copied to the procedural definition area of the program. This process limits the resulting program size since only the subset of the library really needed for the application is added to the program. Developing the library is not easy, but it is easier than regenerating the same routines each time an application stumbles by.

As in the case of the global data, names of the procedures are important. Comments are also helpful. Anything that supports an understanding of the procedures will turn out to be useful in the final analysis.

8.2.5 Main Program

The TIL main program will always turn out to be the final keyword definition in an applications program. There may actually be several interrelated main programs, but this is an exception rather than the rule. The editor vocabulary can be viewed in this context, for example. The more usual situation is to have a single main program. The appearance of the main program as the last entry is consistent with the fact that keywords cannot be used before they are defined.

A TIL main program is often a loop which returns to the outer interpreter only on operator command. Whatever its design, it is a stand-alone program which is not constrained to have the same characteristics as the outer interpreter. The operator's interactions with the program are defined by the program design.

8.2.6 Physical Records

Any TIL application program must exist somewhere as a source code listing. This may be in program screens on disk or it may be on the back of a laundry ticket or it may be only in the mind of the programmer. The above list is in decreasing order of preference. The subtle inference that a disk system is available is embedded in the entry structure discussion. The fundamental advantage to the disk is that it produces a self-documenting file when the entry takes place. This is not true of the other methods of listing generation.

If the mass media supported by your system is cassette storage, source file generation and program retrieval are much more difficult. Usually hand documentation combined with recording of the object file (the entire TIL language with the application program already entered) is required. Other methods that allow saving or loading only the source file could be designed but they usually require fairly large memory blocks for the source code. At that, it is to be preferred over hand documentation.

Given that a disk system is available, one important factor must be raised. Store your applications programs on a disk different from your system disk. The system disk should contain a bootstrap loader for the TIL, the basic TIL language, the operator message block, system utilities such as the editor, and the library routines. An application program should be on a separate disk which contains only the operator message block, applications programs, and possibly the application data files. Intermixing the system and applications programs on a single disk is rarely an advantage.

The physical records of any program determine the long-term utility of the code. Undocumented or poorly documented programs are as useful as a JSW (jump somewhere) assembler mnemonic.

8.3 Program Design

As has been noted, the disadvantage of a TIL is that its interactive nature can lead to poor programming practice. It is so easy to add, check-out, and retain code that program design tends to occur at the keyboard rather than at the desk (the DATK syndrome). Program entry must be bottom-up, but a bottom-up program design leads to a poor design. The design stage must be top-down if a reasonable design is to result.

So much has been written about top-down design that I hesitate to muddy the water with *my* oar. Suffice to say that there are advocates of flowcharts, structure charts, ALGOL-like languages, HIPOs, Warnier-Orr diagrams, and numerous other techniques, all of which are advertised as being the technique for top-down design. Use whatever technique you feel comfortable with. Whatever design approach you use, if it isn't straight-out TIL code, a conversion to TIL code format is necessary before a real design exists. I shall concentrate on the TIL code format.

8.3.1 Vertical Design

The top-down design of a TIL program or procedure (ie: a keyword) should ideally result in both a syntactically and semantically correct design. Although there are no quick and easy rules for determining the total correctness of a given definition, there are some guidelines that help during the design phase. The TIL entry format of tokens separated by spaces does not readily indicate the underlying structure of the definition. During the design phase, I use a vertical format with setbacks to more clearly indicate the structure. For example:

: ■JOB■BEGIN■WORD1■WORD2■TEST■
IF■TASK1■ELSE■TASK2■THEN■FLAG■END■;
: ■JOB
  BEGIN
    WORD1
    WORD2
    TEST
    IF
      TASK1
    ELSE
      TASK2
    THEN
    FLAG
  END
;

Although both definitions are precisely the same, clearly the vertical format with setbacks is far more informative of the keyword structure than the horizontal format. In the vertical format it is much more obvious that the syntax of the constructs is complete. Simple syntax completeness will not prove program integrity, but the lack thereof will assure problems.

Given that the top-level form of the main program keyword is defined, the local (stack) data at the *completion* of each keyword in the definition is noted to the right of each keyword used in the definition. This is a fairly simple way to display the stack input/output requirements. The changes to the global data are every bit as important, but not as evident at any given stage in the program design. It is clear, however, that local data disagreements are fatal. In noting the keyword stack data I/O requirements, I distinguish between flags, numbers, addresses, pointers, and other data types. It is important that the stack depth and types be in agreement with the keyword I/O needs. If the keyword is undefined at the next lower level, the I/O requirements are indicative of the algorithmic transfer function needed to define the keyword. If the keyword is defined, the I/O and computational functions must match the keyword definition.

The identification of the I/O and processing requirements of all the undefined keywords in the main program completes the top level design of the program. The total design of the program is not complete until all of the keywords have been completely detailed. This involves exactly the same techniques as used on the top-level keyword.

At the top-level design stage, the use of macroinstruction secondary keyword definitions greatly simplifies the overall design. A macroinstruction secondary keyword is simply a keyword that serves as an alias for a group of keywords (ie: a subroutine or subprogram). The outer interpreter of Section 5 has several examples of macroinstruction secondaries (eg: ?NUMBER, ?EXECUTE, etc).

The identification of global data requirements is among the more difficult tasks in program design using any language. A threaded interpretive language will not make this aspect any easier. The subject of data structures is so important that many texts are devoted solely to the data structure aspects of program design. A list of the keywords which initialize, use, or change each global parameter is very helpful. This is aided by noting, to the right of the stack I/O for each keyword in the total program, a list of the global parameters used directly by the keyword. Unfortunately there is no ready way for the system itself to aid in the documentation of the global data changes.

8.3.2 Program Executives

A TIL program does not necessarily use the outer interpreter as the controlling executive. It is perfectly feasible to design a TIL program which, when evoked, never returns control to the outer interpreter. This implies that the entire I/O protocol for a TIL program can be redefined and need not follow the interactive protocol established by the outer interpreter for program generation and execution. In short, the TIL is only a resources base for the design of a program and does not constrain the program/user interactions.

A more useful situation involves a program executive which will return control to the outer interpreter only if a specific event occurs. The design of such an executive is not difficult. The fundamental program executive is designed as a loop with a jump out of the loop embedded within an IF construct. Escape code such as this is desirable particularly during the program checkout phase.

A program executive serves as the main program in most designs. This outer executive can cause a lower-level executive to be called as the result of some event. This nesting of executives commonly occurs to cause changes to I/O protocols. As an example, the EDIT command of the EDITOR evokes a lower-level command structure in which a subset of the ASCII control codes is recognized. The CNTL-E (ENTER) command in this structure then evokes a still lower-level executive with an entirely different set of I/O protocols. In both the EDIT mode and the ENTER submode of the EDIT mode, the code design uses the primitive keyword KEY to access the I/O device: the keyboard. The existence of primitive I/O keywords such as KEY is the attribute of the TIL which allows designs of this type to be mechanized.

8.4 Entry and Test

Entering the code really involves more than typing in the keywords. I use a more complex approach in that keyword testing is intermixed with keyword entry. Although the design was top-down, the coding and testing will occur in a bottom-up fashion.

8.4.1 Keyword Contention

The very first step in any program entry after the establishment of the vocabulary linkage is a test for keyword duplication. The proposed keyword names are tested using the sequence ■'■ <name> ■.■. If the keyword is present in the vocabularies, the word address of the keyword will be displayed to the operator. At this point the choice is to rename the keyword or to allow the definition in the new program to take precedence. This latter course will eliminate use of the older keyword in the current program. If the keyword is not present, an error message will be echoed to the operator and the name is known to be acceptable. This simple test avoids grief. More than once I have discovered duplicate keywords and/or contending keyword names simply by not following this procedure.

8.4.2 Keyword Testing

Each keyword is tested as it is entered. If the program is being built on a screen, keyword definitions are added one at a time. After each new definition is added, the current program is deleted from the system using FORGET, and then the screen is reloaded for testing using the LOAD command. The newest keyword is then tested and debugged before the next definition is added to the screen.

Keyword testing is unusually simple for any TIL. First, any global data manipulated by the keyword is initialized. Input stack parameters are then typed in while in the execute mode, followed by the name of the keyword being tested. Any results left on the stack can then be examined using the "." keyword. Always attempt to output one more stack item than is expected. If a stack error message does not result, a problem exists with the definition. Any global data manipulated by the keyword is then examined to confirm data integrity. All keywords are tested including the global parameters.

The most difficult part of keyword testing is the design of the local and global data values needed to completely test the keyword. All possible paths through the keyword code should be exercised and the various extremes of all algorithms should be tested. This usually requires a good deal of thought on the part of the programmer/designer and may explain why most "tested" code comes asunder at embarrassing moments.

When approached in this rather methodical manner, most, but not all, errors of oversight and negligence are revealed. This level of testing will not uncover all possible programming errors. A bad algorithm carefully coded and tested is still a bad algorithm. Further, an exhaustive test of all possible paths through a program may not be feasible. At this point you might as well resort to prayer beads because I can guarantee that if you don't test them all, an error will occur in a path you did not check.

8.5 Tricks of the Trade

As in any programming language, operating system, or other substantial chunk of code that interacts with a user, a degree of familiarity is required to become truly comfortable with the operator protocol. An advantage to designing your own language is that you have complete control over the protocol. There is absolutely nothing sacred about any part of a TIL. If you really want to emulate the operator protocol of some system you are familiar with, do it. It may require a substantial amount of work to design the parser, but it can be done. The capabilities of a TIL are in how ingeniously you can define what you need for your problem, given your environment.

Bibliography and Notes

Part of the problem in writing a bibliography for a text of this nature is the broad range of subjects one would like to cover. This is much easier said than done. The other part of the problem is the dearth of material on threaded interpretive languages.

Of the potential number of subjects which could be covered, a very limited number will be considered. This is partially due to the vast amount of computer-related literature and partially due to my own laziness. The selected references cover most of the threaded interpretive language sources that I used in the development of the TIL I use. I am aware that others exist, but I do not have access to them. The other references are mostly background material or material useful to extending a TIL in new directions.

Interpreters and TILs

The simple utility of interpreters is well-known. The use of interpreters is as old as the art of computer programming. Gries, for example, devotes a chapter in a compiler design text to the subject of interpreters and their utility. Almost all BASIC languages are implemented as interpreters rather than as compilers. Allison, et al, present a fairly simple method for generating an interpreter for Tiny BASIC. It is relatively simple to extend this concept to other languages. The interpretive language or "onion" approach espoused is very similar to the threaded code approach. Forsyth and Howard discuss trade-offs of interpreters, threaded interpreters, and compilers on microprocessors, but conclude that threaded code is "troublesome" to implement on an 8-bit microprocessor. It might be well not to press this point with an experienced FORTH programmer.

Most of the literature on threaded interpretive languages is very FORTH-specific. Variations on basic FORTH semantics and syntax appear in languages such as IPS and in STOIC, a language that I have not investigated. James gives an excellent overview of FORTH and a brief description of how it is mechanized. There is not quite enough description to allow a variation of FORTH to be implemented. The microFORTH PRIMER is also descriptive, particularly with regard to register assignments, but does not come close to a full discussion of the language. I am sure that FORTH has fully descriptive documents, but they are not publically available. The DEC Users' Society Program Library document is available and contains a great deal of mechanization detail for a PDP-11 version of FORTH. Still another version of FORTH is discussed by Rather and Moore (the latter being the original developer of FORTH). The reference gives timing comparisons between BASIC and FORTH, although it is difficult to judge benchmarks when the absolute test conditions are unknown.

Background and Extensions

The design of the screen keywords implies at least a basic understanding of file structures. I have never been particularly enthralled with the screen keywords I designed for ZIPD, my current TIL. Klein explains at least the fundamentals of file structures and management, which could serve as a point of departure for a screen keyword redesign. Files are not my strong point and I can easily envision improvements being made by someone with a better perspective on files.

The design of the assembler is somewhat primitive, mostly because of its intended use simply as a keyword extension tool. Extending the assembler to a fully relocatable, macroassembler would be nice. Fylstra and Emmerichs are references which introduce the assembler problems and offer solutions to some of the more common problems. Both of the texts are tutorial, but present useful approaches.

The extension that I most want is floating-point arithmetic keywords. Time to design the keywords has been the problem. The essentials are available in Hashizume and Rankin and Woziak. The former presents flowchart-level designs for floating-point routines while the latter presents a code design for a 6502. A modest amount of conversion should yield a code design for some other microcomptuer (such as my Z80).

Widget Sorters

The definitive reference to widgets is Kripke. This text depicts the conversion of lignite glop, anthracite glop, and hard glop into high-grade and low-grade muckle by the Acme Muckle Mfg. Co., and the subsequent use of the muckle by the Amalgamated Widget Works to manufacture widgets. Although an overabundance of time is spent discussing the partial derivatives involved in widget production, little thought is devoted to the problem of sorting and grading the widgets produced. If anyone finds the definitive widget sorting reference, please put it in a bottle addressed to the author.

References

Allison, D et al. "Build Your Own BASIC." *Dr. Dobb's Journal of Computer Calisthenics & Orthodontia*, Volume 1, January 1976, page 7.

Allison, D and M Christoffer. "Build Your Own BASIC — Revised." *Dr. Dobb's Journal of Computer Calisthenics & Orthodontia*, January 1976, page 8.

Allison, D et al. "Design Notes for Tiny BASIC." *Dr. Dobb's Journal of Computer Calisthenics & Orthodontia*, January 1976, pages 8 thru 12.

Emmerichs, J. "Designing the Tiny Assember." *BYTE*, April 1977, pages 60 thru 67.

Forsyth, H and R Howard. "Compilation and Pascal on the New Microprocessors." *BYTE*, August 1978, pages 50 thru 61.

Flystra, D. "Write Your Own Assembler." *The Best of Byte*, Morristown, NJ: Creative Computing Press, 1977, pages 246 thru 254.

Gries, D. *Compiler Construction For Digital Computers*. New York: John Wiley & Sons, 1971.

Hammond, H and M Ewing. *FORTH Programming System For the PDP-11*. DECUS Programming Library, Numbers 11 thru 232, 1975.

Hashizume, B "Floating Point Arithmetic." *BYTE*, November 1977, pages 76 thru 78, 180 thru 188.

James, J. "FORTH for Microcomputers." *Dr. Dobb's Journal of COMPUTER Calisthenics & Orthodontia*, May 1978, pages 21 thru 27.

Klein, M. "Files on Parade, Part 1: Types of Files." *BYTE*, February 1979, pages 186 thru 192.

Klein, M. "Files on Parade, Part 2: Using Files." *BYTE*, March 1979, pages 32 thru 41.

Kripke, B. *Introduction To Analysis*. San Francisco: W.H. Freeman and Co, 1968.

Meinzer, K. "IPS, An Unorthodox High Level Language." *BYTE*, January 1979, pages 146 thru 159.

MicroFORTH Primer. Manhattan Beach, California: FORTH, Inc, 1976.

Rankin, R and S Wozniak. "Floating Point Routines for the 6502." *Dr. Dobb's Journal of COMPUTER Calisthenics & Orthodontia*, August 1976, pages 17 thru 19.

Rather, E and C Moore. "The FORTH Approach to Operating Systems." *Proceedings of the ACM*, 1976, pages 233 thru 239.

SUBJECT INDEX